Yoga Escapes

yoga JOURNAL

Yoga Escapes

A Yoga Journal Guide to the Best Places
to Relax, Reflect, and Renew

JEANNE RICCI

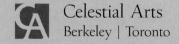
Celestial Arts
Berkeley | Toronto

Yoga Journal
2054 University Avenue #600
Berkeley, California 94704
www.yogajournal.com

in association with
Celestial Arts
P.O. Box 7123
Berkeley, California 94707
www.tenspeed.com

Distributed in Australia by Simon & Schuster Australia, in Canada by Ten Speed Press Canada, in New Zealand by Southern Publishers Group, in South Africa by Real Books, and in the United Kingdom and Europe by Airlift Book Company.

Cover and text design by Nancy Austin
Illustrations by Edward Hee
Photo credits: pp. ii, v, 8 courtesy of Canyon Ranch; pp. x, 4, 183 courtesy of Golden Door; p. 64 courtesy of Red Mountain Spa; p. 138 courtesy of the Wyndham Peaks Resort & Golden Door Spa; p. 162 courtesy of The Sagamore

Library of Congress Cataloging-in-Publication Data

Ricci, Jeanne.
  Yoga escapes : a Yoga journal guide to the best places to relax,
reflect, and renew / Jeanne Ricci.
      p. cm.
Includes index.
  ISBN 1-58761-187-2 (pbk.)
  1. Yoga--Directories. 2. Health resorts--Directories. I. Yoga journal II. Title.
  RA781.7.R514 2003
  613.7'046'025--dc21
                                              2003009465

First printing, 2003
Printed in Singapore

1 2 3 4 5 6 7 8 9 10 - 08 07 06 05 04 03

CONTENTS

Yoga & Healing Retreats

Resorts & Spas

Yoga Inns and B&Bs

Ashrams

ACKNOWLEDGMENTS

Thanks to all past retreat, spa, resort, and ashram guests who gave their time and opinions for this book. Special thanks to Kathryn Arnold, *Yoga Journal* editorial director, for having faith that I could make this idea a reality; the *Yoga Journal* staff for providing background information, firsthand experience, and listing suggestions; Jillian Manus, for shepherding the idea and finding Ten Speed Press/Celestial Arts; and my husband, Don Williams, for his constant support and conducting the bulk of the initial research.

INTRODUCTION

Modern everyday life, which forces us to balance, sometimes unsuccessfully, family and friends with work, can be stressful to say the least. Many Americans now turn to yoga in search of inner peace—or at least an hour or two of tranquility. But oftentimes, this is not enough to redirect our lives in a more healthy direction. That's why more and more yoga practitioners, whether they have a daily practice or go to class once a week, are looking to spend their coveted vacation time at a yoga retreat to combat the effects of the ubiquitous 60-plus-hour workweek and chronic multitasking.

A yoga vacation, like any other holiday, is an opportunity to relax and recharge. This can be a time for reflection and to assess your current life path and the changes you would like to make to live more peacefully in this high-octane world. Or perhaps you simply want to deepen your practice or study with a renowned teacher.

How do you know where to go? And what if you want to bring the family along? In this book, we've included more than 150 properties to match almost every person's style. Whether you're looking for the structured routine of an ashram, a family-friendly destination, a spa experience, or a retreat that attracts the top teachers, you'll find it in *Yoga Escapes*. And we include guest comments with every entry, so you can read an unbiased review before making your decision.

How to Use This Book

The properties featured in this book were recommended by a variety of sources, including yoga teachers and practitioners, *Yoga Journal* editors, and well-seasoned travelers. The goal is to offer something for everyone, from the remote ashram to the posh Caribbean resort. In fact, *Yoga Journal* has covered many of these yoga retreats and vacation spots throughout the years in the pages of the magazine. Now, for the first time, the information is consolidated in an easy-to-use book.

To be listed in the book, each property has to offer yoga to the individual traveler. If your favorite yoga teacher holds a fabulous retreat in Jamaica each winter but that hotel does not offer yoga year-round, it will probably not be in this book. We encourage you to visit your teachers' websites and find out where they are holding workshops. Many of their favorite locations can be found in the upcoming pages.

This book is divided into four main sections: Yoga & Healing Retreats; Resorts and Spas; Yoga Inns and B&Bs; and Ashrams. Properties are arranged by country/state/city in the following order: the Americas (North, Central, and South), Asia, the Caribbean, and Europe. If you want to find a specific facility or look within a particular region, refer to the alphabetical index.

The **Yoga & Healing Retreats** chapter is a directory of yoga retreats and Ayurvedic healing facilities around the world. If you're looking for a place that offers yoga at least twice a day, then a retreat center may be for you. Here, you'll meet other people who are also interested in deepening their practice, improving their health, or exploring spirituality. Most retreat centers exclusively serve vegetarian or vegan food. Alcohol and tobacco are rarely permitted, and lodging is usually dormitory-style, with shared bathrooms. Call in advance to inquire about single or double rooms.

If you prefer a flexible schedule, read the **Resorts and Spas** chapter. You'll find it easy to add some yoga to a family vacation. At most resorts, yoga is offered once or twice daily. Then you can spend time with your family for the remainder of the day, or you can choose to have the kids participate in a youth program, which usually costs $35 to $50 per day, per child.

A spa vacation is often more focused on fitness, health, or weight loss. Some have mandatory exercise schedules. Others allow you to simply receive pampering massages and treatments whenever you wish and exercise as much or as little as you want. Assess your goals before you choose which spa is right for you. Children are rarely welcome at spas.

Yoga Inns and B&Bs combine the intimate quality of a bed and breakfast with yoga and healing treatments. Most of the properties in this chapter offer yoga once or twice daily. Then it's up to you to create your own itinerary for the day. A few combine the inn experience with a yoga retreat. At these places, five to fifteen people get individual attention and a more intense yoga experience. Often, activities and excursions are conducted as a group. If it's privacy you're looking for, this type of inn may not be for you.

The **Ashrams** section supplies a worldwide listing of spiritual centers. At an ashram, you'll experience communal living firsthand. Almost all ashrams have a set daily schedule. Read about the typical day described in each listing and see if it appeals to you. If you are fairly new to yoga, a day consisting of four compulsory yoga and meditation sessions could be overwhelming. In addition, you are often asked to practice karma yoga by contributing to the upkeep of the facility. This could include kitchen duties, gardening, cleaning, and other chores. Most ashrams only serve vegetarian or vegan food. Alcohol, caffeine, and tobacco are not permitted. Guests stay in dormitories with shared bathrooms. Modest dress is usually required at all times. Shorts, short skirts, and sleeveless or sheer tops are not appropriate ashram attire, nor are Lycra leggings and tank tops for yoga. Choose loose pants and a short-sleeved shirt for your practice instead.

Each entry in *Yoga Escapes* has a description of the property, with teacher or guest comments; a list of a few past guest teachers; a description of the yoga classes, their frequency, and cost; a sampling of services, other classes, recreation, and children's programs; an accommodations description; dining information; appropriate attire and what to bring; travel information; rates; and address, phone, fax, and website.

"Planning the Perfect Yoga Vacation," on page 5, will help you get started by providing criteria you should consider before you go. In addition, the in-flight stretches described on page 184 will keep the kinks at bay and help you stay relaxed while traveling. You'll also find sprinkled throughout the book a variety of tips from health and wellness writer Kathleen Finn Mendola for staying healthy on the road. Common yoga, Ayurveda, and spa terms used throughout the book are briefly defined in the glossary.

The information on these pages is as up-to-date as possible. However, places close and phone numbers change, so confirm specifics before you leave home.

Of course, the properties listed in this book represent only a small percentage of retreats, ashrams, resorts, spas, and inns around the world. If you've discovered a special retreat we haven't included, let us know. Your feedback could be valuable in the writing of future editions of this book. Send correspondence to: *Yoga Escapes*, c/o *Yoga Journal*, 2054 University Avenue #600, Berkeley, CA 94704.

PLANNING THE PERFECT YOGA VACATION

Lucielle Hall

Even if this is not your first yoga vacation, choosing among the vast number of offerings can be a challenge. How do you select the experience that's right for you? With a bit of common sense and the right resources (like this book), it's not as hard as it might seem. Ask yourself the right questions, and you'll soon determine the type of yoga vacation that best suits your needs.

Location, Location, Location

You'll want to start by looking for ways to narrow down the field of options. For instance, if you've already found a teacher and yoga technique you like, you're in good shape. If you don't have a teacher or technique that you are committed to—or if you simply want to try out other styles—your range of choices is much broader. You'll find yoga retreats throughout the United States, from the serene mountains of Colorado to the woodlands of New Hampshire, from the lavish beaches of Hawaii to the mystical silence of the red rocks of Sedona, Arizona. Choose the destination, and then check out what's available in that area.

If you have a taste for more far-reaching adventures, set your sights on India, Bali, or Peru—or on vacation staples like the Caribbean Islands, Costa Rica, and Europe. If you do decide to travel to distant shores, take special care to weigh your travel options. Some overseas yoga vacations are packages that include everything from airline tickets to local accommodations, language instruction, and prearranged sight-seeing trips. Others, however, leave you completely on your own.

The advantages of prearranged packages—convenience and comfort— can be especially useful when traveling to developing countries. Having someone else worry about the sanitary conditions of your living space and the safety of the food allows you to relax into the serenity and pleasure of your daily yoga practice. But less structured packages afford benefits, too—namely, lower costs and greater exposure to the local customs and culture.

Although prearranged packages can be very reasonably priced, you can sometimes save up to half the cost by making your own arrangements instead.

You might seek out a special theme vacation, such as a yoga retreat for women, which offers yoga practitioners a safe and supportive environment for exploring deeper levels of the Self. You can also find vacations that focus on mind and body renewal through yoga combined with alternative therapies. At the Raj in Fairfield, Iowa, for example, guests practice yoga as an adjunct to daily Ayurvedic panchakarma treatments, which consist of oil massages, herbal steam treatments, and other therapies.

Retreat, Ashram, or Resort?

In addition to the geographical possibilities, consider this: How much yoga do you want to do on your yoga vacation? Options range from intensive, monthlong retreats in remote spiritual communities with a rigorous daily schedule of yoga, meditation, and other spiritual practices to casual classes held at resort hotels in attractive tourist destinations.

At one end of the retreat spectrum, you'll find a vacation like that offered at the Yoga Oasis near Pahoa on the Big Island of Hawaii, a center which offers weeklong yoga intensives with local and guest teachers. If an intensive is more yoga than you want, you can participate in a yoga class for an hour each morning, enjoy an organic vegan breakfast, and spend the rest of the day hiking, exploring the island, or indulging in whatever other vacation pleasures you discover.

Retreat centers such as White Lotus Foundation in Santa Barbara, California, or Feathered Pipe Ranch in Helena, Montana, lie at the middle of the spectrum. These large retreat centers offer an eclectic assortment of courses in personal and spiritual development—and yoga retreats comprise just part of their offerings. The more demanding daily schedule at retreat centers typically features yoga classes for one to three hours, twice a day. You spend the rest of the day in instructional activities or meditation, and you'll usually have one to three hours off for other recreational activities like music, dance, hiking, swimming, biking, and so on. The courses in these centers often attract a large number of participants, a great plus if you are socially minded, but not so hot if you prefer smaller groups.

At the intensive end of the spectrum of yoga vacations are the ashrams, or spiritual communities, around the world that open their doors to visitors. Whereas retreat centers offer courses taught by teachers from many different traditions, ashrams most often focus on the teachings of one spiritual master. The Expanding Light of Ananda center in California's Sierra

Nevada, for example, is the home of Ananda Village, a large intentional community founded by followers of Paramahansa Yogananda. The daily routine includes yoga sessions and workshops with a focus on self-discovery or healthy living. Similarly, the Sivananda Ashram Yoga Ranch in New York's Catskill Mountains offers retreat programs based on the yoga and Vedanta teachings of Sivananda. Here you'll spend your stay in meditation, asana practice, chanting, readings, and discussion. You'll also be expected to participate in some of the daily work activities around the ranch.

If you're looking for a deeper yoga experience, then the retreat centers and ashrams have the advantage. For many people, the journey to a sanctuary where everyone is focused on yoga and spiritual growth can be a transforming experience. At the same time, you want be sure the more structured routine typical of retreat centers and ashrams won't be too restrictive for you. In some cases, particularly at ashrams, participation in the daily schedule is required. Even when it isn't, you don't want to put yourself in a situation where you feel torn between following a program and fulfilling your own vacation goals.

Accommodations and meals add another dimension to the planning. Many retreat centers and ashrams serve vegetarian or vegan food; coffee and caffeine-containing teas are often forbidden—a welcome bonus for some, a challenge for others. Ashrams usually offer dormitory accommodations (four to seven people per room), with shared bathrooms. If you don't mind a little communal living, the low cost of retreat vacations makes them a persuasive option.

If you want the freedom to plan your day the way you want, choose the resort vacation. This is also the best bet if you're combining a yoga adventure with a family vacation, as few retreat facilities offer child care or options for a nonparticipating spouse.

Whichever option you choose, any yoga vacation can be a deeply transforming experience that helps you develop a new sense of yourself and what's important in your life. Peace, strength, serenity, renewed vigor, and better health are just some of the souvenirs that you'll bring home. Yoga retreats enable you to meet fellow travelers on the spiritual path, learn new techniques for creating greater inner balance, and above all, have fun and explore both the outer and the inner wonders of life.

Lucielle Hall is a freelance writer living in Iowa who specializes in natural health–related topics and whose work has appeared in several magazines, including Yoga Journal.

Yoga & Healing Retreats

CALIFORNIA

Esalen Institute   Big Sur, California

The Esalen Institute was founded in 1962 as an alternative educational center for the exploration of what the British writer Aldous Huxley called the "human potential": "unrealized human capacities that lie beyond the imagination." Esalen soon became known for its blend of Eastern and Western philosophies; eclectic workshops; visiting philosophers, psychologists, artists, and religious thinkers; and natural hot springs. Esalen is on 27 acres of Big Sur coastline that was once home to a Native American tribe called the Essalen.

Overnight visits and weekend and five-day workshops are offered. The Experiencing Esalen workshop, available periodically, offers an overview of practices such as Gestalt psychology, massage, sensory awareness, and meditation. The pool, hot springs, and massage areas are clothing optional.

Guest Yoga Teachers? Yes. Including Lilias Folan, Thomas Michael Fortel, Deborah Anne Medow, Chuck Miller, Shiva Rea.

Types of Yoga Classes Hatha. Once daily (more often during yoga retreats). No extra charge.

Services Craniosacral therapy, deep-tissue massage, Hellerwork, Feldenkrais, Rolfing.

Other Classes Dance, Continuum Movement, meditation, qigong.

Recreation Hiking, mineral springs, swimming.

Children's Program? Yes. For ages one to six.

In the United States, Esalen is probably the most extraordinary retreat center because of its location right on the cliffs of Big Sur. The forest, rock formations, and ocean all surround Esalen—it is an amazing combination. The gardens seem like something out of a Dr. Seuss book—the dahlias were the size of sunflowers! There is some special qi surrounding Esalen. Besides being one of the most beautiful places in the world, the massage is amazing, and there is nothing better than watching the sun set and the moon rise from the hot springs. Usually three or four retreats are going on at once, so you have a sense of being part of a larger community. A river runs through the grounds to the ocean and the meditation center sits next to it. And the history. . . Esalen has been a major force in America's spiritual development.

—Shiva Rea, yoga instructor, Venice, California

Accommodations 94 beds in double and triple rooms, 16 bunk beds, 12 sleeping bag spaces.

Dining Included. Vegan, vegetarian, some fish and chicken.

Attire/What to Bring Standard yoga attire, sun/insect protection, hiking boots, swimsuit, flashlight, earplugs.

Travel Information Esalen is about 100 miles from San Francisco International Airport and 30 miles from the Monterey airport; $30 shuttle service from Monterey airport available on Friday nights (reservations required).

Rates $130–$150 per person per night. Weekend $485 per person. Five-day stay $885 per person.

Contact Highway 1, Big Sur, CA 93920; tel: 831-667-3000, 831-667-3005 (reservations); fax: 408-667-2724; www.esalen.org.

The Growing Edge Retreat   Big Sur, California

The Growing Edge is a very intimate retreat center. The view is amazing, overlooking the ocean. The Ayurvedic treatments are wonderful. I highly recommend this retreat center for individuals and small groups.

—Shiva Rea, yoga instructor,
 Venice, California

The Growing Edge is an unpretentious retreat center poised on a cliff overlooking the Pacific that offers a private beach cove and miles of trails. The land, once home to the Essalen Native American tribe, is still considered sacred. An extended "family" of practitioners and a small residential staff work to create a supportive, healthy environment. The intimate guest house is ideally situated at the water's edge.

From May through October, stays of two nights or more are available. Each one-of-a-kind room has a view of the ocean and the Big Sur coastline. An organic continental breakfast is included. The fully stocked, communal kitchen is available to those who wish to prepare meals. (Cooking meat or fish is not allowed.)

Extended stays of one to three months are also possible. Visitors share the common space in the guest house and on the grounds, including an expansive living room, dining sunroom, communal kitchen, patio, grassy lawn, and private beach cove. Each person is responsible for his or her own food. Rooms are generally reserved on a one person–one room basis, although the master suite and the patio room can accommodate a couple.

From November through April, six-month winter residencies are offered—an ideal amount of time for completing a stalled novel or recovering from intense stress. Personal interviews are required.

Ayurvedic lifestyle consultations are available from David Howard, who draws on elements of Ayurveda (the Indian science of self-healing practiced for over 5,000 years), a wide range of botanical knowledge, and contemporary Western nutritional science. Or take an aromatherapy steam treatment followed by a warm oil massage. Morning yoga classes for all levels or a personalized introduction to basic yoga and meditation are taught by Ana Poirier.

Guest Yoga Teachers? Yes. Including Chitra Giauque, Beth Greenfield, Shiva Rea.

Types of Yoga Classes Hatha. Once daily. No extra charge.

Services Ayurveda, massage, steam room, Jyotish (Indian astrology).

Other Classes Ayurveda, meditation.

Recreation Hiking.

Children's Program? No.

Accommodations Four guest rooms that can accommodate a total of nine people; a yurt with a double bed and two group rooms.

Dining Breakfast included. No alcohol permitted.

Attire/What to Bring Standard yoga attire, hiking boots, sun/insect protection, rain gear, flashlight.

Travel Information The Growing Edge is located on the ocean side of the Pacific Coast Highway (Highway 1), about an hour's drive (40 miles) south from the Carmel/Monterey airport.

Rates January–April $95–$165 per night. May–December $140–$225 per night. Two-day minimum stay.

Contact Abalone Gulch, Big Sur, CA 93920; tel: 831-667-2366; fax 831-667-0237; www.growingedge.org.

Tassajara Zen Mountain Center   Carmel Valley, California

Tassajara is the perfect place for those drawn to the contemplative rhythms of monastic life and community. Located on cliffs above the Pacific, Tassajara is a Zen Buddhist community established by San Francisco Zen Center in 1966. From May through August, Tassajara offers workshops and retreats and public use of its hot springs. From September through April, the monastery is closed to the public for traditional monastic training. Three vegetarian meals are served daily in the dining room. The bathhouse complex contains separate facilities for men and women. (Mixed bathing takes place in the men's bathhouse at scheduled times.) Each bathhouse includes a tiled plunge, decks, steam room, showers, and an enclosed tub

Some come to Tassajara simply for the gourmet food, hot springs soaks, and hikes to a narrow canyon swimming hole. But guests can also join the Zen students and teachers in daily zazen practice and chanting. Tassajara also offers "guest practice" slots each season for those who want to make their stay more affordable—and deepen their experience of Tassajara's Zen community—by working half the day. When I went as a guest practitioner, I spent a lot of time in Tassajara's famous kitchen doing culinary meditation and picking up some great cooking techniques.

—Colleen Morton Busch, *Yoga Journal* senior editor

room for private baths. Bathing suits are required in the swimming pool. Guests are asked to wear clothing over their bathing suits while walking around Tassajara. Area hiking is exceptional, especially in the spring, when wildflowers cover the hills and meadows.

Guest Yoga Teachers? Yes. Including Victoria Austin, Edward Brown, Deirdre Carrigan, Judith Hanson Lasater, Patricia Sullivan.

Types of Yoga Classes Iyengar. Twice daily. No extra charge.

Services Traditional Japanese tea ceremony.

Other Classes Meditation, Zen philosophy, cooking.

Recreation Swimming, hiking, mineral baths, sauna, plunge pools.

Children's Program? No.

Accommodations 36 cabins (six with Japanese shikibuton foam mattresses and tatami mat floors), all equipped with kerosene lamps; one suite.

Dining Included. Vegetarian.

Attire/What to Bring Modest yoga attire, boots, long pants, and a long-sleeve shirt for hiking, swimsuit, sun/insect protection.

Travel Information Access to Tassajara from Jamesburg (135 miles south of San Francisco International Airport and 30 miles south of the Monterey airport) is a 14-mile dirt road that takes more than an hour to drive and cannot be safely navigated by all cars. You can take the Tassajara eight-passenger, four-wheel-drive stage. Park your car at Jamesburg and board the stage. The stage boards at 10:30 AM and departs Jamesburg daily at 10:45 AM. The stage usually departs Tassajara daily at 3 PM. Roundtrip fare is $35 per person. Reservations are required.

Rates $85–$150 per person per night, double occupancy. Dormitory $70–$84 per person per night. No credit cards.

Contact 39171 Tassajara Road, Carmel Valley, CA 93924; tel: 415-865-1899; fax: 415-865-1892; www.sfzc.com.

Harbin Hot Springs   Middletown, California

Harbin Hot Springs is a nonprofit retreat center located on 1,160 acres of woodlands in Northern California's wine country. In the 1880s, people suffering from dyspepsia, rheumatism, or gout came to "take the waters." The natural spring pools are still the main attraction, but now they're clothing-optional. Guests can also receive massages, attend workshops and daily yoga classes, and hike.

Guest Yoga Teachers? Yes. Including Tim Thompson.

Types of Yoga Classes Hatha, Standing Wave (combines a deep diaphragmatic breath practice with postures). Three times daily. No extra charge.

Services Massage, reflexology, acupressure, facials, aromatherapy, watsu.

Other Classes Dance, Twelve Step.

Recreation Hiking, soaking pools, swimming.

Children's Program? No. Minimum age 18 to stay in rooms.

Accommodations Camping, dormitory, and rooms with private and shared bathrooms.

Dining Not included. Health food store and three restaurants: Stonefront Restaurant, Blue Room Café, Poolside Café la Sirena.

Attire/What to Bring Standard yoga attire, bedding, towels, flashlight, sandals, hiking boots, sun/insect protection.

Travel Information Harbin Hot Springs is 100 miles north of San Francisco International Airport.

Rates Dormitory $35–$50 per person per night. Rooms $55–$220 per night. Additional adult per room $30–$40. On weekends and holidays, a two-night minimum stay is required for rooms. Camping $25–$30 per person per night.

Contact PO Box 782, Middletown, CA 95461; tel: 707-987-2477; www.harbin.org.

The yoga classes at Harbin are solid enough for advanced practitioners, yet not overwhelming for beginners. And the surrounding landscape is amazing. You can see why Native Americans thought this to be a sacred place. I recommend hiking the nearby trails. Afterward, going from the hot pool to the cold plunge can be a transformative experience. You can still sense the '60s and '70s here—you'll definitely overhear talk about crystal use and raw food diets. But even if you're not into that sort of thing, you'll enjoy Harbin—though you do have to be comfortable with nudity, since the pool and hot tub area are clothing-optional.

—Todd Jones, *Yoga Journal* senior editor

White Lotus Foundation   Santa Barbara, California

White Lotus Yoga is the collaborative effort of Ganga White and Tracey Rich, who meld two eclectic backgrounds and years of experience into a non-dogmatic teaching approach dedicated to helping students develop a well-balanced personal practice. At their 40-acre retreat in the Santa Ynez Mountains of Santa Barbara, California, this husband and wife team offers a complete yoga-immersion experience with programs ranging from weekend and weeklong getaways to teacher training programs.

White Lotus yoga is a flowing yoga practice that ranges from gentle to vigorous, depending on your ability or comfort level. In addition, class formats incorporate alignment, breath, and the theoretical understanding of yoga.

A personal retreat, available Monday through Thursday, includes accommodations in any of six yurts. Visitors can also stay in the loft, which accommodates three people, or camp along the creek or in the surrounding forest.

The grounds at the White Lotus are fabulous! You can pick fruit from the trees and the flowers are exquisite. On the property is a waterfall and swimming holes. When you stay in one of the yurts near the waterfall or at the point, you get a great walk each morning, where you can look out at the ocean and Santa Barbara.

At White Lotus, everyone—the staff and the participants—forms a strong, nurturing, and loving community. Beverly, in the office, asks that each participant send a photo before arriving. Then she greets everyone by name. I have never eaten so well in my entire life. Beatrix, the chef, creates the most amazing vegan meals, everything from sushi to tempeh burgers. You can't go hungry at the White Lotus. The kitchen is open, and everyone participates in "kitchen karma," where you wash your own dishes after each meal and help in the kitchen a few times during your stay. It's a wonderful opportunity to learn more about cooking.

—Julie Hooker, fourth grade teacher and yoga instructor, Sundance, Utah

Guests participate in daily hatha yoga classes, hike, swim, meditate, read in the library, and visit the many attractions in Santa Barbara. If you would like to study with Ganga and Tracey, call in advance to inquire about their schedules.

Guest Yoga Teachers? Yes. Including Seane Corn, Saul David Raye, Steve Ross.

Types of Yoga Classes White Lotus yoga. Once or more daily. No extra charge.

Services Therapeutic massage, deep tissue, stone therapy, Thai and other body therapy treatments.

Other Classes Pranayama, NIA.

Recreation Hiking, swimming.

Children's Program? No.

Accommodations Six yurts.

Dining Included in workshops. Personal retreatants are welcome to use the vegetarian kitchen.

Attire/What to Bring Towels (bath and beach), swimsuit, hiking or running shoes, shorts and long pants, toiletries, travel alarm, a flashlight with extra battcries, water bottle, hat and day pack for hikes, and jacket for cool evenings, sun/insect protection.

Travel Information White Lotus is 20 minutes from the downtown Santa Barbara airport.

Rates $65 per person per day; $120 per couple per day. One class per day included.

Contact 2500 San Marcos Pass, Santa Barbara, CA 93105; tel: 805-964-1944; fax: 805-964-9617; www.whitelotus.org.

Green Gulch Farm Zen Center   Sausalito, California

Green Gulch Farm Zen Center, located north of San Francisco in Marin County, is a Buddhist practice center in the Japanese Soto Zen tradition founded by Shunryu Suzuki Roshi. There is a temple, an organic farm and garden, and a guest house and conference center on the property.

Traditional Zen meditation retreats (one-, five-, and seven-day) are held each month. In addition, a number of weekend retreats include meditation, lectures, and group discussion. Some of the retreats are even designed for families.

A traditional Japanese teahouse is also on the farm property. Tea ceremony classes in the Urasenke tradition are offered weekly. Private viewings of the teahouse and tea ceremonies can be arranged.

The Green Gulch garden and nursery are open every day. Classes in organic gardening, pruning, flower arranging, and herb culture are offered throughout the year, and Green Gulch offers an apprenticeship in organic farming each summer.

Accommodations are available in the Lindisfarne Guest House, an octagonal building. Twelve rooms and six bathrooms encircle a 30-foot sunlit atrium where guests can gather to read or sit by the fire. Snacks and tea are available in the guest house kitchen. In addition, the Wheelwright Center has a suite with a kitchen and living area for families.

Guests join residents in early morning meditation and other activities until noon; afternoons and evenings are free. This program is available from Sunday through Thursday nights and requires a three-night minimum stay.

Guest Yoga Teachers? No.

Types of Yoga Classes Guests practice karma yoga by volunteering to help with the upkeep of the farm. This includes kitchen duties, gardening, cleaning, etc.

Services Tea ceremony.

Other Classes Zen meditation, writing, gardening, sewing, Twelve Step, sensory awareness.

Recreation Hiking, gardening.

Children's Program? Yes. Young people's lecture first Sunday of each month for ages 10 and above; ongoing Coming of Age program for ages 11 to 13.

Accommodations 12 rooms, one cottage.

Dining Included. Three vegetarian meals daily.

Attire/What to Bring Comfortable clothes for meditation, hiking boots, sun/insect protection.

Travel Information Green Gulch is 27 miles from San Francisco International Airport.

Rates $75–$105 per night, single occupancy. Cottage $200 per night. Two-night minimum stay.

Contact 1601 Shoreline Highway, Sausalito, CA 94965; tel: 415-383-3134; fax: 415-383-3128; www.sfzc.org.

One of the best features of Green Gulch is undeniably its food—the amazingly fresh salads and simple but sumptuous soups. On retreat at Green Gulch, in addition to eating the fruits of the garden, you can wander through rows of flowers, vegetables, and fruit trees as the seasons change, or walk along the ridge trail overlooking the Pacific Ocean. One of the best New Years I ever had was spent at Green Gulch, meditating in a zendo with wall-to-wall zafus, listening to the lapping waves on Muir Beach, and ringing a giant bell 108 times as one year gave way to another.

—Colleen Morton Busch, *Yoga Journal* senior editor

There's always something going on at Spirit Rock—from classes to daylong or monthlong retreats—to help us tap into our innermost selves. A busy place—it doesn't feel busy, but rather, dedicated to creating a practice space where Buddhist teachings are experienced and embodied. Opportunities for kindness lurk around every corner: My battery went dead at Spirit Rock once, and the caretaker came readily to my rescue with a jump start and some conversation to pass the time.

—Colleen Morton Busch, *Yoga Journal* senior editor

Spirit Rock Meditation Center   Woodacre, California

Spirit Rock Meditation Center is dedicated to the teachings of the Buddha and vipassana meditation. The center offers ongoing classes and daylong and residential retreats. The Spirit Rock land was purchased in 1987 from the Nature Conservancy. In 1990, a meditation hall, administrative office, and caretaker's quarters were completed. In 1994, a kitchen/dining hall was built that can seat more than 100 people. The residential retreat center opened in July 1998 and currently hosts retreats that range from two nights to two months. The Spirit Rock property covers more than 400 acres, with forests, meadows, grasslands, pastures, and creeks.

Guest Yoga Teachers? No. Guest vipassana teachers.

Types of Yoga Classes Hatha. On Mondays and Wednesdays. $10 per class.

Other Classes Meditation, Buddhist philosophy.

Recreation Hiking.

Children's Program? Yes. Monday evening class for kindergarten to 6th-grade level. Teen meditation program for ages 12 to 18.

Accommodations 80 rooms. All bathrooms are shared.

Dining Included. Vegetarian.

Attire/What to Bring Modest yoga and meditation attire, layers of comfortable clothing, shoes that slip on and off easily, a pair of tennis or hiking shoes, sun/insect protection.

Travel Information Spirit Rock Meditation Center is located 40 miles north of the San Francisco and Oakland airports.

Rates $67–$87 per person per night. Two-night stay minimum.

Contact 5000 Sir Francis Drake Blvd., Woodacre, CA 94973; tel: 415-488-0164; fax: 415-488-0170; www.spiritrock.org.

Nourish Your Body A sound dietary regimen can be difficult to maintain when traveling. Prepare for skipped meals and altered schedules by packing small bags of dried fruit, seeds, nuts, energy bars, and firm fruits such as apples and oranges, according to Elson Haas, M.D., author of *The Staying Healthy Shopper's Guide: Feed Your Family Safely* (Celestial Arts, 1999). Dehydrated miso soup packets can help quell a queasy stomach as well as provide a nutritional boost.

—Kathleen Finn Mendola

COLORADO

Shambhala Mountain Center   Red Feather Lakes, Colorado

Shambhala Mountain Center, located on 600 acres in northern Colorado, is a center for beginning and advanced students of Buddhist teachings, yoga, and other contemplative disciplines. Weekend, weeklong, and monthlong yoga retreats are offered throughout the year.

Shambhala means "enlightened society"; it is also the name of the legendary Tibetan utopia. Shambhala Mountain Center is affiliated with Shambhala International, a network of 140 urban communities and seven rural retreat centers whose members believe that human beings are inherently wise, compassionate, and good, thus an enlightened society is possible.

Over the last few years the center has grown, adding more than 35,000 square feet of program, dining, and housing space. Shambhala Mountain Center is now able to accommodate more than 500 people during the summer season and 150 in the winter. Guests are asked to participate in rota (rotating work assignments).

Many guests will want to take the 20-minute walk to see the Great Stupa of Dharmakaya—a symbol of hope for peace, harmony, and equanimity for all beings. Stupa is a Sanskrit word that means "to heap" or "to pile up" and refers to the moundlike shape of the earliest stupas. The Buddha instructed his students to cremate his body and place his ashes and the remains of his bones in a stupa. There are many types of stupas, and they are a key element of Buddhist life in all countries where Buddhism is practiced. Most stupas are sealed monuments, but the first level of the Great Stupa of Dharmakaya is open to the public.

Guest Yoga Teachers? Yes. Including Katharine Kaufman, Claudia Kuhns, Tias Little, Sarah Powers, Jill Satterfield.

Types of Yoga Classes Hatha. Once daily. No extra charge.

Services N/A.

Other Classes Meditation, Shambhala training, shamanism, chanting.

Recreation Hiking.

Children's Program? Yes. Shotoku Children's Center for ages 3 to 15.

Accommodations Shambhala Lodge can host 60 program participants in 29 single and double rooms with 30 private full baths; the Red Feather Conference Center can host up to 75 guests; large, two-person tents.

I like teaching at the Shambhala Mountain Center. The facilities are nicely maintained and clean. The food is good, especially the vegetarian dishes. The accommodations are comfortable, and the land is breathtaking. There are opportunities to be close to wildlife. The hiking trails lead to really beautiful views, and the Great Stupa of Dharmakaya is truly a great work of art.

—Claudia Kuhns, yoga teacher, Denver, Colorado

Dining Included. Three meals daily. Vegetarian and vegan. Meat options are provided at some lunches and dinners.

Attire/What to Bring Modest yoga attire, mats, props, sun/insect protection, layered clothing, flashlight, bedding (if in tent or dorm), meditation shawl and cushion, battery-operated alarm clock, hiking boots.

Travel Information The center is 108 miles from Boulder. Greyhound Bus from Boulder to Fort Collins is $12 one way. Bus fare from the Denver airport to Fort Collins is $21 cash each way, paid to the driver, and Shambhala Mountain Center travel service between Fort Collins and the center is $30 each way.

Rates $110–$278 per person for two nights; prices vary with each program.

Contact 4921 County Road 68C, Red Feather Lakes, CO 80545; tel: 970-881-2184; fax: 970-881-2909; www.shambhalamountain.org.

HAWAII

Kalani Oceanside Retreat — Hilo, Big Island, Hawaii

Kalani's grounds and simple buildings seem less like a posh spa and more like an unusually nice summer camp transported to an idyllic tropical setting. Couple that with a variety of one-week yoga retreats, and you understand why yoga practitioners flock here throughout the year. Kalani is the only coastal lodging in Hawaii's largest conservation area, so you won't see high-rises from the nearby cliffs. Instead, watch turtles, dolphins, and migrating whales.

Seminar fees for most six-night Kalani-sponsored events range from $600 for campsite facilities to single occupancy in a monkeypod tree house with private bath for $1,600. Daily classes in hatha, Yin, Ashtanga, or Iyengar yoga are also available. Most classes take place in the Rainbow Assembly Room and four other wood-floor studios. Kalani, a nonprofit educational organization, also offers free hula classes and self-guided native plant treks.

You might initially be lured to Kalani for the yoga, but be sure to explore the surrounding rain forest, volcanic slopes, and dramatic coastline. Generally sunny days, light breezes and mild, year-round 60° to 80°F temperatures make it easy to enjoy Hawaii's southeast coast. The natural setting, healthful meals, and relaxed pace make Kalani an ideal setting for yoga.

Guest Yoga Teachers? Yes. Including Tracey Coddington, John Fliessbach, Marla Leigh, Lynn Minton, Dana Rae Pare, Yogi Raj, Shiva Rea, Diane Roberts, Kathy Vasquez.

If you're looking for Club Med-style pampering, Kalani might not be your cup of tea. You won't find a poolside bar or a gung ho activities director (although the staff is more than willing to turn you on to secret spots you'd never find on your own). But if your soul craves serenity, quiet, simplicity, and intimate communion with nature, Kalani will more than satisfy your desires.

—Todd Jones, *Yoga Journal* senior editor

Types of Yoga Classes Hatha with Kathy Elder year-round. Once or twice daily. $10 per class.

Services Massage, lomi lomi, watsu, craniosacral therapy, aromatherapy, Reiki method, energy work.

Other Classes Hawaiian storytelling, lauhala weaving, dance.

Recreation Kayaking, hiking, swimming, snorkeling.

Children's Program? No.

Accommodations Tree house, lodge, cottage, camping. Sleeps 117 guests.

Dining Included with yoga retreat. Vegetarian and vegan. Buffet: breakfast ($8), lunch ($10), dinner ($16).

Attire/What to Bring Standard yoga attire, yoga mat, sneakers/hiking shoes, a long-sleeve shirt and pants, flip-flops, shorts, T-shirts, swimsuit, sun/insect protection, flashlight, snorkel-mask-fins.

Travel Information Kalani is a 45-minute drive from the Hilo airport.

Rates Two-night yoga retreat $310–$450 per person, double occupancy. Accommodations only: $30 for camping to $240 for tree house per night, double occupancy.

Contact RR2 Box 4500, Pahoa, HI 96778; tel: 800-800-6886, 808-965-7828; fax: 808-965-0527; www.kalani.com.

Yoga Oasis   Pahoa, Big Island, Hawaii

As is evident from its name, Yoga Oasis is a yoga-centered retreat, offering both six-day workshops and daily yoga classes. The retreat center is on 26 acres of rain forest ripe with coconut palms, papaya, banana, mango, avocado, macadamia nut trees, and fragrant flowering plants. The solar-powered facility has a 1,600-square-foot yoga room with two screened walls that afford views into the jungle. The organic fruit orchard and garden are harvested to prepare the vegetarian cuisine. Yoga and food programs are designed to detox the body, build the immune system, heal injuries, reduce stress, and increase flexibility, stamina, and strength.

Yoga Oasis is 45 minutes from Hawaii Volcanoes National Park, home of Kilauea, an active volcano that continues to add new land to the Big Island, and a short drive from the ocean, natural thermal hot springs, sauna steam caves, a black sand beach, surfing, snorkeling, tide pools, Lava Tree State Park, and hiking along Green Mountain and Green Crater Lake. The retreat center is near the ocean yet in a remote area, so renting a car is recommended.

I loved the canopy of trees as you approach Yoga Oasis, which gives the feeling of going somewhere unique and hidden.

My wife and I stayed in the "tree house" apartment with a king-size bed, private bathroom, kitchen, and living room. We were very comfortable there, resting and reading. The food was mostly fresh and vegetarian, original, and delicious. The chef was very kind to work around my food allergies. (As an omnivore, I would have liked to have seen at least some fish on the menu.)

We did take yoga, as complete beginners, but the structure of the class allowed us to participate easily for most of the class, until they moved into more advanced stuff. At that point, we were given special attention and other exercises to do. The yoga space with the sprung floor and a floor-to-ceiling view of the jungle on two walls was terrific.

We each took a watsu treatment from Terry Cooke, an amazing woman we booked through the Oasis. At dawn, we went to the nearby hot ponds and were floated, moved, and caressed in the lava-heated water.

There are many activities off property. Green Lake was spectacular to swim in. The black sand beach was beautiful and rugged. And a day trip to walk on hot lava at Hawaii Volcanoes National Park is a must.

—Chris Magee, cinematographer,
Santa Monica, California

Work-study is available. Participants provide support to guests and staff and help with daily operations and maintenance. In return, you receive a room or tentalow accommodations, vegetarian meals, and five yoga classes per week. The positions are designed for energetic and responsible people, healthy in body and mind.

Guest Yoga Teachers? Yes. Including Wilbert Alix, Judith Alston, Glenn Butcher, Hayward Coleman, Victor Dubin, Ulrika Engman Felder, Shelli Morrison, Ira Rosen, Zofia.

Types of Yoga Classes Chi, hatha, partner. Once or twice daily. No additional charge.

Services Massage, lomi lomi, watsu, body treatments.

Other Classes Pranayama, meditation, acrobatics.

Recreation Natural thermal hot springs, sauna steam caves, swimming, surfing, snorkeling, hiking, tide pools, Hawaii Volcanoes National Park, eco-tours.

Children's Program? No.

Accommodations Rooms, jungle tentalows, pine cabin with shared and private baths. 30 guests total.

Dining Breakfast included in mini retreat. Two vegetarian meals per day in six-day retreat.

Attire/What to Bring Yoga mat, props, standard yoga attire; sunscreen, bathing suit, flashlight, beach towel, umbrella, snorkel, mask, boogie board, fins, hat, rain poncho, flip-flops, sweater, mosquito repellent.

Travel Information Yoga Oasis is 45 minutes from the Hilo airport.

Rates Mini yoga retreat $50–$125 per night, single occupancy; two-night minimum stay. Six-day retreat $950 single occupancy, $1,700 double occupancy.

Contact PO Box 1935, Pahoa, HI 96778; tel: 800-274-4446, 808-965-8460; www.yogaoasis.org.

Bamboo Mountain Sanctuary   Ha'iku, Maui, Hawaii

Bamboo Mountain is a contemplative sanctuary for pilgrims and travelers not interested in the tourist area on the other side of the island. This Japanese plantation house was built 50 years ago and later converted into a Zen monastery and the home of Robert Aitken Roshi's Maui Zendo of the Diamond Sangha. During the past few decades, this reclusive hide-away has attracted Zen students, artists, writers, poets, surfers, healers, dancers, and musicians.

The retreat's 62 acres are surrounded by groves of bamboo, palms, and eucalyptus. You can practically subsist off the garden's coconuts, bananas, papayas, passion fruits, and guavas. Bamboo Mountain, on the edge of the Ko'olau Forest Preserve, which stretches all the way to Hana, is close to jungle and volcano hiking, snorkeling, surfing, and windsurfing.

The main building has six guest rooms with queen beds and either a private or semiprivate half bath (the full bath is shared). There is a communal vegetarian kitchen, an organic vegetable garden, an ocean-view outdoor hot tub, a common room, and group meditation room.

A daily meditation (zazen-style) takes place in the zendo each morning and is open to all residents or guests. Since Bamboo Mountain Sanctuary has its roots in both Zen Buddhism and classical yoga, it welcomes all forms of devotional service.

The residential community sponsors a weekly kirtan (devotional celebration). Classes in yoga, tai chi, and hula are offered regularly on the premises. Healing therapies such as massage, lomi lomi, and acupuncture are also available. A weekly Lakota-style sweat lodge ceremony on the volcano is open to all guests.

Guest Yoga Teachers? No.

Types of Yoga Classes Hatha. Once daily.

Services Massage, lomi lomi, acupuncture.

Other Classes Meditation, tai chi, hula, Hawaiian chanting.

Recreation Hiking, snorkeling, surfing, windsurfing, hot tub, sweat lodge.

Children's Program? No.

Accommodations Six rooms, one deluxe apartment suite. One full bath.

Dining None. Vegetarian kitchen available for guest use.

Attire/What to Bring Modest yoga attire, sneakers/hiking shoes, swimsuit, sun/insect protection.

Travel Information Bamboo Sanctuary is a 30-minute drive from the Kahului airport.

Rates $60 per night, single occupancy. $80 per night, double occupancy.

Contact 1111 Kaupakalu Road, Ha'iku, HI 96708; tel: 808-572-4897; fax: 808-572-8848; www.maui.net/~bamboomt/.

I found little-known Bamboo Mountain by a unique intuitive process. I knew at once it would provide the ideal setting for my inner work and monthlong retreat. This is a small community of yogis and Zen practitioners near quiet Ha'iku, Maui. I had the freedom to pursue my own schedule with the option of yoga classes, zendo meditation, and bodywork available.

For my room I chose the 20-foot canvas dome perched on a ridgetop overlooking a guava and kukui grove, with a stunning view of Haleakala. It had a mosquito-netted double bed, chair and ottoman, desk, and small altar table. The slender wraparound deck led to a small screened kitchen and bath with blue roof tiles. Food shopping and preparation was my responsibility.

I participated in twice-weekly pranic yoga classes with instructor Margo Gal in Bamboo Mountain's gorgeous yoga room, the Kali Temple of Spiritual Emergence. It was a nice complement to my Anusara practice. Margo is attentive, highly skilled, and also a certified Ayurvedic bodyworker. Acupuncture, Hawaiian hot rock massage, and Ayurvedic bodywork are some of the modalities I enjoyed at Bamboo Mountain, as well as watsu at nearby Mana Le'a Gardens.

—Patricia Berger, yoga teacher, Coeur d'Alene, Idaho

Hale Akua Shangri-La   Ha'iku, Maui, Hawaii

Driving to the gate of Hale Akua Shangri-La, I felt all of my tension and worries literally wash away with the sounds of the Pacific Ocean. The grounds are charming, including lush gardens and fruit you can pick straight off the vine. The views are tremendous, and you can spend the whole day hanging on a hammock or exploring nearby waterfalls or hikes. Practicing yoga here was truly magical; the groundskeeper and manager, Madhava, has an eclectic background; he lived on a Sivananda ashram for many years and has studied with many great teachers. It is a quiet and introspective place; there is even a cave if you really want some-place to contemplate. The overall feeling of this hidden gem is that of an extended family; we even had a Saturday night potluck dinner, with people from the community bringing their favorite vegetarian dish, and we shared stories and a great meal.

—Nora Isaacs, *Yoga Journal* managing editor

This hideaway has been attracting spiritual seekers for decades. The center began as a community living space in the 1980s and over time went through several incarnations, from tantric learning center to a bed and breakfast to its current form, a 16-room retreat center. The director, manager, and yoga teacher is Madhava D'Addario, who trained in the Sivananda, Kripalu, Ashtanga, and Iyengar yoga traditions for 30 years before settling at Shangri-La in 1993. D'Addario teaches six Vinyasa-based flow classes each week, as well as private lessons in yoga, breathing, and meditation. Shangri-La, surrounded by mango, papaya, guava, and coconut palms and perched on a cliff 300 feet above the Pacific Ocean, is ideal for retreating from the world. A labyrinth, two clothing-optional hot tubs, and ozone-treated pool further aid contemplation and relaxation.

Guest Yoga Teachers? Occasionally. Consult retreat listing in website.

Types of Yoga Classes Vinyasa-based flow yoga daily. No extra charge.

Services Massage, polarity therapy, craniosacral therapy, Trager therapy, lomi lomi.

Other Classes Pranayama.

Recreation Nature walks, horseback riding, swimming, hot tub.

Children's Program? No.

Accommodations 16 rooms.

Dining Breakfast included. Kitchen facilities available for cooking.

Attire/What to Bring Standard yoga attire, yoga mat, sneakers/hiking shoes, swimsuit, sun/insect protection.

Travel Information Hale Akua Shangri-La is 18 miles from the Kahului airport.

Rates $60–$165 per room per night. Add $25 for each additional person per night.

Contact Star Route 1, Box 161, Ha'iku, Maui HI 96708; tel: 888-368-5305, 808-572-9300; fax: 808-572-6666; www.haleakua.com.

Mana Le'a Gardens   Ha'iku, Maui, Hawaii

Mana means the "spiritual power of life" and le'a is the Hawaiian word for "happiness and joy." Mana Le'a provides just that: a spiritual and nurturing environment where it seems impossible not to be joyful.

This private conference center is located on 55 acres of lush gardens, rolling hills, and ocean-view meadows. From the minute you step on the grounds, you are surrounded by the aroma of exotic flowers, the beauty of the tropical gardens, and the sounds of flowing waterfalls.

The retreat center offers comfortable, simple lodgings and vegetarian food. Although miles away from any town, it is within minutes of world-famous windsurfing and swimming beaches such as Ho'okipa Beach and Baldwin Beach in Paia. About 25 yoga retreats are offered each year. Make sure you sign up for one before you arrive—drop-in classes are not available.

Guest Yoga Teachers? Yes. Including Wendy Andersen, Baron Baptiste, Mary Bersagel, Laurie Broderick-Burr, Georg Feuerstein, Thomas Fortel, JJ Gormley, Lee Guerreri, Jeanne Heileman, Mark Horner, Bryan Kest, Gary Kraftsow, Maya Lev, Judy Louie, Janet McLeod, Rosanna Nager, Dave Nelson, Mary Paffard, Kate Potter, Simone Simon, Amanda McMaine Smith, Gary Springfield, Max Strom, Rod Stryker, Rodney Yee.

Types of Yoga Classes Consult retreat listing on website; Bikram, Iyengar, Power, Ashtanga, raja, to name a few.

Services Watsu, massage, lomi lomi, shiatsu.

Other Classes Consult retreat listing on website; meditation, pranayama, body work, art, Alexander Technique, Pilates, to name a few.

Recreation Swimming, bath house, hot tub, Native American sweat lodge, volcano crater exploration, whale watching, snorkeling, scuba, sea kayaking, deep-sea fishing.

Children's Program? No.

Accommodations Private as well as dormitory rooms. Sleeps 36 guests.

Dining Included with yoga retreat. Vegetarian.

Attire/What to Bring Standard yoga attire, yoga mat, swimsuit, flashlight, beach towels, biodegradable bath articles, sun/insect protection, clothing for rain and possible cool evenings.

Travel Information Mana Le'a Gardens is 15 miles from the Kahului airport.

I decided to hold my retreat at Mana Le'a because I found it to be perfect in several ways: the accommodations are neither too fancy nor too funky; there is a wonderful pool surrounded by greenery, with a great slide; the food is nothing short of fabulous; it is reasonably priced; and the staff is very easy to work with. And Mana Le'a has a very nice studio for yoga. It's large enough to easily fit 20 people or more, is stocked with most of the props we use, has a wood floor, good lighting, and heat, and does not have many distracting features, such as mirrors or pictures.

Mana Le'a has a couple of cottages that are somewhat separate from the other rooms, which allow the group leader to have some privacy and space. The grounds are lush and green because Mana Le'a is located on the wet side of the island, which is also the less developed, less touristy side, far from the big hotels. There are not a lot of open grassy places, but the hot tub is a short walk from the main building, and the pool is a bit farther up the path, and there is a garden beyond that.

There is snorkeling and all the usual beach pleasures, plus plenty of hiking, either in a jungle setting or to Haleakala, the volcano.

—Maya Lev, owner, Yoga Center, Santa Cruz, California

Rates Varies with retreat. Rodney Yee's one-week retreat $1,500 per person, dorm-room occupancy, $1,725 per person, double occupancy.

Contact 1055 Kaupakalua Road, Ha'iku, HI 96708; tel: 800 233-6467, 808-572-8795; fax: 808-572-3499; www.maui.net/~mlg/.

INDIANA

Orbis Farm Retreat Center   Mauckport, Indiana

The Orbis Farm is a year-round retreat center, offering a variety of yoga workshops. It is located at the southernmost tip of Indiana, just 45 miles west of Louisville, Kentucky, on 75 acres of woodlands with plenty of walking trails. In the garden, beds of vegetables and 75 scented herbs provide much of the food for the farm's vegetarian cuisine. Yoga and tai chi are taught in the Yoga Pavilion. All guests stay in dormitory lodgings.

Guest Yoga Teachers? Yes. Including Thomas Fortel, Amanda McMaine Smith.

Types of Yoga Classes Kudalini, Hatha. Twice daily. No extra charge.

Services N/A.

Other Classes Tai chi, meditation.

Recreation Swimming, hot tub.

Children's Program? No.

Accommodations Dormitory; sleeps 20.

Dining Included.

Attire/What to Bring Standard yoga attire, mat, props, swimsuit, walking shoes, sun/insect protection.

Travel Information Orbis Farm is 45 miles west of the Louisville, KY, airport.

Rates Weekend retreat $200. Daylong workshops $60–$65.

Contact 8700 Ripperdan Valley Road SW, Mauckport, IN 47142; tel: 812-732-4657; www.orbisfarm.com.

I decided to hold a retreat at Orbis Farm because I was invited there for a "teacher's day" with Helen McMahan and fell in love with both the place and the two women who make it what it is—Helen and Betty. They had a vision that I was inspired by, and I wanted to be a part of it.

The dorm is cozy and turns into a slumber party of sorts at night. Men and women have separate facilities. I never cease to be amazed at the quality of delicious vegetarian foods presented, and with such love; much of the food is grown there in the huge organic garden.

A typical day consists of classes and meals flowing gracefully into each other, with a break in the afternoon after lunch. The workshop presenters have the option of bringing their own bodyworkers. This works well, as the therapist is then suited to the specific workshop participants.

Orbis Farm is situated on acres and acres of beautiful wooded land. There are hiking trails galore, an outdoor swimming pool, Jacuzzi hot tub, and ample space for relaxing alone or with friends.

—Amanda McMaine Smith, yoga teacher, Richmond, Kentucky

IOWA

The Raj   Fairfield, Iowa

Surrounded by 100 acres of meadows and woodlands, the Raj offers Ayurvedic beauty and healing treatments in a peaceful environment. Ayurveda is an ancient Indian health-care system, and its purification treatments are said to alleviate the damaging effects of stress and environmental toxins, thereby stimulating the body's natural healing abilities. Case studies on the Raj website show the wide range of benefits guests have experienced, including relief from arthritis and hypertension. However, you can also visit the Raj for its yoga classes and pampering spa. The first step if trying to treat a condition is a consultation with a medical doctor, who will prescribe treatments and lifestyle changes. Supplements are on sale in the Herb Room, along with teas, spices, and massage and essential oils. In the library on the second floor, guests can read, watch informative videos about Ayurveda, or relax on the adjoining balcony. All activities take place in a French-style main building. The lobby sets the tone with paintings from India coupled with elegant furniture. Suffice it to say, you won't be roughing it. The Raj is more of a healing sanctuary that focuses on clearing the toxins from the body than a traditional spa or yoga retreat.

Guest Yoga Teachers? No.

Types of Yoga Classes Hatha. Twice daily. No extra charge.

Services Ayurvedic health evaluations, aromatherapy, massage, facials, body treatments, shirodhara, herbal steam bath.

Other Classes Meditation, Vedic sound therapy, pranayama.

Recreation Gym available, walking.

Children's Program? No.

Accommodations 16 rooms with private bath.

Dining Included. Vegetarian.

Attire/What to Bring Standard yoga attire, walking shoes, sun/insect protection.

Travel Information The Raj is 108 miles from the Des Moines airport.

Rates $150 per night, double occupancy. Royal Skin Rejuvenation Program $645 per day.

Contact The Raj, 1734 Jasmine Avenue, Fairfield, IA 52556; tel: 800-248-9050, 641-472-9580; fax: 641-472-2496; www.theraj.com.

The food at the Raj is really good. The menu is all Ayurvedic and dosha balancing. It's really flavorful—you don't feel like you're starving. The Raj is very relaxing partly because there are no televisions. You are encouraged to relax in between treatments, which are intense but not painful. You can see your skin improve, which is the most noticeable way you can tell you're detoxing. And I lost five pounds without trying. One of the best sensory moments of my life was a synchronized massage with two massage therapists. There are some classes explaining Ayurveda, which are really informative, and the surrounding farmland is very beautiful and peaceful and good for long walks.

—Jennifer Barrett, editor, *Herb Quarterly*, West Hartford, Connecticut

I decided to go to the Paracelsus Clinic at Foxhollow because I desperately needed a retreat experience different from a Canyon Ranch-type of experience. Paracelsus Clinic is an extraordinary healing center. Having the Foxhollow spa down the road was the icing on the cake. The clinic and the spa are 1/2 mile from each other. I was given a bicycle to travel from one to the other. Both are situated on the same magnificent Kentucky farm. The green cornfields, endless blue sky, and symphony of birds chirping in the trees can calm most nervous conditions alone.

The clinic is a single-story, unassuming building. It was built entirely of organic materials. From every window there is a beautiful view of the gardens. The clinic houses a state-of-the-art medical facility that is fully licensed by the state of Kentucky. Near the clinic is the Manor House, where some people can lodge. I found the Manor House as well as the other small cottages for housing in need of updating aesthetically.

My room was a small, spare cottage with a comfortable king-size bed. The food was exemplary. Every lettuce leaf was grown on the property, and every loaf of bread kneaded and baked daily. There was no red meat, sugar, preservatives, or artificial sweeteners. Fresh fish and chicken alternated with tofu and tempeh.

I practiced yoga every day with Chaz Rough. His video, *Yoga for the Kid In All of Us,* is a favorite among my friends with small children. Chaz and I practiced a mixture of hatha, Iyengar, and Ashtanga. I enjoyed what Chaz calls "savasana unplugged." I meditated while he played his guitar.

—A Baltimore, Maryland, mother of two

KENTUCKY

Foxhollow   Crestwood, Kentucky

Some people visit Foxhollow to enjoy its spa services, yoga classes, pool, nature trails, and gourmet vegetarian cuisine. Others may come to stay for a week or two of analysis and treatment at the Paracelsus Clinic of Integrated Biological Medicine, which has two M.D.s and an osteopath on staff and utilizes a broad spectrum of alternative medicine disciplines to address your health problems. Nutritional evaluations for metabolic irregularities and food allergies are available. Other services include comprehensive blood/urine/saliva tests, hair mineral analysis, cardiovascular risk assessment evaluation, heavy metal detoxification, juicing therapy programs, hormonal balancing, and stress management counseling. Healing is complemented with spa services, vegetarian meals, and outdoor activities on the 1,300-acre working farm.

Guest Yoga Teachers? No.

Types of Yoga Classes Blend of Ashtanga, Iyengar, and Bikram. Thursday and Friday. $10 per class.

Services Facials, massage, reflexology, acupressure, craniosacral therapy, Reiki method, body treatments, hydrotherapy, shirodhara, bindi treatment, ear candling, aromatherapy, nail care, alternative medicine.

Other Classes Pilates, art therapy, pottery.

Recreation Golf, hiking, biking, horseback riding, tennis, swimming.

Children's Program? No. Minimum age over 10.

Accommodations 19 rooms, 4 cottages.

Dining Breakfast included. Other meals eaten in the restaurant. Vegetarian, with fish and chicken upon request.

Attire/What to Bring Standard yoga/workout attire, walking shoes, swimsuit, sun/insect protection.

Travel Information Crestwood is 20 miles from the Louisville airport.

Rates $57 to $150 per night, double occupancy.

Contact 8909 Highway 329, Crestwood, KY 40014; tel: 800-624-7080, 502-241-8621; fax: 502/241-3935; www.foxhollow.com.

MASSACHUSETTS

Kripalu Center for Yoga and Health   Lenox, Massachusetts

Kripalu, one of the largest centers for yoga in the U.S., began as an ashram for followers of Yogi Amrit Desai, who resigned as spiritual leader in 1994. Although Kripalu still has full-time residents, it is now more of a retreat center, offering workshops in a variety of yoga disciplines. If not participating in a specific workshop, a visitor's typical day includes two sessions of Kripalu yoga, meditation, and DansKinetics, a blend of yoga and dance.

Kripalu was formerly a Jesuit seminary, so accommodations are very simple. Drugs and alcohol are not tolerated, and lights must be out by 9:30 PM, although there are all-night lounges for those in dormitory accommodations. Breakfast is taken in silence between 7 AM and 8:30 AM.

Guest Yoga Teachers? Yes. Including Baron Baptiste, Rama Berch, Ana Forrest, Judith Lasater, Cyndi Lee, Esther Myers, François Raoult, Shiva Rea, Rod Stryker, Rodney Yee.

Types of Yoga Classes Kripalu. Twice daily. No extra charge.

Services Acupuncture, massage, positional therapy, shiatsu, reflexology, aromatherapy, Reiki, craniosacral therapy.

Other Classes Meditation, pranayama, DansKinetics.

Recreation Horseback riding, biking, hiking, cross-country skiing, swimming, sauna, Jacuzzi, gym.

Children's Program? Yes. For ages 5 to 12 and 9 to 19.

Accommodations Dormitory and double rooms. Sleeps more than 400 guests.

Dining Included. Vegetarian/vegan.

Attire/What to Bring Modest yoga attire, swimsuit, sun/insect protection hiking boots, cold weather gear in winter.

Travel Information Kripalu is about 45 miles from the Albany, NY, airport. Kripalu offers reduced-fare limousine service every Friday and Sunday.

Rates $89–$265 per person per night. Two-night minimum stay.

Contact West Street, Route 183, Lenox, MA 01240; tel: 800-741-7353, 413-448-3152; fax: 413-448-3384; www.kripalu.org.

The staff at Kripalu is uniformly friendly and helpful; the vegetarian cuisine is tasty and nourishing; the accommodations, which tend to be on the spartan side, are nonetheless serviceable—and affordable. If you go to attend a specific retreat or program, you also have access during your stay to a cornucopia of other classes and services, as well as special events like evening concerts. If you do visit Kripalu, be sure to treat yourself to at least one of their justly famed bodywork sessions (first-timers should do a one-hour Basic Kripalu Massage). Book your appointment in advance, and try to schedule it at the beginning of your stay, to help put you in the relaxed, peaceful, slow-paced, open-hearted frame of mind that will be most receptive to what Kripalu—both the place and its programs—offers. And if you're going to be there for more than a couple of days, allow time to explore some of the many local attractions, including Stockbridge Bowl, a lovely lake right across the road from Kripalu; Tanglewood music center, summer home of the Boston Symphony Orchestra, also right across the road; the historic towns of Lenox, Williams, and Stockbridge, and the beautiful Berkshires.

—Phil Catalfo, *Yoga Journal* senior editor

MONTANA

Feathered Pipe Ranch   Helena, Montana

Feathered Pipe is surrounded by national forests, so there is great hiking in the area. There is a tepee next to the lake at the bottom of a hill on the property. I found that area very soothing and calming—a good place to meditate. There is excellent vegetarian cuisine, and I like the way it is served—you sit on a cushion on the floor in the great room and eat at low tables. I studied with Judith Lasater when I was there, and they always attract a number of good yoga teachers. After a long day of hiking and yoga, the hot tub is a popular destination.

—Tim Noworyta, copywriter, editor, and yoga teacher, Chicago, Illinois

Feathered Pipe Ranch has been offering yoga and holistic programs for almost 30 years. Located in the Montana Rockies, the retreat center sits on sacred Native American land and is surrounded by miles of forested mountains, wildlife, and healing plants. Only one program is offered at a time, so plan your stay accordingly. Because most accommodations are tents, tepees, and yurts, visit Feathered Pipe May through September. You can swim in the on-property lake during the hottest days of summer.

If the spirit of the ranch is captured anywhere, it is in the kitchen. Gourmet natural food is the specialty, and whole, organic ingredients are used.

Guest Yoga Teachers? Yes. Including Kausthub Desikachar, Mary Dunn, Lilias Folan, JJ Gormley, Judith Lasater, Cyndi Lee, Dean Lerner, Shiva Rea, Erich Schiffmann, John Schumacher, Lois Steinberg, Patricia Walden, Rodney Yee.

Types of Yoga Classes Hatha, Ashtanga, Iyengar. Twice daily. No extra charge.

Services Massage.

Other Classes N/A.

Recreation Hiking, swimming, volleyball.

Children's Program? No.

Accommodations 6 cabins, 12 dorm beds, tepees, tents, and yurts.

Dining Included. Primarily vegetarian; occasionally chicken or fish is served.

Attire/What to Bring Standard yoga attire, hiking or athletic shoes, swimsuit, sun/insect protection.

Travel Information Feathered Pipe is 14 miles from the Helena airport. Roundtrip van transportation is available for $40. Schedule in advance.

Rates $1,000–$1,650 per person per week. Double room with a private bath is an additional $300 per person. Double room with shared bath is an additional $200.

Contact PO Box 1682, Helena, MT 59624; tel: 406-442-8196, fax: 406-442-8110; www.featheredpipe.com.

NEW MEXICO

Ten Thousand Waves   Santa Fe, New Mexico

When you arrive at Ten Thousand Waves, a Japanese-style hot springs resort, you are given a cotton kimono and sandals to wear as you go between the communal areas and the many hot tubs. All tubs are maintained at 104° to 106°F (except Waterfall, which is body temperature) and have nearby cold plunges. During the hottest months, two regular tubs are also brought down to body temperature. Premium tubs cost $23 to $27 per person for 55 minutes. Four regular tubs are outdoors, have redwood decks, accommodate up to six people, and cost $19.75 per person for 55 minutes. Communal tubs are $13.50 per person with no time limits. (Communal tub access is included with body treatment prices.) Bathing suits are optional in all tubs during the day, but are required after 8:15 PM in the communal tub and while receiving aquatic massage (watsu). Bathing suits can be rented at the front desk for $1.50.

At the spa, facials, massages, hand, foot, and scalp treatments, body treatments, and watsu are available. Although there are no yoga classes, the Thai massage combines yoga-like stretches, pressure points, and lengthening of the muscles. Reservations are recommended. Ten Thousand Waves is basically a day spa, although there are nine guest rooms. If you want to stay overnight, book well in advance.

Guest Yoga Teachers? No.

Types of Yoga Classes N/A.

Services Facials; massage; hand, foot, and scalp treatments; body treatments; watsu; Thai massage, body wraps, four hands massage.

Other Classes N/A.

Recreation Hot tubs.

Children's Program? No.

Accommodations Nine guest rooms. Japanese-style detached guesthouse, Japanese-style traditional room, Japanese adobe-style rooms.

Dining Not included. Light snacks, baked goods, fresh fruit, bottled water, drinks, and sodas can be bought in the lobby.

Attire/What to Bring Swimsuit, sun/insect protection.

Travel Information Ten Thousand Waves is 68 miles from the Albuquerque airport.

It was a cool fall evening when we arrived at Ten Thousand Waves, a Japanese-style hot springs resort, after a lovely drive through the mountains outside of Santa Fe. The facility includes numerous tubs, massage and spa treatment rooms (both private and communal), and Japanese-style lodging.

The spa looks like it was lifted from Kyoto and dropped into the New Mexico hills. When we checked in we were given cotton kimonos and sandals to use. In a few minutes we were on our way to the dressing rooms, which included lockers and showers. Just a short walk away were the tub facilities.

Once we finished soaking and warming in the tubs, we went back to the lodge, where we waited for our treatment. Tea and water were available, and a retail shop with Japanese-style spa goods is close at hand. There are a variety of treatments offered, and I selected a private hot rock massage. In a simple room with a view of the hillside, I received an extensive and thoroughly relaxing treatment. I waited for a while in the room after my treatment, not quite wanting to get up. It was late at night when we walked down the hill in a light drizzle, the mist rising up from the bamboo-lined walk. It was a lovely experience and one that led to a very good night's sleep.

—Michael Kleeman, environmentalist, San Francisco Bay Area

Rates $190–$285 per night, double occupancy. Additional person or pet $15 per night.

Contact 3451 Hyde Park Road, Santa Fe, NM 87501; tel: 505-992-5025, 505-982-9304 (reservations); fax: 505-989-5077; www.tenthousandwaves.com.

NEW YORK

Omega Institute   Rhinebeck, New York

When Omega was founded in 1977, Americans, especially Baby Boomers, were becoming more interested in health, psychology, and Eastern spirituality. Omega became a utopia for those embracing the "Me decade" and continues to be one of the country's largest holistic learning centers. Every year, more than 20,000 people attend workshops, retreats, and conferences at the 140-acre facility in Rhinebeck, New York, and at other sites around the country. The Rhinebeck location is closed during the winter, from November through April.

Omega is not affiliated with any specific spiritual or yoga tradition. There are more than 40 yoga programs each year from a variety of teachers instructing in different disciplines. The Omega Institute offers a large number of other workshops as well, in such diverse topics as body-centered approaches; career, leadership, and community; dance and movement; fine arts and crafts; food and cooking; intuitive development; mind-body transformation; music, rhythm, and voice; native wisdom and shamanism; nature and environment; theater and performance art; and writing and language. At the Omega Wellness Center, you can use the sauna or have a massage or facial. Choose from various types of bodywork and consultations offered by licensed holistic health practitioners.

Guest Yoga Teachers? Yes. Including Baron Baptiste, Beryl Bender Birch, Thom Birch, Kofia Busia, TKV Desikachar, Lilias Folan, John Friend, Sharon Gannon, Gary Kraftsow, Cyndi Lee, David Life, Sarah Powers, Shiva Rea, John Schumacher, David Swenson, Rodney Yee.

Types of Yoga Classes Iyengar, Ashtanga, Power, Bikram, Kundalini, Vinyasa, Jivamukti. Twice daily. No extra charge.

Services Massage, facials, bodywork, reflexology, shiatsu, Reiki method, acupuncture.

Other Classes Meditation, tai chi on regular basis, plus other workshops.

Recreation Basketball, canoeing, jogging, tennis, volleyball, sauna.

I've been to Omega eight times, although not for a yoga retreat every time. Once I took knitting with the actress Karen Allen! But the yoga workshop with John Schumacher was a great experience. Iyengar teachers from New York City were taking John's class because he is so good. Omega attracts very good teachers, but even their staff yoga teachers are good. If you attend another type of workshop, you can still take Omega staff-taught yoga in the morning and evening—it is just a more general class for all levels.

The dorms are rustic, and the single and double rooms are like your basic motel/hotel accommodations—simple but nice. Omega has great vegetarian food, a fabulous bookstore where you can always get ice cream, and a cafe open until 11:30 PM. Basically it's like an adult camp. Because there are five or six different workshops going on at once, if you don't like your class, you can always switch. The grounds are beautiful—there is a lovely meditation garden and a swimming lake. Omega attracts all types of people: I've hung out with 16 and 17 years olds and also with some grandmothers studying shamanism.

—Cynthia Kling, writer and serious yoga student, New York

Children's Program? Yes. Including Family Weeks and Run Camp.

Accommodations 208 rooms and cabins, 11 dorms, 50 camping sites.

Dining Included. Vegetarian buffet with some dairy and fish.

Attire/What to Bring Towel, pillow, and bed linens if sleeping in the dorms or tent cabins; swimsuit, standard yoga attire, hiking boots, sun/insect protection.

Travel Information Omega is 90 miles north of New York City. Charter bus service from New York (near Penn Station) is $25. Call 800-944-1001. The closest airport is Stewart Airport in Newburgh, NY. Airport shuttle service is $30. Call 800-944-1001.

Rates $155–$750 per person per night. Camping $120–$320.

Contact 150 Lake Drive, Rhinebeck, NY 12572; tel: 800-944-1001, 845-266-4444; fax: 845-266-3769; www.eomega.org.

NORTH CAROLINA

DeerHaven Hills Farm & Yoga Eco-Center   Columbus, North Carolina

At DeerHaven Hills Farm & Yoga Eco-Center in the rolling foothills of the Blue Ridge Mountains, owners Michael and Barbara Gail Blate have created a sustainable center complete with organic vineyards and vegetable garden. A teacher of spiritual yoga since 1986, Michael emphasizes that yoga is not a practice but an entire way of life, and teaches a version of jnana yoga, or the way of wisdom and knowledge. DeerHaven is open year-round and can accommodate up to 10 people at a time. Barbara also provides instruction in cooking and quilting.

Guest Yoga Teachers? Yes. Including Patricia Streit.

Types of Yoga Classes Jnana, Ananda, hatha. Included in retreat fees.

Services Acupressure.

Other Classes Cooking, quilting, chanting.

Recreation Hiking, gardening.

Children's Program? No.

Accommodations Four rooms.

Dining Included in retreat fees. Vegetarian/vegan available.

Attire/What to Bring Standard yoga attire, hiking boots.

DeerHaven is for people who wish to spend some quality time reading, meditating, communing with nature, and learning more about spiritual aspects of yoga with Michael, who is a wise and experienced teacher. You can help prepare the farm's main, noon-time vegan meal. There is nothing scheduled in the afternoons, since this is the permanent residents' time of siesta, meditation, and turning inward. This leaves time for guests to explore the nearby Blue Ridge mountain scenery or just walk the farm's 100 acres of woods and vineyards. Evenings are usually spent doing hatha yoga, qigong, or singing bhajans (sacred chants). I see visiting DeerHaven Hills Farm as a kind of immersion experience into the lives of full-time yogis.

—Barry Sultanoff, M.D., holistic physician and author, Maui, Hawaii

Travel Information The farm is 45 minutes from the Greenville, SC, and Asheville, NC, airports and 90 minutes from the Charlotte, NC, airport.

Rates Cabin for three days and two nights $250. Weekend retreat $397.

Contact PO Box 1460l, Columbus, NC 28722-1460; tel: 800-747-0306, 828-863-4660; fax: 828-863-4575; www.yogafarm.com.

OREGON

Breitenbush Hot Springs Retreat   Detroit, Oregon

Breitenbush is a little haven of healing deep in the Oregon forest. Make sure to walk out to the Meadow Pools, where you can rest your head on the rocks in natural, sand-bottom pools and gaze at the Breitenbush River rolling by or at a star-studded sky if it's nighttime.

—Colleen Morton Busch, *Yoga Journal* senior editor

At Breitenbush Hot Springs, you can soak in the healing waters 24 hours a day. Located in the Cascade Mountains, this retreat has one of the largest concentrations of hot springs in the area. Relax in the natural rock–lined Meadow Pools overlooking the Breitenbush River, or make the rounds at the Medicine Wheel Tubs—four tubs offering four different temperatures and a cold plunge. There is also a natural spring-fed sauna.

The hot springs at Breitenbush were created by a combination of volcanoes and glaciers thousands of years ago. Many Native American tribes visited the springs to hunt, fish, pick berries, and use the springs for healing and rituals.

The lodge was built 70 years ago, and the facility attracts a large number of yoga teachers each year who come here to hold retreats. Even if you don't come for a workshop, you can participate in any of the various classes, hikes, and events hosted by Breitenbush. Free one- to two-hour classes are led by Breitenbush staff every day of the week and include yoga, meditation, hiking, nature walks, ecstatic dance, drum circles, sweat lodge ceremonies, and dharma talks.

On the Breitenbush land and surrounding area you can camp, jog, bike, swim, and kayak. Hiking and cross-country skiing are available on one of the many area trails.

Visit the Vista Healing Arts Center for a massage, hydrotherapy, or Reiki method session. Or visit the greenhouse, where spices and other plants are sometimes grown for use in the kitchen. Vegetarian cuisine in served in the dining room.

Guest Yoga Teachers? Yes. Including Ana Forrest, Hanneli Francis, Geoffrey Gordon, Jean Hindle, Sarahjoy Marsh, Vin Martí, Shannon McCall, Ki McGraw, David Newman, Jeffrey "Page" Redman, Lorilee Schoenbeck, Bob Smith, Lama Somananda Tulku, Jai Uttal, Winky Wheeler, Laura Yon-Brooks, Nan Yurkanis.

Types of Yoga Classes A blend of Hatha, Kundalini, and restorative. Usually once daily. No extra charge.

Services Watsu, Reiki method, trigger point release, hydrotherapy, massage.

Other Classes Meditation, dance, drumming, dharma talks.

Recreation Hiking, hot tubs, biking, swimming, skiing, sweat lodge.

Children's Program? Family retreats.

Accommodations 42 cabins, 20 tents.

Dining Included. Three vegetarian meals daily.

Attire/What to Bring Standard yoga attire, hiking boots, swimsuit, sun/insect protection, cold weather/ski attire in winter, bedding (or you can rent bedding for $15).

Travel Information Breitenbush is about 110 miles from the Portland airport.

Rates $40–$90 per person per night.

Contact PO Box 578, Detroit, OR 97342; tel: 503-854-3314; fax: 503-854-3819; www.breitenbush.com.

SOUTH CAROLINA

Hilton Head Health Institute   Hilton Head Island, South Carolina

Hilton Head Health Institute is more of a medical retreat than a vacation. Founded in 1976, it was created for serious weight loss, behavioral modification, and stress reduction. The three programs, for male and female adults of all ages, are Weight Control, Disease Prevention, and Stress Management (and who couldn't use more ways to deal with stress?). If none of those appeal, there are also six specialty theme weeks: Healthy Table; Mindful Eating; Making Peace with Mind, Body, and Food; Making Order out of Chaos; Living Consciously and Creating a Balanced Life; and Healthy Retreat. Each guest is encouraged to establish healthier eating and exercise habits and accept personal responsibility for change.

Spouses and companions who are not participating in the program can accompany attendees and only have to pay for meals, which cost $55 per day or $350 per week. They can also enjoy golf and tennis at preferred rates.

Guest Yoga Teachers? No.

Types of Yoga Classes Hatha. Once daily. No extra charge.

Services Nutrition assessment, fitness assessment, blood/cholesterol screening, massage, reflexology.

We decided to go to Hilton Head Health Institute because of its reputation. We called ahead and talked with the program consultants, who addressed our particular needs and goals. Yoga classes at the institute can be modified for the beginner, intermediate, and advanced. We were definitely beginners. As a matter of fact, we were skeptics. We're two big blokes that thought we would feel silly on the floor, since we are so inflexible. We really received a surprise. We could really feel what our instructor was teaching. She demonstrated how to stretch on one side, and it felt like one leg was longer on that side . . . just amazing. She had us practice a stretch at home, and within days we got into a posture we never thought possible. We are so impressed with yoga to stay fit that we are planning on hiring an instructor to teach at our company.

−Peter Blake Turner and Roy Clegg, coworkers, London, England

Other Classes Aerobic walking, aquatic fitness, tai chi, Pilates, mindful eating.

Recreation Golf, tennis, swimming, biking.

Children's Program? No.

Accommodations 40 villas.

Dining Included. Three meals daily. Vegetarian options available.

Attire/What to Bring Standard yoga/workout attire, sun/insect protection, beach towel, swimsuit, flashlight, walking shoes, golf/tennis attire.

Travel Information The Savannah, GA, airport is 35 miles away.

Rates $2,795–$3,595 per person per week.

Contact 14 Valencia Rd., Hilton Head Island, SC 29928; tel: 800-292-2440, 843-785-7292; fax: 843-686-5659; www.hhhealth.com.

TENNESSEE

Gray Bear Holistic Retreat Center   Hohenwald, Tennessee

I go to Gray Bear once or twice a year for Doug Keller's workshops. Gray Bear has a lodge and a few cabins. Most students sleep in the lodge, dorm-style. Adam's father built the lodge in the '70s from a kit, and it has a big log cabin feel. The center of the building is where the yoga used to be done (they recently built a separate yoga facility), and they've decorated the lodge with gifts people have given them throughout the years. It's big, but you feel like you're in someone's house—it has a personal, family feeling. The owners, Adam and Diann, live downstairs.

Meals are cooked by a gourmet vegetarian chef from Nashville who comes in for the workshops. The meals, served buffet style, are very vegan-friendly and everything is organic. The last night of a workshop they have a big dinner, and they set up the hall with tables and there's dancing and singing.

People are very open and gentle with each other because of the atmosphere created by Adam and Diann. You want to be kind to people. There is a gentleness in the air.

—Laura Miller, speechwriter, Nashville, Tennessee

Tucked away in west Tennessee, Gray Bear Holistic Retreat Center focuses on yoga, with retreats conducted by visiting teachers offered throughout the year. Workshop participants can enjoy 150 acres of thick forest for hiking, natural springs, a waterfall, and a wood-fired sauna. The lodging is rustic, but owners Adam Schumaker and Diann Fuller make sure guests feel right at home. Most rooms are double occupancy with shared baths. Vegetarian meals are prepared with organic ingredients.

Guest Yoga Teachers? Yes. Including JJ Gormley, Doug Keller, Mary Paffard, Kenneth Robinson, Laura Tyree, Rodney Yee.

Types of Yoga Classes Iyengar, Anusara, and others. Twice daily. Included in workshop fee. Some individual retreats available.

Services Massage, Breema, watsu.

Other Classes Meditation, pranayama. Workshops in vegetarian cooking, drumming, Ayurvedic Thai massage, and juicing/fasting.

Recreation Hiking, sauna, hot tub.

Children's Program? No.

Accommodations Dorm and double occupancy rooms, shared baths; sleeps 35 maximum. Private cabins with private bath.

Dining Included. Three vegetarian meals daily.

Attire/What to Bring Standard yoga attire, yoga mat and props, hiking boots, sun/insect protection, flashlight.

Travel Information Gray Bear is 80 miles from the Nashville airport.

Rates Weekend retreats $165–$350. Seven-day retreat $500–$1,250.

Contact PO Box 682, Hohenwald, TN 38462; tel: 615-782-0469; www.graybear.org.

UTAH

Inner Harmony Retreat Center   Brian Head, Utah

Yoga teachers from around the world have been holding workshops and retreats at Inner Harmony Yoga Retreat Center for more than 20 years. Maybe it's the location, four miles outside of Brian Head Ski Resort in Southern Utah between Bryce Canyon and Zion National Parks. Or the renowned vegetarian food. One thing is for sure: Inner Harmony attracts a steady stream of yoga practitioners.

A typical day begins at 7 AM with a guided pranayama and meditation practice, followed by a light breakfast. At 9:30 AM a 2^1/$_2$- to 3-hour asana practice begins, which gradually builds in depth and intensity through the week. After lunch, you can hike with the group in one of the nearby national park areas or spend free time on your own. At 4:30 PM there is usually another yoga session. Dinner follows at 6:30 PM. On some evenings, there are scheduled programs; you can also enjoy the sauna or hot tubs, or get a massage. Winter retreats include cross-country skiing and snowshoeing instead of hiking.

Guest Yoga Teachers? Yes. Including Seane Corn, Krishna Das, Maty Ezraty, Angela Farmer, Richard Freeman, John Friend, Ann Greene, Suzie Hurley, Cyndi Lee, Tias Little, Mary Beth Markus, Chuck Miller, Elise Browning Miller, Tim Miller, Todd Norian, Shiva Rea, Desiree Rumbaugh, Robert Svoboda, David Swenson, Jai Uttal, Victor van Kooten.

Types of Yoga Classes Common offerings include Vinyasa, Ashtanga, Anusara, Iyengar. Twice daily. No extra charge.

Services Massage.

Other Classes Meditation, pranayama, chanting.

Recreation Hiking, cross-country skiing, snowshoeing, hot tubs, sauna.

I met John Friend at a Yoga Journal conference and have been studying with him ever since. He often teaches at Inner Harmony, so I've been there three times. It's a wonderful location at 9,000 feet with views of three different mountain ranges. The big house is an A-frame with a great room that has a fireplace and reading/study area. This building is where teachers stay, as well as the owners of the property. Adjacent to the A-frame is the building with the yoga room, which has sliding glass doors that open onto a patio. Lunch and dinner are served on the patio when the weather permits. The food is vegetarian and outstanding. Above the yoga room are the better guest rooms, but I always stay in the dorm. There are also yurts and tent areas. The two hot tubs have great views of the mountains, and there is also a sauna on the property. Usually, with John Friend, we begin the day with two hours of meditation and pranayama, followed by a break and three hours of yoga. Then we go hiking in the afternoon. Before dinner, there is more yoga. I highly recommend the place.

—Tim Noworyta, copywriter, editor, and
   yoga teacher, Chicago, Illinois

Children's Program? No.

Accommodations Tents, dorms, yurts, private rooms for 58 people.

Dining Included. Vegetarian available.

Attire/What to Bring Yoga attire, yoga mat and props, hiking boots, cold weather/ski attire in winter, flashlight, sun/insect protection.

Travel Information Inner Harmony is 200 miles from Las Vegas and 250 miles from Salt Lake City. Guests who fly into Cedar City (30 miles away), St. George (90 miles away), and Las Vegas can be picked up by a shuttle. Winter guests are carried in three miles from the road by snowcat.

Rates Seven-day retreats $675–$1,495.

Contact PO Box 190086, Brian Head, UT 84719; tel: 800-347-5633, 435-677-9923; www.innerharmonyyoga.com.

The Last Resort   Cedar City, Utah

The Last Resort is a yoga and meditation retreat center run by Abhilasha and Pujari Keays near Pah Tempe hot springs and Zion and Bryce Canyon National Parks. The Keays have studied in India with B. K. S. Iyengar and have been holding workshops at the Last Resort since 1984. Programs, focusing on yoga, meditation, or both, are offered at different times of the year. Workshops include a seven-day yoga retreat, a 5-, 7-, 10-, and 21-day vipassana retreat, a four-day relationship workshop, and an eight-day detoxification and spring cleaning of the body.

Guest Yoga Teachers? No.

Types of Yoga Classes Iyengar. Twice daily. No extra charge.

Services Massage.

Other Classes Meditation, vipassana, relationships, natural foods, cleansing/juice fasting.

Recreation Hiking, snowshoeing, cross-country skiing, hot springs.

Children's Program? No.

Accommodations Five rooms for 10 people; shared baths.

Dining Included. Vegetarian.

Attire/What to Bring Standard yoga attire, sun/insect protection, hiking boots, swimsuit, cold weather/ski apparel.

The Last Resort is near the Brian Head Ski Resort, but it feels like it is a world away. The "resort" is an A-frame house on the side of a mountain. Abhilasha and Pujari really believe that yoga is practiced to support a meditation practice. The yoga was good, but meditation was the focus. We ate in silence, and we had three meditation sessions a day and two yoga sessions a day. The last day of the retreat was completely silent. They hold a few silent retreats each year.

–Tim Noworyta, copywriter, editor, and yoga teacher, Chicago, Illinois

Travel Information Cedar City is about 160 miles from the Las Vegas airport and 46 miles from the St. George airport.

Rates Seven-day yoga retreat $850 per person.

Contact PO Box 707, Cedar City, UT 84721; tel: 435-682-2289.

WYOMING

HF Bar Ranch   Saddlestring, Wyoming

The HF Bar Ranch, a century-old dude ranch, caters to all levels of horse-back riders, from city slickers to experienced equestrians. It has more than 180 saddle horses, and its 9,000 acres include a vast number of trails over varied terrain. The ranch offers lessons for new to experienced riders, and wranglers lead small groups on half- or full-day rides and overnight camping trips. Experienced riders may also go out and ride alone.

Yoga does take a backseat to the horses here, but it ultimately becomes an important aspect of the experience. Since most people can get sore from a full day of riding, taking a yoga class soothes and stretches out the body for the next day. Yoga instructor Alyssa Pickerton teaches a daily Ashtanga hybrid class, adjusting its intensity to the ability of her students. She has designed her sequence to help the body recover from bouncing on a horse all day and often focuses on hip openers, abdominal work, and thigh stretches. Classes are held in the ranch's main log house, built when the great outdoorsman Teddy Roosevelt was president.

Guest Yoga Teachers? No.

Types of Yoga Classes Power yoga.

Services None.

Other Classes None.

Recreation Horseback riding, sporting clay, fly fishing, swimming.

Children's Program? Yes.

Accommodations 30 cabins, ranging from one to six rooms.

Dining Included. Rustic gourmet.

Attire/What to Bring Casual, yoga attire, riding boots.

Travel Information Fly into Sheridan, WY, via Denver, CO, which is 35 minutes from the ranch. The ranch provides transportation from the airport to the ranch for a small fee.

We've been going to the ranch for six years, but I just started taking the yoga classes offered at HF Bar two years ago. It is wonderful to practice yoga after three hours of riding to really stretch the muscles, especially if you're not used to being in the saddle. Yoga is part of what I look forward to when I go to the ranch. I've always done a lot of stretching, aerobics, and Pilates, but yoga has had a tremendous affect on me both mentally and physically. It helps me keep my head together as a mother of a toddler. Now yoga is part of my everyday life.

—Laurie Richardson, management training consultant, Washington, D.C.

Rates $200 per person per day. No charge for children under age five.

Contact 1301 Rockcreek Road, Sattlestring, WY 82840; tel: 307-684-2487; fax: 307 684-7144; www.hfbar.com; www.hfb@wyoming.com.

CANADA

Mountain Trek Fitness Retreat & Health Spa

Ainsworth Hot Springs, British Columbia

I wanted to go to a place where I would be pampered but also get some exercise. When I arrived at Mountain Trek, I immediately felt the stress in my shoulders and neck start to melt away. The grass was freshly mowed and the various gardens blossomed with flowers. I saw chairs facing the lake and couldn't wait to grab my book and start relaxing.

Inside the lodge is a huge fireplace and comfy couches that were calling out my name. I was in a bit of a dilemma about where to read my book—outside enjoying the landscape or around the fireplace snuggled up in the couch! My room was spacious and always clean, with its own bathroom. You don't spend much time in your room, except to sleep at night. The food was always good. But be ready to go without coffee, because there isn't a drop in the lodge.

I am not experienced with yoga, but I had a blast with Tesh, the instructor. It doesn't matter if you have never done yoga—Tesh will make it so easy for you that before you know it you will be up on his feet flying in the air. I can't say enough good things about Tesh and the great influence he was on my life. We did yoga at the hot springs, after a bike ride, at the tops of mountains, and every morning to start the day off right.

Three massages come with the seven-day Yoga Boot Camp. I paid extra and had massages every night. After a day of hiking and yoga, there is no better way to end the day.

—Amy Zeller, senior paralegal, San Francisco, California

Mountain Trek Fitness Retreat & Health Spa offers all-inclusive three-, four-, and seven-day packages that can include a wide variety of activities geared toward the outdoor sports enthusiast including hiking, kayaking, biking, rock climbing, and skiing. Almost all programs include yoga as part of the daily routine. The 8,000-square-foot lodge is surrounded by 34 acres of forest and is just a five-minute walk from Ainsworth Hot Springs. A typical day begins at 6 AM with a wake-up knock on the door. Herb teas and fruit are available in the dining room. An hourlong yoga class begins at 6:30. A full breakfast is served at 7:30. Afterward, you depart for your scheduled activity in a four-wheel-drive vehicle. Premade lunches are packed by each hiker. The group is led by guides who are trained in first aid and who carry radios and telephones in case of emergency. Lunch is often eaten beside an alpine lake, waterfall, or meadow. You return to the lodge at 5 PM and have two hours of free time until dinner is served. There are no phones or TVs in guest rooms. Seven-night programs include three Swedish massages (55 minutes each), and three-night and four-night programs include two Swedish massages. Extra massages and activities are available for additional cost.

Mountain Trek offers a Challenge Yoga Boot Camp each summer that is led by Nateshvar Ken Scott. It includes Kripalu-style yoga throughout the day as well as challenging mountain hiking, biking, kayaking, and massage.

Guest Yoga Teachers? No.

Types of Yoga Classes Hatha, Kripalu, Contact (a dynamic and physical practice involving two people). Once or twice daily. No extra charge.

Services Massage, aromatherapy, reflexology.

Other Classes Hiking, biking, kayaking, skiing, snowshoeing.

Recreation Jacuzzi, sauna, gym.

Children's Program? No.

Accommodations 12 rooms with private baths.

Dining Included. Vegetarian and vegan available. No caffeine or alcohol. Supervised fasting available.

Attire/What to Bring Standard yoga/workout attire, hiking boots, sandals/moccasins/slippers, hiking shorts and long pants, second skin or moleskin blister aid, one medium-weight long-sleeve shirt, small folding umbrella, one top for warmth (Polarfleece, wool), sun/insect protection, rain jacket, swimsuit, light pair of gloves (even in summer), Teva-like sandals for kayaking, cold-weather attire in winter, snowboots that are high on the calf for snowshoeing. Provided by lodge: sweat suits, T-shirts, bathrobe, hair dryer, water bottles, and a day pack.

Travel Information Fly into the Spokane airport. Van shuttle service is available every Friday from Spokane airport to Mountain Trek, $175 roundtrip.

Rates Four-night stay $1,495 per person.

Contact Box 1352, Ainsworth Hot Springs, B.C. V0G 1A0 Canada; tel: 800-661-5161, 250-229-5636; fax: 250-229-5246; www.hiking.com.

Hollyhock   Cortes Island, British Columbia

Hollyhock was designed as a center for the "cultivation of human consciousness and well-being." It is not affiliated with a specific spiritual tradition. Hollyhock is a learning center dedicated to "holidays that heal" and offers a variety of workshops, including half a dozen or so yoga programs per year. In addition, resident yoga teachers conduct early morning yoga classes and three- and four-day workshops. Meditation is also available each morning. The center is surrounded by ocean, forest, and mountains. Guests can join resident naturalists for daily morning rows, afternoon walks, and evening star talks. No phones or televisions in the rooms.

Guest Yoga Teachers? Yes. Including Jocelan Coty, Ram Dass, Catherine Garrigues, David Garrigues, Yvonne Kipp, Nateshvar Ken Scott, Jai Uttal.

Types of Yoga Classes Hatha, Ashtanga, Kripalu, Iyengar, karma. Once daily. No extra charge.

Services Craniosacral therapy, massage, body wraps, facials, acupressure, reflexology.

Other Classes Other workshops include dance, health and healing, shamanism, writing, art, spiritual development, meditation, music.

Hollyhock has yoga classes every day. The staff-taught yoga was a bit slow for me. I stayed in something called the carousel, which is a round house, and I had a slice-of-pie-shaped room. It was very basic accommodations. Every week they have a different sort of workshop. They bring in guest yogis, potters, and music people. I was there as a panelist for a special session called the Social Venture Institute, which features seminars on social venture business. I had a great time and thought the place was magical. I can't wait to return.

—Mara Manus, executive director,
  the Public Theater, New York City

Recreation Kayaking, sailing, hot tub (clothing optional), walking, and hiking.

Children's Program? Yes. Family Nature Adventure, programs for ages 12 and over.

Accommodations Dormitories, private rooms, and camping for 100 people.

Dining Included. Vegetarian.

Attire/What to Bring Standard yoga attire, flashlight, water bottle, layered clothing, alarm clock, beach towel, rain wear, walking shoes and shoes that slip on easily (no shoes are worn in the buildings), footwear that can get wet (for kayaking), sun/insect protection.

Travel Information Hollyhock lies on Cortes Island, British Columbia, about 100 miles north of Vancouver. The trip from Vancouver takes one hour by seaplane, six hours by car and ferry.

Rates $64 per person per night for a shared dorm to $153 per person per night for a single with private bath. Camping $51.

Contact PO Box 127, Manson's Landing, Cortes Island, B.C. V0P 1K0 Canada; tel: 800-933-6339, 250-935-6576; www.hollyhock.bc.ca.

Maple Ki   Tamworth, Ontario

Maple Ki is on 33 acres of forest with more than 1,600 feet of private waterfront at the shore of Cade Lake. Guests can canoe or kayak on Salmon River, or novice paddlers can head for the calmer lake. There are also plenty of trails to explore in the woodlands that surround Maple Ki.

The inn has cathedral ceilings, hardwood floors, a floor-to-ceiling brick fireplace, Jacuzzi, a library filled with reading material, and four guest rooms that share two and a half bathrooms. Yoga is held each morning in the new studio or outside by the lake, and massages, facials, and reflexology are available on site.

Guest Yoga Teachers? No.

Types of Yoga Classes Hatha. Once daily. No extra charge.

Services Shiatsu, reflexology, aromatherapy, facials.

Other Classes N/A.

Recreation Hiking, swimming, canoeing, kayaking.

Children's Program? No.

Accommodations Four guest rooms.

My husband and I first visited Maple Ki when it was located near Owen Sound. My husband had cancer, and we were looking for a vacation spot that would be beneficial to him. We went two years in a row. We loved our time there, and I developed a friendship with the owner, Julianna, during those visits. After he passed away, Maple Ki was the first (and only) place on my mind. My visit to Maple Ki this past August was my first time to visit Julianna's new location on Cade Lake. I was not disappointed. It was even more beautiful than her previous location.

Sometimes, at night, when I have had a stressful day and am having trouble falling asleep, I go to Maple Ki in my mind and I just fall asleep.

—Susan Akimoto, software developer, Waterdown, Ontario

Dining Included. Three vegetarian meals.

Attire/What to Bring Standard yoga attire, personal toiletries, layered clothing, flashlight, water bottle, beach towel, swim suit, rainwear, walking shoes/hiking boots and slippers.

Travel Information Maple Ki is $2^1/2$ hours from Toronto.

Rates $58–$78 per person per night.

Contact RR #2, Box 159, Tamworth, Ontario K0K 3G0 Canada; tel: 613-379-2227; www.mapleki.com.

MEXICO

Mar de Jade   Chacala, Mexico

Mar de Jade, an oceanfront vacation and retreat center, is in Chacala, a small fishing village on the Pacific coast of Mexico, 90 minutes north of Puerto Vallarta. The center, created in 1983, is surrounded by a tropical forest and groves of coconut, mango, and banana trees.

The Mediterranean-style main building overlooks the ocean and houses the kitchen, a classroom, offices, terrace lounge, activity room, and a library. The outdoor dining room and a covered pavilion-lounge almost touch the ocean. A swimming pool, wading pool, and large Jacuzzi sit in the middle of a palm grove and also offer ocean views. Yoga takes place in a thatched-roof, open-air palapa.

The kitchen staff prepares both authentic Mexican meals (chile rellenos, mole, enchiladas, salsas) and international dishes using fish, chicken, dairy products, vegetables, and tropical fruits. Vegetarian options are also available. Meals are served three times a day, buffet-style, in the outdoor dining room.

When not in yoga class, guests can swim, snorkel, kayak, surf, hike, bird-watch, or ride horseback. In addition, Mar de Jade offers a Spanish instruction program taught by native speakers, which costs $80 per week.

A percentage of Mar de Jade's profits go toward local community projects, such as a primary-care community clinic, a legal-aid project, a scholarship fund for young people, an emergency fund for families in distress, a local house-building project for low-income families, and a children's library.

Guest Yoga Teachers? Yes. Including Kat Allen, Cintra, Mishabae Edmond, Barbara Luboff, Emily Navar.

Types of Yoga Classes Hatha. At least once daily during retreats. No extra charge. No yoga is offered when retreats are not in session.

Mar de Jade is at the end of one of the loveliest beaches in all of Mexico. The beach is palm tree-lined, and there are palapa (thatched-roof) restaurants scattered along the beach and a small fishing village. Mar de Jade itself has palm trees, a pool, a large beachside hot tub, and attractive buildings. Especially nice is the dining area, which is open-sided but covered and right next to the beach. All types of accommodations are available, from rather basic four-person rooms to new deluxe rooms with raised wooden-platform alcoves for yoga or meditation, as well as private terraces.

The food is plentiful and very good. There is always a great variety served at each of the three meals. Usually chicken or fish is served, but there are plenty of choices for vegetarians.

Two local women offer massage at Mar de Jade. People can sign up for them, and the cost is only $25 per hour. One of the best features of Mar de Jade is the large, wooden-floored yoga/meditation room with great wall space. It can very easily accommodate 30 yoga students. It is open at all times for students to use for their own practice.

—Barbara Luboff, a yoga teacher now living in Mexico

Services Massage.

Other Classes Aerobics, dancing, Spanish.

Recreation Hiking, swimming, fishing, water sports, snorkeling, whale watching, surfing, horseback riding, dancing, Jacuzzi, kayaking, bird watching, boating.

Children's Program? Yes. Child care and Spanish lessons for kids.

Accommodations Rooms, suites, and penthouse apartment; can sleep 60 maximum. Most groups are of 30 people or fewer.

Dining Included. Traditional Mexican. Vegetarian available.

Attire/What to Bring Traditional yoga attire, sun/insect protection, rain coat, rain shoes, towels, beach towels, toiletries, flashlight, water bottle, Spanish dictionary, walking shoes.

Travel Information Fly into Puerto Vallarta. Mar de Jade will arrange for airport pickup on the starting dates of its three-week programs. The cost of the transportation will range from $15 per person to $75 for one person alone, depending on the number of people sharing the taxi or van.

Rates $85–$150 per person per night. No credit cards.

Contact PMB 078-344, 827 Union Pacific, Laredo, TX 78045-9452; tel: 011-52-322-222-1171, 011-52-322-222-3524, voice mail only: 011-52-322-294-1163; www.mardejade.com.

Casa Iguana   Platanitos, Mexico

Anusara yoga teacher Barbara Luboff has opened up her home in Platanitos, Mexico, to offer personalized yoga vacations. Obviously some amenities are not offered, like other classes, massage therapists, or children's programs. But people can choose their own dates and get individual attention, private yoga classes, and free transfers to and from the airport. Before guests arrive, Luboff writes to them and asks about their yoga goals and dietary preferences. Besides being an Anusara teacher, Luboff has taken therapeutic yoga training, so a private yoga vacation might be just the thing for someone interested in studying but limited by an injury or intimidated by a group situation.

Casa Iguana is in a gated community of eight homes on a peninsula jutting out into the sea. There is a large swimming pool on the property, as well as a small cliffside infinity pool. The house sits next to a 12-mile-long beach that is great for walking, running, surfing, and swimming. Boats can be rented for whale watching, fishing, snorkeling, sightseeing, and exploring the local 2,500-acre estuary. Luboff and her husband, Ken, often take guests exploring in the area. Favorite activities include a nearby hike to a waterfall and natural pool, a jungle cruise, and sightseeing in the seaside town of San Blas.

Guest Yoga Teachers? No.

Types of Yoga Classes Anusara. Daily. No extra charge.

Services N/A.

Other Classes N/A.

Recreation Swimming, whale watching, fishing, snorkeling, hiking, surfing.

Children's Program? No.

Accommodations One large guest bedroom with private bath can accommodate one, two, or three people. If a larger group wants to come, bedrooms in a neighboring house can be rented.

Dining Included. Fruits, vegetables, chicken, fish. Vegetarian available.

Attire/What to Bring Standard yoga attire, swimsuit, sun/insect protection, hiking boots.

Travel Information The nearest airport is in Puerto Vallarta, about 90 minutes away. Roundtrip airport transportation included.

Rates $150 per day, single occupancy. $200 per day, double occupancy. No credit cards.

Contact PO Box 2442, Santa Fe, NM 87504; tel: 505-983-7245, 011-52-322-101-4019; www.yogainmexico.com.

My husband was going on a mountain biking trip with a friend, and I wanted to do something relaxing and alone. I was looking for self-indulgence with a few hours of yoga a day. I wanted to be a "spoiled only child" for the week, and that is exactly what I got!

I rented a room from Barbara and Ken at their home, Casa Iguana. My room overlooked the sea and was so beautiful. It had a private bathroom, and I would watch the sunset from the shower in the evenings. The sound of the waves crashing against the cliff was awesome. I could see the spray of the water from the bed. The food was great. Barbara and I emailed each other many times before I arrived, and discovered we both liked similar foods. We cooked together sometimes (my choice) and shared some of our favorite recipes.

I had private lessons in Anusara yoga. I usually did a couple hours of instruction in the morning (after coffee and breakfast) and then an hour before sunset. Sometimes we'd go over areas of weakness and helpful hints in the evening over a glass of wine.

My husband and I are going back in February and will rent the same room. I'll do some yoga, and we will plan on more activities, such as bird watching, hiking to waterfalls, and maybe whale watching.

—Sally Haddow, emergency room nurse, Tacoma, Washington

Villas Shanti — Puerto Morelos, Mexico

Villas Shanti, a popular retreat with students and teachers alike, is in the small fishing village of Puerto Morelos just 20 minutes south of the Cancún airport. Jean and Jack Loew first came to Puerto Morelos in 1974. Attracted to the small-town atmosphere, they returned each year and finally opened Villas Shanti in 1990. Jean, a certified shiatsu therapist, has been studying and teaching yoga for more than 20 years.

Yoga is practiced in a 1,350-square-foot thatched-roof structure with fans and a sound system. Since 1990, many yoga teachers have held workshops at Villas Shanti. During most workshops, a yoga class in the morning

Villas Shanti is located in a small fishing village, Puerto Morelos, away from the typical Yucatán tourist destinations, which was an attraction for me. We were welcomed into the enclosed villa and led through a lush courtyard with a pool. The buildings are very attractive, surrounded by beautiful trees and flowers. The rooms are spacious, with a full kitchen, private bath, fans and air-conditioning, balcony or patio, and a comfortable queen or two double beds. They keep a regular supply of purified drinking water in the rooms.

The meals are excellent—fresh, local Mexican dishes. There were both vegetarian and nonvegetarian choices. I liked it all, particularly the guacamole and the fresh squeezed watermelon juice.

During my workshops, we start with a two-and-a-half-hour active morning class, followed some days with brunch. Then we are free to relax in the pool, hammocks, enjoy the beach, swimming, snorkeling, etc. The evening yoga class is usually more passive/restorative. We often take one day off to go on a tour of Mayan ruins. We then either have a catered group dinner or go to the center of town (a five- to ten-minute walk or short cab ride) for dinner at one of the small local restaurants.

One of the owners, Jean, offers shiatsu massage, and there are some local massage therapists who will come to your room. There is also a native-style sweat lodge nearby.

—Michael Doyle, yoga teacher and telecommunications/network analyst, Portland, Maine

is followed by brunch in the courtyard. After breakfast, guests can explore the coast of the Yucatán, snorkel, scuba dive, or enjoy the beach. Then there is another yoga class in the late afternoon.

Several restaurants within walking distance of Villas Shanti serve seafood, Yucatecan food, Italian, and Asian cuisine. There is also a grocery store for those who choose to make use of their own kitchen at Villas Shanti. Guests can also go down to the docks in the early afternoon and bargain with the fishermen for their catch of the day, and then return to cook the fish out on the barbecue grill.

Guest Yoga Teachers? Yes. Including Laurie Blakeney, Kristin Chirhart, JoAnn Connington, Kari Cotton, Annalisa Cunningham, Michael Doyle, Alexander Spaith Evans, Angela Farmer, Dana Flynn, Gabriel Halpern, Paula Kout, Vickie Labbe, Sylvie Lemelin, Janet Macleod, Amanda McMaine Smith, Victor van Kooten, Susan Van Nuys, Kathleen Wright.

Types of Yoga Classes Iyengar on Tuesday and Thursday mornings when Jean Loew is in town (December 6 to May 15). Check workshop schedule on the website for other options. $5 per session.

Services Massage, shiatsu, chiropractor.

Other Classes N/A.

Recreation Water sports, hiking, Mayan ruins.

Children's Program? No.

Accommodations Eight units, each with kitchenette and private bath; one two-bedroom villa.

Dining Included in workshops: Breakfast is available upon request, with a vegetarian Mexican dinner on the first and last evening of the workshop.

Attire/What to Bring Standard yoga attire, walking shoes, swimsuit, sun/insect protection.

Travel Information Villas Shanti is 20 minutes south of Cancún.

Rates Seven-day workshops average $925, double occupancy, or $1,225, single occupancy.

Contact PO Box 789, Cancun, Q. R., Mexico 77500 (December 6–April 30), PO Box 464, Glen, NH (May 1–December 5); tel: 011-52-998-871-0040, 011-52-987-871-0041 (December 6–April 30), 603-383-6501 (May 1–December 5); www.villasshanti.com.

Maya Tulum   Tulum, Mexico

Maya Tulum, on the Yucatán Peninsula, is right at the entrance of the Sian Ka'an Biosphere Reserve, the second-largest protected area in Mexico, making it an ideal location for nature-lovers seeking a quiet retreat.

Twice-daily yoga classes are open to all guests, even if they are not participating in a workshop. Private lessons in various types of bodywork, yoga, and traditional Mayan healing practices are available.

Most guests will want to visit Tulum, seven kilometers north of Maya Tulum and the largest Mayan ruin on the Caribbean coast. Those interested in archeology will also want to see the pyramids of Cobá, located in the jungle 30 miles west of Maya Tulum.

Other activities include swimming, snorkeling, sailing, fishing, scuba diving, or indulging in one of the many spa treatments offered by Maya Tulum.

Guest Yoga Teachers? Yes. Including Denise Benitez, Kelly Blaser, Seane Corne, Ana Forrest, Jenni Fox and Paul Gould, Jonny and Milla Kest, Jordan and Martin Kirk, Kelly Morris, Mark Stephens, Julia Tindall, Barbara Voinar, Kimberly Wilson.

Types of Yoga Classes Hatha. $10 per class. No extra charge if attending a workshop.

Services Massage, shiatsu, reflexology, body treatments.

Other Classes Meditation.

Recreation Snorkeling, swimming, sailing, fishing, diving, boat trips, Mayan ruin tours, eco-parks, hiking.

Children's Program? No.

Accommodations 43 cabanas with private bathrooms.

Dining Meal plan available. $33–$40 per person per day. Primarily vegetarian. Fresh fish and seafood are served à la carte.

Attire/What to Bring Standard yoga attire, swimsuit, sun/insect protection, walking shoes.

I brought a group of yoga students down to Maya Tulum. My workshop combined yoga with salsa dancing and conversational Spanish, so this was a perfect setting. It is a gorgeous place with good energy. The cabanas are really well-screened palapas with tile floors. There are fans, but no air-conditioning. Fresh water is in every room, and some rooms have traditional hanging beds. There are two main yoga halls (the larger one can accommodate 100 yogis) with plenty of mats and props available.

The food was vegetarian with some nights Mexican-themed. There is a spa there too, and massage is available. One of the staff, Maria, took three people at a time for a special day that included a mud massage, an exploration of the ruins, and a watsu treatment.

—Kelly Blaser, yoga teacher, Santa Cruz, California

Be Sun Savvy No matter where your travels take you, pack sunblock with an SPF of 15 or higher. In case you do suffer from sunburn or windburn, aloe vera gel helps soothe the pain and heal damaged skin. Use it as an overall moisturizer for your body and face. –K.F.M.

Travel Information Maya Tulum is 90 minutes south (80 miles) of the Cancún airport.

Rates $80–$180 per night, double occupancy. Credit cards are not accepted at Maya Tulum, but credit cards are accepted in the U.S. office for deposits only.

Contact Km. 7 Carr. Tulum-Boca Paila, PO Box 99 Tulum, Q. R., Mexico 77780; tel: 011-52-984-877-8638, 888-515-4580, 770-483-0238; www.mayatulum.com.

Solstice Mexico   Zipolite Beach, Mexico

Solstice is an intimate yoga and vacation center on the Oaxaca coast, known for its mountainous jungles.

One-week workshops with Brigitte Longueville are available and include lodging, a daily morning yoga class that lasts three hours, one hour of meditation, and one hour of pranayama each morning, three meals daily, one massage, and one afternoon trip. During the week, your practice builds slowly, whether you are a beginner or more advanced. Classes are for all levels of ability. Brigitte teaches traditional South Indian hatha yoga in both English and Spanish. Because groups are small (fewer than 16 people), there is an emphasis on individual attention and correct body alignment. Students learn to relax both physically and mentally before they start to stretch.

Brigitte Longueville began practicing yoga in India 19 years ago with Clive Sheridan. In Amsterdam, she obtained a teacher certificate after completing a three-year course at the Bharata Institute of Yoga under the guidance of Gert van Leeuwen. She has given workshops in the Netherlands, Belgium, India, Antigua (West Indies), and Mexico.

Guests stay in the dormitory or bungalows with private bathrooms, hammocks, and views of the Pacific Ocean. Nonparticipating spouses and children are welcome.

Guest Yoga Teachers? No.

Types of Yoga Classes Hatha. Twice daily. Non-workshop: $6 for 90 minute-session.

Services Massage.

Other Classes N/A.

Recreation River tubing, snorkeling, sea fishing, horseback riding, dolphin

I attended Solstice's one-week intensive in March 2002. I wanted a retreat that offered one three-hour yoga session. Solstice was also very affordable. I don't like resorts. I prefer quaint and charming places with character, and Solstice is just that. The compound was artistic and clean, welcoming and warm.

You can see the ocean from the second floor yoga studio, which faces the ocean. The open design of the studio allows ocean breezes into the class, which is a welcome reprieve from all the heat generated by the practice. We would all run from class to our rooms to change, then straight into the ocean to cool off before lunch. Zipolite Beach is beautiful, and the sunsets are nothing short of magical.

I had done only a few yoga classes prior to Solstice, so I wasn't used to the intensity of Brigitte's three-hour class, but we did not do headstands and only embarked on handstands and full wheels toward the very end, and even then the instructor assisted every student up. It really is ideal for both beginners and advanced practitioners. I have kept up my yoga practice since returning from Solstice and plan to go back again. We practiced pranayama every day for an hour in the morning before the asanas. An aromatherapy massage was included in the package and was the perfect complement to my aching body.

—Margaret Song, new media consultant, New York City

boat tour, hikes, visit to the Punta Cometa Sanctuary, turtle museum, wildlife viewing (crocodiles, iguanas, and birds).

Children's Program? No.

Accommodations Dormitory, two studios, three bungalows; sleeps 18 people.

Dining Included. Three meals daily. Vegetarian available.

Attire/What to Bring Standard yoga attire, swimsuit, insect/sun protection, walking shoes.

Travel Information Zipolite is located at the southernmost tip of the state of Oaxaca, about two kilometers west of Puerto Ángel. To reach Zipolite you can either fly to Huatulco or to Puerto Escondido (both with international and daily flights from Mexico City). From Huatulco it's a 40-kilometer drive to Zipolite, from Puerto Escondido about 70 kilometers. You can take a bus from Oaxaca City (6 hours) or from Mexico City (14 hours). Airport pickup is available.

Rates $490–$840 per person per week.

Contact Calle del Amor #94, Zipolite, Oax. Mexico 70902 (mail: apdo #18, Puerto Ángel, Oax., 70902 Mexico); www.solstice-mexico.com.

CENTRAL AMERICA

Nosara Yoga Institute   Guanacaste, Costa Rica

The Nosara Yoga Institute, overlooking the Pacific and the white sandy beaches of Costa Rica, trains yoga teachers and practitioners.

Don and Amba Stapleton are the owners and directors of Nosara Institute. They met when they were residents at Kripalu in Lenox, Massachusetts, where they both studied yoga in 1977. Don and Amba moved to Costa Rica and created Nosara Institute in 1995. Their brand of yoga combines Amba's more traditional approach to hatha yoga with Don's prana-oriented (using breathing) direction. If you plan to go and take public classes outside the workshop schedule, call ahead to make sure Don and Amba are in town.

Nosara Yoga Institute is a short walk from the beach, so guests can soak in the Pacific after a day of yoga. Most programs begin at 6:30 AM, followed by a two-hour lunch break, and end in time to watch the sunset. There are no classes on weekends. Students stay at nearby small hotels, all within a short walk. Nosara can assist with hotel reservations.

Guest Yoga Teachers? No.

I went to Nosara to become certified as a yoga instructor with Don and Amba Stapleton. How lucky for me that they happened to be located in Costa Rica. My first impression was that I had arrived in paradise. The countryside is quiet and pastoral, covered with lush jungle vegetation right down to the wide open beaches. Nosara Yoga Institute itself is a work of art and a wonderful example of creating sacred space. The yoga pavilion where we practiced every day was open on all sides, with a thatched cathedral ceiling. The howler monkeys would hang in the trees and make their presence known by literally laughing at us while they sat in the trees, until they got used to us being there every morning.

Together Don and Amba represent years of combined wisdom, experience, and dedicated practice. I came home with a very exciting yoga practice to offer students. When not in yoga class, you can go horseback riding, surfing, or take walks on the beach and laze around.

—Mishabae Edmond, yoga instructor, writer, and massage therapist, Bainbridge Island, Washington

Types of Yoga Classes Hatha. $10 per class.

Services N/A.

Other Classes Pranassage training (combines yoga and bodywork).

Recreation N/A.

Children's Program? No.

Accommodations Available at Hotel Cafe de Paris, which also has a French bakery, restaurant, cappuccino bar, Internet cafe, pool, and many other services. Private and shared rooms are available.

Dining Not included. Meal plan at Hotel Cafe de Paris: three meals daily for five days $150 (vegetarian, fresh fish, and tropical fruit plates).

Attire/What to Bring Toiletries, flashlight, beach attire, standard yoga wear, walking shoes, sandals, yoga mat, backpack, sun/insect protection.

Travel Information Nosara is a six-hour bus ride from San José ($9 one way). The bus leaves daily at 6 AM from San José. There is also a daily 35-minute commuter flight to Nosara from San Jose ($67 one way). Hotel Cafe de Paris offers complimentary shuttle service to and from the airport or bus station in Nosara.

Rates Monthlong teacher training $2,300, not including lodging.

Contact Nosara Yoga Institute, c/o Don and Amba Stapleton, Interlink 979, PO Box 02-5635, Miami, FL 33102; tel: 866-439-4704, in Costa Rica: 506-682-0071; fax: 506-682-0072; www.nosarayoga.com.

Samasati Nature Retreat   Puerto Viejo, Costa Rica

Samasati is an eco-resort and retreat center located on 250 acres of tropical rain forest with views of the Caribbean Sea. Guests stay in Caribbean-style bungalows complete with large porches and hammocks. Hatha, Iyengar, Ashtanga, and Vinyasa yoga classes are offered throughout the day, and a guided meditation is held just before dinner. When not participating in a class, guests can receive a massage, surf, swim, trek, kayak, scuba dive, horseback ride, or bird watch. (The surrounding property has one of the most rich and varied populations of birds in the country.) A vegetarian buffet is served three times a day, and tropical cocktails, beer, and wine are available at the bar.

Guest Yoga Teachers? Yes. Including Debi DiPeso-Anna, Stephanie Langbein, Joe Palese, Elizabeth Saguna Pedersen, Shiva Rea, Carrie Schneider, David Walker.

Types of Yoga Classes Hatha, Vinyasa, Ashtanga, Iyengar. At least twice daily. $12 per class. No extra charge if attending a retreat.

Services Massage, craniosacral therapy, Reiki, shiatsu.

Other Classes Meditation.

Recreation Bird watching, nature hikes, swimming, river and sea kayaking, scuba diving, surfing, horseback riding, swimming with dolphins, snorkeling.

Children's Program? No.

Accommodations Nine bungalows with private baths, guest house with shared bath, and three private houses.

Dining Included. Three vegetarian meals daily.

Attire/What to Bring Standard yoga attire, swimsuit, hiking shoes, waterproof sandals, sun/insect protection.

Travel Information Samasati Nature Retreat is located 130 miles south of San José, the capital of Costa Rica. Samasati schedules a private taxi to pick you up upon arrival at the airport at San José. The driver will take you to the Caribbean bus terminal in the city, where four times a day a direct bus runs to the village of Puerto Viejo, right next to Samasati. The taxi driver will help you buy the ticket and get into the right bus. Taxi fare from the airport is $20 and a bus ticket is $7. Samasati's entrance gate and reception area is about 800 meters from the main road. Samasati staff will transport you with four-wheel-drive vehicles up the hill to Samasati's restaurant and accommodations.

Rates $62–$148 per person per day.

Contact 4883 Ronson Court Suite R, San Diego, CA 92111; tel: 800-563-9643, in Costa Rica: 506-224-1870; fax: 858-279-5094; www.samasati.com.

When I go to Costa Rica, I want to get off the beaten path. That's why I like Samasati, which is a getaway on the Caribbean side. The asana room is an octagon that is screened in on all sides. I was there with Jai Uttal, and we had some really magical moments in that room because you can hear the sounds of the jungle while you're practicing. And the main dining hall overlooks the ocean. The grounds are so green and lush that when you leave you feel naked without having the jungle surrounding you. The beauty of Samasati is that you have access to both the lush rain forest and the ocean.

—Shiva Rea, yoga instructor, Venice, California

Pura Vida Retreat Center   San José, Costa Rica

Pura Vida (which means "pure life") is located on a private mountain estate surrounded by coffee plantations. The tropical grounds are lush with gardens, fountains, pools, flowers, fruit and ornamental trees, colorful birds, and butterflies. Yogis will want to look into the Mind/Body/Spirit Adventure Package, which includes seven nights' accommodations in a chalet tent, three vegetarian meals (chicken and fish available), daily yoga classes, movement

One of the most attractive aspects of Pura Vida is that it's secluded enough that you get the feeling of isolation, but you are just 20 minutes away from downtown San José. Along with practicing yoga surrounded by rain forests, there are also opportunities to interact with nature. Pura Vida offers full- and half-day eco-adventures, such as white-water rafting down 18 miles of the Pacuare River or hiking through Waterfall Gardens, which is located in the heart of the rain forest and has the largest butterfly sanctuary in the world, as well as a hummingbird garden. If you stand still and are patient, dozens of the tiny birds will venture close enough for you to feel the breeze of vibrations from their wings.

—Matthew Solan, *Yoga Journal* senior editor

classes, guided meditations, one-hour therapeutic massage, roundtrip airport pickup, two half-day eco-adventure tours in the rain forest, one all-day white-water rafting trip or day at the beach, guided hikes in the surrounding hills, and three antiaging seminars that focus on proper nutrition, vital supplements, targeted exercises, total fitness, and antistress techniques. There are five facilities for yoga: the Ananda Hall, which has ceiling-to-floor windows and can hold up to 85 people; Lila Hall, which has an almond-wood floor and is surrounded by a sunken garden; Bhakti Hall (up to 30 people); Shanti Hall (up to 16 people for Bikram); and Satya Hall (open-air studio, holds 30 people).

Guest Yoga Teachers? Yes. Including Susi Hately Aldous, Susan Apthorp, Jimmy Barkan, Michael and Laura Benton, Carol Bloch, Mark Epstein, Ana Forrest, Roseanna Frechette, Leslie Harris, Guruatma Khalsa, Cyndi Lee, Sudhakar Ken McRae and Kathleen Knipp, Matt Taylor, Cybele Tomlinson, Kim Valeri.

Types of Yoga Classes Hatha. Twice daily. No extra charge.

Services Massage, aromatherapy, acupuncture, facial, body treatments, shiatsu, Reiki method, reflexology, nail care, craniosacral therapy.

Other Classes N/A.

Recreation White-water rafting, eco-tours, coffee tours, hiking, hot tub.

Children's Program? No.

Accommodations 50 villas, suites, cabanas, luxury tents, and pagodas.

Dining Included. Three meals daily. Mostly vegetarian with some chicken and fish.

Attire/What to Bring Standard yoga attire, flashlight, swimsuit, walking or hiking boots, alarm clock, beach towel, warm sweater/sweatshirt, sun/insect protection, day pack, rain gear, waterproof sandals.

Travel Information Pura Vida is 20 minutes from the international airport at San José. Call in advance to schedule a van pickup.

Rates Seven-night stay $2,000 per person, double occupancy.

Contact Villas Pura Vida Retreat Center, Apartado 1112, Alajuela 4050, Costa Rica, 700 metros al sur de salon Apolo 15, Pavas de Carrizal, Alajuela, Costa Rica; tel: 888-767-7375, in Costa Rica: 506-392-8099; fax: 506-483-0041; www.puravidaspa.com.

SOUTH AMERICA

Willka T'ika Garden Guest House   Urubamba, Peru

Willka T'ika was specifically created as a yoga, meditation, and spiritual retreat. The heated yoga studio has a hardwood floor, the food is vegetarian, and three outdoor stone baths provide a place for yoga practitioners to soak after a workout.

Individual yoga students can participate in a yoga intensive program led by certified yoga teachers. Morning and afternoon yoga sessions are suitable for all levels. Each day, you will enjoy tours to major ancient sites in the Sacred Valley, Cuzco, Machu Picchu. You will also have the opportunity to meet local Peruvians, visit their homes, learn about Andean medicinal herbs, and attend workshops on Andean spirituality and cosmology. Willka T'ika also has created a 10-day package for yoga teachers who wish to bring a group of their own students.

Guest Yoga Teachers? Yes. Including Sibylle Baughan, Mary Dunn, Bryan Kest, Judith Lasater, Leslie Manes, James Murphy, Julian Neil, Larry Schultz, India Supera, Rodney Yee.

Types of Yoga Classes Hatha. Once daily. No extra charge.

Services Massage, herbal spa treatments.

Other Classes Andean spirituality, herbs, cosmology, healing.

Recreation Hiking, tours of ancient sites.

Children's Program? No.

Accommodations 17 rooms with private bathrooms.

Dining Included. Vegetarian, organic.

Attire/What to Bring Standard yoga attire, hiking boots, swimsuit, sun/insect protection, clothing for cool evenings.

Travel Information Fly into Cuzco via Lima. Willka T'ika is located on the outskirts of the village of Urubamba, 1 hour and 15 minutes from the Cuzco airport. Airport pickup is included.

Rates 10-day intensive $2,750.

Contact Willka T'ika/Magical Journey, 5905D Clark Rd., Paradise, CA 95969; tel: 888-737-8070, 530-538-9309; www.travelperu.com.

Willka T'ika is a paradise that allows you to slip into the Peruvian culture with a deep ahhh! The gardens, the staff, and the owner, Carol Cumes, are exquisite like the unexplainable walls of Machu Picchu. It feels so right to stay in a guest house retreat that supports the local community, that promotes organic sustainable farming, and that nourishes its guests with the wisdom of Peru.

—Rodney Yee, yoga teacher, Oakland, California

ASIA

Purple Valley Yoga Centre   Goa, India

I practice Ashtanga, and the teaching at Purple Valley was of a high caliber and in alignment with Pattabhi Jois's teachings, the master teacher of the tradition. The grounds are beautiful, lush, and relaxing. You can hear birds chirping. The rooms are colonial style, with all the amenities, very comfortable and homey. I had a nice spacious kitchen in which to prepare my own food. So, meals were great—there's lots of fresh, good food to chose from in Anjuna, even organic and brown rice, tofu, fresh fruit, and vegetable juices.

I loved my trips to the beach and playing in the waves, and motorcycle rides to out-of-town beaches, and shopping at the fairs.

—Maia Hess, dancer, choreographer, and yoga teacher, New York City

Purple Valley Yoga Centre is located at the Hotel Bougainvillea, a traditional Goan country guest house created from a 200-year-old mansion. The hotel is about two kilometers from the beaches of Vagator and North Anjuna and three kilometers from Anjuna's flea market. It is 15 minutes from the resorts of Baga Beach and Calangute Beach and 20 minutes from Candolim.

The center offers drop-in Ashtanga yoga classes four times a day, open to the public as well as those staying at the hotel. Purple Valley attracts many international teachers, including Gabriella Pascoli, who lived in Mysore and studied with Sri. K. Pattabhi Jois for many years. In fact, all teachers have considerable experience teaching and have studied under Pattabhi Jois.

The hotel has lush tropical gardens and a swimming pool that can be used by both visiting yoga practitioners and hotel guests. The hotel restaurant serves juices, lassis, snacks, and meals using organic ingredients when possible.

Purple Valley offers a package that includes accommodations at the Hotel Bougainvillea, unlimited yoga classes, and airport transfers for $240 to $320 per week. Also available is a guest house (20 minutes away by foot) for $180 to $240 per week, including yoga and airport transportation.

Goa is on the western coast of India, with sandy beaches and temperatures in the eighties from October to April. It was once a Portuguese territory, as reflected in the colonial houses and the names of the locals. In fact, most Goans don't consider themselves typical Indians.

Purple Valley Yoga Centre is closed during monsoon season, from the beginning of April through the end of October. At press time, the center was in the process of building a new facility, the Purple Valley Retreat, which will offer two-week retreats year-round, excluding April and May. The workshops will include visits by prominent Ashtanga teachers and teachers of other forms of yoga, plus meditation. The new building is located about three kilometers from the Purple Valley Yoga Centre. Rates will start at $400 per week, including accommodations. Guests stay in local Goan houses with families.

Guest Yoga Teachers? Yes. Including Kate Graham, Charlotte Lindstrom, Denise Martin-Harker.

Types of Yoga Classes Ashtanga. Four classes a day, six days a week (Monday to Saturday). No extra charge with package.

Services N/A.

Other Classes Meditation.

Recreation Swimming.

Children's Program? No.

Accommodations Hotel Bougainvillea or guest house.

Dining Not included. The Hotel Bougainvillea Restaurant uses organic ingredients whenever possible.

Attire/What to Bring Standard yoga attire, swimsuit, sunblock, mosquito repellent (antimalarial pills are optional: This is not a high risk area; avoiding the bites is the best precaution), flashlights, locks for hotel rooms and luggage, photocopies of all essential documents (in case of theft), electrical adapters if you are using electrical items (Indian voltage is 220V, and the plugs have three flat prongs), comfortable footwear, insurance against accident and theft, trousers, and long-sleeve shirt for the evenings to protect against mosquitoes.

Travel Information Fly into Dabolim Airport. Purple Valley provides airport transfers.

Rates Hotel Bougainvillea $240–$320 per week. Guest house $180–$240 per week.

Contact Purple Valley Yoga Centre, Goa, India; tel: 011-91-832-269-643, 011-91-98-22-133-977 (011-44-777-802-3177 and 011-44-173-636-4787 during monsoon season); www.yogagoa.net.

Steady Your Stomach Do not leave home without the all-around travel herb: ginger. Not only does it quell motion sickness, but it also helps to ease digestive disturbances, according to Sharol Tilgner, N.D., an herbalist based in Creswell, Oregon. Hops and valerian do double duty as digestive aids and relaxants. Hops, a bitter, helps stimulate poor digestion and calm the nerves when taken prior to eating. Valerian, taken after meals, dispels gas and soothes the nervous system. –K.F.M.

I've been to several Ayurvedic resorts here in the States, and they are so expensive. Ideal was reasonable, and I liked the treatment offerings. I did a three-week intense panchakarma regime.

Ideal was very clean, which is nice when you're in India. All the meals were included in my program. I did a strict Ayurvedic diet with lots of dahl, rice, fruits, and vegetables. Everything was extremely fresh. I did not take malaria pills like I have during other trips to India. I was told it is not a problem in that area of the country. I even had some of the local water, and I had no repercussions. I did a little bit of yoga every day, but the majority of my day was devoted to treatments, which lasted four hours. Every day a doctor would check my progress and adjust the many herbs I was taking. They also have an herbalist on staff. The family of the main Ayurveda technician has been administering these treatments for 500 years.

—Jeff Peters, record producer, Los Angeles, California

Ideal Ayurvedic Resort   Kerala, India

Ideal Ayurvedic Resort, run by J. Christudas as guided by spiritual leader Sri Sri Ravi Shankar, combines a vacation with Ayurveda and yoga. The Ayurvedic center employs doctors and therapists and offers about 40 treatments, including Ayurvedic massage and panchakarma (treatments to remove toxins). Yoga is available daily for a small fee, and cultural shows are scheduled on a regular basis.

Guest Yoga Teachers? No.

Types of Yoga Classes Hatha. Twice daily. $7 per session.

Services About 40 Ayurvedic treatments.

Other Classes Meditation.

Recreation Cultural shows, tours, mountain trips.

Children's Program? No.

Accommodations Rooms and cottages.

Dining Included in packages. Two restaurants serve regional, Indian continental, Chinese cuisine, seafood, and typical Kerala dishes.

Attire/What to Bring Standard yoga attire, swimsuit, sun/insect protection.

Travel Information Daily flights from Bombay (Mumbai), New Delhi, and Madras (Chennai) to Trivandrum (Thiruvananthapuram) are available. The resort offers pickup service.

Rates $25–$45 per night, double occupancy.

Contact Chowara Beach, Chowara P.O., (Via) Balaramapuram, South of Kovalam, Trivandrum - 695 501, Kerala, South India; tel: 011-91-471-26-8632; fax: 011-91-471-26-8396; www.idealayurvedicresort.com; www.panchakarmakerala.com.

Somatheeram Ayurvedic Beach Resort   Kerala, India

The 15-acre Somatheeram Ayurvedic Beach Resort is on the Malabar coast overlooking the Arabian Sea. Guest accommodations—traditional wooden houses, stone bungalows, and cottages—dot the hills among coconut groves. More than 28 Ayurvedic treatments are available at the Somatheeram Ayurvedic Beach Resort. The resort offers treatments designed to strengthen your immune system and prevent disease. A special program is created for each individual after an evaluation by an Ayurvedic physician.

Guest Yoga Teachers? No.

Types of Yoga Classes Hatha. Twice daily. $9 per session.

Services More than 28 Ayurvedic treatments, massage.

Other Classes Meditation, massage classes.

Recreation Swimming, fishing, boating.

Children's Program? No.

Accommodations 59 rooms in houses, stone bungalows, cottages.

Dining Not included. Restaurant serves regional, Indian, tandoori, grilled, continental, and Chinese cuisine. Meal plan: breakfast $5; lunch and dinner $10.

Attire/What to Bring Standard yoga attire, swimsuit, sun/insect protection.

Travel Information Daily flights from Bombay (Mumbai), New Delhi, and Madras (Chennai) to Trivandrum (Thiruvananthapuram) are available.

Rates $15–$200 per night, double occupancy.

Contact Chowara P. O., South of Kovalam, Trivandrum - 695 501, Kerala, South India; tel: 011-91-471-226-8101 or 011-91-471-226102; fax: 011-91-471-26-7600; www.somatheeram.com.

I am an author of beauty and wellness books and articles, so I was drawn to Somatheeram Ayurvedic Beach Resort to deepen my knowledge of Ayurveda. I was inspired to meet so many doctors, healers, massage therapists, spa architects, and people from around the world who wish to integrate Ayurveda into their work.

The yoga, which took place every morning, was an important part of the retreat. The yoga was pretty dynamic compared with the other Ayurveda spas I had visited in India. It was more Vinyasa flow, with standing postures, headstands, forward bends, and meditation.

Each day, you receive two hours of treatments, depending on the program you are on. Since I was researching, I got to test quite a few. The shirodhara is heaven—40 minutes of medicated warm oil continually pouring over your forehead sends away worrying thoughts. The oil bath is 40 minutes of shirodhara on your whole body!

–Judy Chapman, author of several aromatherapy books, Australia

Skyros   Ko Samet, Thailand

Skyros runs three retreat centers: the Skyros Centre and Atsitsa, on the Greek island of Skyros (see page 58), and a winter community on the Thai island of Ko Samet. In these dramatic settings, Skyros offers more than 200 courses in yoga, writing, personal development, cooking, sailing, art, and more. Guests can choose three courses in the first week and, if they wish, another three in the second.

Skyros-in-Thailand is located in the Ao Prao resort on Ko Samet, an island about 200 kilometers southeast of Bangkok. Its air-conditioned chalets are a few steps away from the beach.

Guest Yoga Teachers? Yes. Including Rosslyn Albright, Jo Attwood, Costas Chrysikakis, Thomas Claire, Peter Guttridge, Vaya Hanou, John Hardstaff, Ulrike Harris, Jane Morgan-Jones, Michael Stewart, Lisehanne Webster.

Types of Yoga Classes Hatha, Ashtanga. Twice daily if taking yoga workshop. No extra charge.

The accommodations in Ao Prao in Thailand are beautiful. I fell asleep each night to the wonderful sounds of nature–the waves, birds, and bats. The staff at Ao Prao are the most beautiful people I have ever been blessed enough to meet; they reflect the Buddhist way of calmness, helpfulness, and playfulness. The pool at Ao Prao is luxurious; I swam at night watching the full moon over the sea. The food is absolutely delicious, extremely healthy and plentiful. I teach a variety of floor and standing postures, emphasizing that yoga is meditation in motion–relaxation and breath are the main focus. I also teach massage. Beginners learn a full body sequence, mainly based on Swedish massage techniques, with acupressure points and Reiki. Other activities outside of the Skyros schedule include scuba diving with Dave and his team at Ao Prao, Thai cooking, Thai vegetable carving, and walks across the island to temples, beaches, and shops.

–Jo Attwood, yoga teacher at Skyros

Services N/A.

Other Classes Windsurfing, sailing, dance, theater, painting, music, writing, qigong, reflexology, tai chi, Pilates, Alexander Technique, Reiki method, and more.

Recreation Swimming, sailing.

Children's Program? No.

Accommodations Double and shared rooms. Single rooms available for an extra fee.

Dining Breakfast and lunch included.

Attire/What to Bring Standard yoga attire, swimsuit, sun/insect protection, flashlight, walking shoes.

Travel Information Fly to Bangkok on Sunday. Participants are picked up from the airport and taken to the Sofitel Hotel, where they spend the night. The three-hour coach and a 30-minute ferry to Ko Samet is scheduled for Monday midday. On the return trip, participants leave Ko Samet on Friday morning, arrive in Bangkok early afternoon, spend the night at the Sofitel Hotel, and depart for home Saturday morning. Cost for transportation and room in both locations is about $150.

Rates Two-week retreat $698–$1,530.

Contact 92 Prince of Wales Road, London NW5 3NE, England; tel: 011-44-207-267-4424, 011-44-207-284-3065; fax: 011-44-207-284-3063; www.skyros.com.

EUROPE

European College of Yoga and Therapy   Kloster Gerode, Germany

In the foothills of the Harz Mountains lies the town of Kloster Gerode. Here, in a former Benedictine monastery built in 1124, is the European College for Yoga and Therapy (ECYT), founded by Daya Mullins, Ph.D. The monastery has classrooms, a dining hall, and guest rooms. Healing and yoga take priority, and the center includes a staff of doctors, herbalists, yoga teachers, and mind-body therapists to attend to guests. People visit Kloster Gerode to study, receive treatment, or participate in health and wellness programs.

ECYT was founded under the auspices of Weg Der Mitte Non-Profit Organization for Holistic Medicine, Health Education and Social Services, one of the oldest holistic healing centers in Berlin. ECYT combines Eastern and Western healing traditions. A clinic for natural medicine on the premises offers different forms of massage, Chinese medicine, acupuncture, and homeopathy. Americans on the board of directors include Georg Feuerstein, Yoga Research and Education Center, Middletown, California; Larry Payne, Ph.D, Samata Yoga Center, Los Angeles, California; and Lilias Folan, Tri Yoga, Loveland, Ohio.

All teachers in the ECYT team have been teaching hatha yoga for many years. How often yoga is offered to the guests depends on the program they have booked. There are hatha yoga–intensive days, or if you come for relaxation, there is one hour of hatha yoga in the morning and meditation in the evening. The Ayurveda, yoga, and wellness program offers two daily yoga sessions.

ECYT is well known for its vegetarian cuisine and uses seasonal, organic, and homegrown ingredients.

Guest Yoga Teachers? Yes. Including Georg Feuerstein, Lilias Folan, Larry Payne.

Types of Yoga Classes Hatha. Once or twice daily. No extra charge.

Services Naturopathy, massage, Chinese medicine, acupuncture, homeopathy.

Other Classes Nutrition, meditation, Ayurveda, chanting.

Recreation Hiking.

Children's Program? Yes. Kindergarten.

Accommodations Single and shared rooms sleep 70 guests.

Dining Included. Vegetarian.

Attire/What to Bring Standard yoga attire, walking/hiking shoes, warm clothing.

Travel Information The nearest airports are Frankfurt and Hannover.

Rates Single room $69 per person per night. Two-bed room $49 per person per night. Three-bed room $38 per person per night.

Contact Kloster Gerode, D-37345 Gerode, Anreisebeschreibung; tel: 011-49-360-72-8200; fax: 011-49-360-728-2024; www.wegdermitte.de.

I have a 22-year relationship with the European College for Yoga and Therapy founder Daya Mullins and have given workshops there over a number of years. The grounds are unique; the school is in a centuries-old monastery. All the guest rooms have been remodeled with simple Danish furniture. The cuisine is made from vegetables grown organically at the center, and there are great cooks on staff.

All styles of yoga and yoga therapy are welcomed, and there are many forms of bodywork and healing, as well as psychological and spiritual counseling. The European College for Yoga and Therapy provides a rich melting pot of people from many paths.

−Larry Payne, Ph.D., author and yoga teacher, Los Angeles, California

Yoga Plus is a very simple kind of place. But the smallness and the simplicity are what make it so divine. You realize how little one really needs to be happy.

My husband and I brought our three kids, so the five of us shared a room. We were initially a bit freaked out by this setup—our whole family in one relatively small room with five white cots, a small desk, and a tiny bathroom. But it ended up being quite fantastic. This is not a plush resort, but what it lacks in material plushness it makes up for in spades in soul-enriching plushness.

The yoga is strictly Ashtanga. I would highly recommend Yoga Plus for all levels, whether you've never done yoga in your entire life or you're a devoted Ashtangi, well into the second series.

I had one heavenly massage in a room overlooking the sea, and we attended art class every day with the kids. We spent the rest of our days hanging out at the gorgeous beaches, exploring, and playing countless games of backgammon. I recommend going for two weeks. We were there one, and it just wasn't enough!

—Amy Krouse Rosenthal, writer, Chicago, Illinois

Yoga Plus   Crete, Greece

If you want to mix Mediterranean sun, sand, and water with yoga, visit Yoga Plus on the remote southern coast of Crete. The center is run by Radha and Pierre, two students of Pattabhi Jois. Typical classes include Ashtanga, Vinyasa, Iyengar yoga, African dance, tai chi, salsa, art, Cretan history, massage, and more. It's open May 4 to November 1. Brunch and dinner menus are based on vegetarian, vegan, and macrobiotic principles.

Guest Yoga Teachers? No.

Types of Yoga Classes Ashtanga, hatha. Once daily. No extra charge.

Services Shiatsu, massage, Alexander Technique, nutrition.

Other Classes Tai chi, Pilates, meditation.

Recreation Swimming, salsa, line dancing, art.

Children's Program? No.

Accommodations Shared double and triple rooms with private baths.

Dining Included. Twice daily. Vegetarian, vegan, macrobiotic.

Attire/What to Bring Standard yoga attire, swimsuit, sun/insect protection, walking shoes.

Travel Information Yoga Plus is a two-hour drive from the airports in Heraklion and Hania.

Rates Two-week package $856–$1,060 per person.

Contact 011-44-127-327-6175; www.yogaplus.co.uk.

Skyros   Skyros, Greece

Skyros runs three retreat centers: the Skyros Centre and Atsitsa, on the Greek island of Skyros, and a winter community on the Thai island of Ko Samet (see page 55). In these dramatic settings, Skyros offers more than 200 courses in yoga, writing, personal development, cooking, sailing, art, and more. Guests can choose three courses in the first week and, if they wish, another three in the second.

Atsitsa, which can host 80 people, is set in a pine forest on the west coast of the island, nine miles from Skyros village. The main stone villa, just a few yards from the sea, was built at the beginning of the twentieth century. Most guests are accommodated in on-site bamboo huts.

The Skyros Centre is at the edge of the village and accommodates 45 people. Guests stay in houses right in the village. This encourages integration into the local Greek community.

At the Skyros Centre and Atsitsa, guests are asked to participate in karma yoga (selfless service) by helping with food preparation and minor cleaning each day.

Guest Yoga Teachers? Yes. Including Rosslyn Albright, Jo Attwood, Costas Chrysikakis, Thomas Claire, Peter Guttridge, Vaya Hanou, John Hardstaff, Ulrike Harris, Jane Morgan-Jones, Michael Stewart, Lisehanne Webster.

Types of Yoga Classes Hatha, Ashtanga. Twice daily if taking yoga workshop. No extra charge.

Services N/A.

Other Classes Windsurfing, sailing, dance, theater, painting, music, writing, qigong, reflexology, tai chi, Pilates, Alexander Technique, Reiki method, and more.

Recreation Swimming, sailing.

Children's Program? No.

Accommodations Double and shared rooms. Single rooms available for an extra fee.

Dining Included. Three meals daily.

Attire/What to Bring Standard yoga attire, swimsuit, sun/insect protection, flashlight, walking shoes.

Travel Information Arrive in Athens on Friday, stay overnight in the Dorian Inn Hotel, and travel to the island on Saturday by coach and ferry. It is not possible to fly directly to Skyros island from or to arrive in Athens in time for a same-day transfer. A domestic small plane flies to Skyros from Athens, but its flights are irregular. At the end of the session, participants leave Skyros on Friday to take a flight home Friday evening, after 6 PM.

Rates Two-week retreat $699–$1,531.

Contact 92 Prince of Wales Road, London NW5 3NE, England; tel: 011-44-207-267-4424, 011-44-207-284-3065; fax: 011/44/207-284-3063; www.skyros.com.

I always dreamed of working for Skyros, as it symbolizes the ideal way of living to me—a beautiful location surrounded by like-minded people searching for ultimate happiness, clarity, peace, and understanding. The courses are all set up to help people express themselves, become creative, try new things, and overcome fears. There are plenty of options, and participants are encouraged to choose what they want to do and leave enough time for simply relaxing and being. I love staying in the huts in Atsitsa—it takes me back to nature.

The style of yoga I teach is called integral yoga hatha—a deep, gentle style similar to Sivananda. The classes are aimed at beginners and those with previous experience. I sometimes teach the class on the balcony outside the studio, so we can listen to the approaching waves below. I also teach massage, mainly based on Swedish techniques, with acupressure points and Reiki method.

—Jo Attwood, yoga teacher at Skyros

I chose Slí na Bandé because I wanted to get out of Dublin and stay somewhere in the countryside that I knew was a dedicated center for workshops. The center sits on a hillside overlooking land that sweeps down to the sea. The yoga studio is "Swiss chalet" style and has a wonderful potbellied stove. The main house has an attic sleeping area with several beds. There are also twin and triple bedrooms downstairs. Out in the courtyard are three other sleeping chalets for three and four people. Notable also are the wind turbine and solar panels, which provide electricity and hot water respectively. And the central heating runs on vegetable oil!

The food is all handmade, and the only word to describe it is delicious. Breakfast is homemade porridge, fresh-baked brown bread, yogurt, and fruit. Lunch is a different homemade soup every day, more lovely bread, and a selection of salads. Dinner is a hot meal with a grain or potato and vegetable dish. It could be buckwheat pancakes filled with mushroom and bean sauce or amazing vegetable lasagna.

Yoga class was held in the morning after breakfast and again in the late afternoon. Before breakfast there was meditation for an hour. The atmosphere was one of care and attention to one's own body, with an emphasis on safe movement. Class was two hours long and finished with a 20-minute guided relaxation session.

—Claire Haugh, shiatsu practitioner, yoga teacher, and part-time editor, Dublin

Slí na Bandé — Dublin, Ireland

Less than an hour's drive from Dublin lies Slí na Bandé, a pine chalet overlooking the sea and surrounding countryside. Here, yoga teacher Marlene Ffrench Mullen offers individual or small groups meditation, pranayama, yoga, vegetarian meals, and a variety of other activities, including sweat lodge ceremonies. Residential yoga weekends happen once a month and include meditation, breathing practices, journaling, hatha yoga, partner work, and a sweat lodge ceremony.

Guest Yoga Teachers? Yes. Including Dawn Cartwright, Granville Cousins, Geraldine Doyle, Joe Mulally.

Types of Yoga Classes Hatha, Iyengar. No extra charge during weekend workshops.

Services Shiatsu, sweat lodge.

Other Classes Meditation, pranayama.

Recreation Hiking, golf, horseback riding, fishing.

Children's Program? No.

Accommodations Six rooms and a dormitory; 20 beds. Three communal bathrooms/shower rooms and five toilets.

Dining Included. Vegetarian, organic.

Attire/What to Bring Standard yoga attire, hiking boots, cool weather attire, rain gear.

Travel Information About an hour's drive from the Dublin Airport.

Rates Weekend $214.

Contact Slí na Bandé, Kilmurry, Newtownmountkennedy, Co. Wicklow, Ireland; tel: 011-353-1281-9990, 011-353-1284-2777; fax: 011-353-1284-2814; www.slinabande.com.

Burren Yoga and Meditation Centre — Galway, Ireland

The Burren Yoga and Meditation Centre rests on two acres at the foot of the Burren Hills in west Ireland. It offers weekend and weeklong courses in yoga, Pilates, detoxification, and holistic health. The types of yoga taught include Ashtanga, Iyengar, Bikram, and Satyananda yoga (a gentle practice that includes breathwork, relaxation, and meditation).

The center, which has wood floors, underfloor heating, and large ceiling-to-floor windows, accommodates 15 people. It was designed using feng shui, with an emphasis on natural light and fresh air. Some workshops and events are held outside, weather permitting.

A local masseuse who practices a combination of deep-muscle massage, aromatherapy, and Reiki method is available to guests. A 70-minute session costs $32. A glass-enclosed Japanese bath, which will hold 10 people, is being built and should be completed by February 2004.

Guests can swim and sail at Lough Bunny Lake, five miles away.

Guest Yoga Teachers? Yes. Including Kevin Gardiner, Brian Potts, Richard Spahn.

Types of Yoga Classes Ashtanga, Iyengar, Satyananda, Hatha. Twice daily. No extra charge.

Services Massage, aromatherapy.

Other Classes Pilates, cooking, yoga-dance, shiatsu courses, detox courses, stress management, chanting, writing.

Recreation Swimming, horseback riding, hiking, sailing.

Children's Program? No.

Accommodations Rooms for two, four, or six people.

Dining Included in retreat package. Vegetarian. Vegan upon request.

Attire/What to Bring Standard yoga attire, towels, house slippers, walking shoes, rain gear, swimsuit, sun protection.

Travel Information The center is a 50-minute drive from Shannon Airport.

Rates Weekend course $213–$245. Weeklong course $638.

Contact Lig do Scith, Cappaghmore, Kinvara, Co. Galway, Ireland; tel: 011-353-9-163-7680; www.burrenyoga.com.

A low, wooden picket fence and wide open gateway mark the entrance to Burren Yoga and Meditation Center. Inside is a standing stone that depicts a yogi in meditation posture and bids one to "take one's ease" in Gaelic. The site is a natural haven, with a stone dolmen and a large stone circle. The main building is nestled among trees. The yoga room is spacious, bright, and airy, with views of the surrounding Burren hills.

The food was exquisite. The chef is a gourmet vegetarian chef, and although none of the course participants were fully vegetarian, the meals received high acclaim.

The particular course I had chosen was Satyananda yoga. There were two types of classes, breathwork and meditation class, and a posture class. Instruction in the postures was clear and concise. The postures and their focus and benefits were described. Students were observed closely and corrected as necessary.

Each morning after breakfast, the group participated in a walk by the sea, in the Burren hills, or to one of the many ancient and beautiful sites in the Burren region. There was also swimming in a nearby lake and visits to the local villages and towns. On one day the group took a ferry to the Aran Islands, another area of outstanding beauty.

—Dr. Siobhan Hennessy, public health medicine practitioner, Kilmaley, Ennis, County Clare

Sunflower Retreats — Casperia, Italy

Sunflower Retreats offers yoga, accommodations, and breakfast in the Italian village of Casperia. Guests stay in local houses, each with a small terrace. Casperia, in the heart of the Sabina Mountains, is a totally pedestrian village, with fewer than 1,000 occupants, and largely untouched by tourism.

Upon arrival, guests receive a weekly program describing which activities are available during the week in addition to yoga. Maps of walking and cycling routes you can do on your own are also provided. Most summer events are also available during the winter, except swimming and canoeing.

Sunflower is in a pedestrian-only medieval hilltop village. It is family run—the wife is the yoga teacher and the husband oversees the management. The yoga is gentle hatha yoga, geared toward the beginning student. It is a good way to be introduced to yoga or combine yoga with a vacation. The yoga teacher was very attentive. Afterward, the day is planned out. We went to the hot springs, horseback riding, and another medieval hilltop village. There were about 10 of us—mostly women and one couple. Usually we all went out to dinner together. The food is the best in Europe, and the most expensive meal with wine was $20.

—Leia Kline, traveling yoga student,
  Big Island of Hawaii

Excursions to Orvieto, Assisi, and other historic towns can be arranged with a private driver. Nearby sulfur hot springs and thermal baths, plus a variety of massage therapies, are part of the Sunflower experience.

Yoga classes, taught Friday through Tuesday, are suitable for beginning and intermediate yoga practitioners and are held outdoors or in the yoga studio. They last one to two hours. Classes are taught by Lucy Bremner, who has studied yoga in the U.K., India, Nepal, and Italy for the past 14 years, or with guest yoga teachers from around the world.

Retreat prices include yoga, breakfast, guided walks, use of bicycles, plus accommodations.

Guest Yoga Teachers? Yes. Including Sheila Coombes, Monica Daboneiti, Sara Rossi, Aldo Salvotori.

Types of Yoga Classes Hatha. Friday–Tuesday. No extra charge.

Services Massage, reflexology, shiatsu, aromatherapy, acupressure, chakra balancing, Indian head massage, Bach flower remedies, aloe vera skin treatments.

Other Classes Pranayama, meditation.

Recreation Swimming, canoeing, walking, biking, skiing, sauna, horseback riding, hot springs.

Children's Program? No.

Accommodations Single and shared rooms for 15 people.

Dining Breakfast included.

Attire/What to Bring Standard yoga attire, swimsuit, walking shoes, sun/insect protection.

Travel Information Casperia is located about 90 minutes from Rome's airports. The easiest and most economical way to reach Casperia is by train from Fiumicino Airport. A frequent direct train runs from the airport to nearby Poggio Mirteto Scalo and costs about $5. (Trains running to Orte also stop at this station.) Sunflower can pick up guests from the station, provided they call before boarding the train and leave a message.

Rates Twin room $432 per person for six nights. Twin with private bathroom $620 per person for six nights.

Contact c/o The Manor House, Kings Norton, Leicestershire LE7 9BA U.K.; tel: 011-39-0765-639015 (Italy), 011-44-116-259-9422 (U.K.); www.sunflowerretreats.com.

Molino del Rey   Jorox, Spain

Molino del Rey, only 50 minutes from the tourist attractions of Costa del Sol and the city of Ronda, was built from two ancient water mills. An on-site spring provides water for the center's bathing facilities. Adjacent to a national park, the area is excellent for hiking. Molino del Rey regularly hosts workshops in yoga, meditation, healing, tai chi, qigong, creativity, voice work, dance, and art.

The yoga studio is built into the mountainside, and remains cool during even the warmest months. Natural caves that lead off from the studios are used for meditation, chanting, and more.

Guests can take day trips by car to Granada (about two hours), with its famous Alhambra Palace (a famous example of Moorish architecture dating back to the 13th century), Sevilla, Nerja, with its famous caves, Cordoba, Gibraltar, Marbella, and Ronda. The nearby national park, Sierra de las Nieves, contains the Abies Pinsapo Boissir, the oldest known species of European fir tree.

Guest Yoga Teachers? Yes. Including Robin and Emma Catto, Sue Delf, Nic Freeman, Simon Low, Gemma Mallo, Panilla Marott, Dago Paz, Jilly Rosse.

Types of Yoga Classes Vinyasa, hatha, Ashtanga. No extra charge if you buy yoga package.

Services Massage.

Other Classes Meditation, tai chi, qigong, voice work, dance, art.

Recreation Swimming, hiking, sauna, horseback riding.

Children's Program? No.

Accommodations Seven double rooms, one single room. Sleeps 15.

Dining Included. Breakfast and dinner. Vegetarian.

Attire/What to Bring Standard yoga attire, swimsuit, walking/hiking shoes, sun/insect protection.

Travel Information Fly to Malaga. Price of car service to the center is often included in yoga packages.

Rates Shared room $58 per person per day. Single room $72 per day. Yoga package $777 per person per week.

Contact Valle de Jorox, E-29567, Alozaina - Málaga - Spain; tel: 011-34-95-248-0009; www.molinodelrey.de/; www.freespirituk.com.

At Molino del Rey there are visiting yoga teachers throughout the summer. I studied with Sue Delf, an incredible vinyasa-style teacher from England. No one there was really a beginning student. The center is tucked into this little valley and built right into the hillside. The yoga and massage rooms were built into caves—it's amazing the way they are constructed. They also have beautiful views and remain cool even in August. The area waterways converged at the retreat center, although the surrounding area is arid.

The food is all traditional Spanish fare but vegetarian. The guest rooms had views of the valley and featured Spanish tile floors and balconies. We went on excursions to a lake about an hour away, to Granada and Alhambra Palace, which was an experience of a lifetime, and Ronda, a traditional Spanish town with the oldest bull ring in Spain.

—Leia Kline, traveling yoga student, Big Island of Hawaii

Resorts & Spas

The Boulders   Carefree, Arizona

At the aptly named Boulders, tawny adobe casitas are almost indistinguishable among the 12-million-year-old terra cotta–colored granite boulders in the desert foothills. As you walk from your casita to the Golden Door Spa, you're bound to encounter saguaro cacti, deer, and jackrabbits.

Guests can enjoy tennis, swimming, hiking, horseback riding, and golf on the 36-hole Jay Morrish championship course. The resort also has its own festival marketplace, with galleries, cafes, and a Native American art museum. The 33,000-square-foot Golden Door Spa has 24 treatment rooms, a labyrinth (meditative maze), a 2,000-square-foot fitness center, Vichy showers, a spa cafe, yoga studio, Pilates, and a watsu pool.

Guest Yoga Teachers? No.

Types of Yoga Classes Viniyoga, yoga flow and stretch, yoga for golf. One to two classes daily. $10 per class.

Services Watsu, massage, aromatherapy.

Other Classes Tai chi, qigong, Pilates, aerobics, Spinning, meditation.

Recreation Rock climbing, mountain biking, hiking, golf, horseback riding, tennis, Jacuzzi, sauna, whirlpool.

Children's Program? No.

Accommodations 215 rooms and villas, three suites.

When you drive up to the Boulders, it is a bit surreal. These huge orange-brown boulders sit on top of each other to create rock formations; it's like they were stacked by an artistic giant. And in between sit adobe casitas that are the same color as the boulders. When the sun rises, the whole place has a golden, mystical glow. The casitas are appropriately decorated with Mexican and Indian art, wood beams, stucco walls, and tiled fireplaces. The desert cools down quickly in the winter, so it is actually chilly enough at night to burn the aromatic logs in the fireplace. I was reminded that I was really out in the desert when a snake crossed my path on the way to the fitness room one morning.

—Jeanne Ricci

Dining Not included. Six restaurants: the Latilla (upscale regional American), Palo Verde (Southwestern), Boulders Club, Bakery Cafe, Cantina del Pedregal (casual Mexican), Golden Door Spa Cafe.

Attire/What to Bring Standard yoga/workout attire, sun protection, hiking boots.

Travel Information The Boulders is 30 miles from Phoenix Sky Harbor Airport.

Rates $250–$595 per night, double occupancy.

Contact 34631 North Tom Darlington Drive, PO Box 2090, Carefree, AZ, 85377; tel: 480-488-9009; fax: 480-488-4118; www.wyndhamluxury.com.

Miraval   Catalina, Arizona

The main concept at Miraval is that we need to slow down and not be in such a rush. It's about really thinking about what you do. Miraval teaches you mindful exercising. There is even a class on mindful eating. You are taught to eat slowly and in silence. It's amazing how you really taste the flavors in food when you eat that way. And the food is amazing—low fat but you would never believe it. You can have a glass of wine with dinner—Miraval is not about deprivation.

You even learn how to ride a horse mindfully. The horse barn is run by a psychiatrist. You learn how to ride a horse without kicking it or yelling at it—you communicate with your body. It is one of the most phenomenal experiences. You actually feel that you bond with the horse without ever saying anything. It is like in the movie The Horse Whisperer. On the last day, I mentally called to my horse, and he came to me without my ever saying a word.

There are lots of activities to challenge you—Outward Bound-like activities to break through your fears. I climbed a rock wall, and I was terrified because I'm afraid of heights. It gave me a burst of confidence, and I was really proud of myself after that.

—Carol Isaak Barden, contributing editor, *Travel & Leisure* magazine, Houston, Texas

Miraval is a luxury resort and spa on 135 acres in the high desert of southern Arizona near Tucson. Miraval combines challenging self-discovery activities like rock climbing with pampering spa treatments and innovative cuisine. Try horseback riding, rock climbing, tennis, golf, meditation, and yoga techniques to help alleviate stress. Usually, three to four yoga classes are offered per day. Morning yoga class focuses on sun salutations, while the restorative class allows you to explore supported poses for better breathing, posture, and tension relief. There is also a level two hatha yoga class for more advanced practitioners.

Guest Yoga Teachers? No.

Types of Yoga Classes Yogilates, fundamentals, restorative, partner, Ashtanga, energetic. Three to four times daily. No extra charge.

Services Massage, hydrotherapy suites, facials, Ayurveda, acupuncture, chi nei tsang massage, shiatsu, jin shin jyutsu, Trager, reflexology, craniosacral therapy, Reiki method.

Other Classes Meditation, tai chi, dietary management, qigong, Pilates, golf, tennis, Zen boot camp, water conditioning, yoga philosophy, introduction to Ayurveda, pranayama.

Recreation Hiking, biking, golf, tennis, rock climbing, horseback riding.

Children's Program? No.

Accommodations 92 rooms, 14 suites

Dining Included. Three meals daily. Low-fat, low-calorie. Vegetarian available.

Attire/What to Bring Standard yoga attire, swimsuit, hiking boots, sun protection.

Travel Information Miraval is 32 miles from the Tucson airport.

Rates $365–$1,145 per person per night.

Contact 5000 E. Via Estancia Miraval, Catalina, AZ 85739; tel: 800-232-3969, 520-825-4000; fax: 520-792-5870; www.miravalresort.com.

CopperWynd   Fountain Hills, Arizona

CopperWynd is a European-inspired resort in the Sonoran Desert, 30 miles north of downtown Phoenix. European body and facial treatments are offered along with classes in tai chi, meditation, aerobics, Spinning, yoga, and Pilates. You can use the fitness and free-weight equipment to work out on your own, or consult the professionally trained fitness trainers to design an individualized program. Afterward, relax in the steam room or whirlpool spa.

Guest Yoga Teachers? No.

Types of Yoga Classes Hatha, Power. No extra charge.

Services Massage, aromatherapy, facials, body treatments, nail care.

Other Classes Spinning, Pilates, aquaerobics, tai chi, stretching, meditation, step aerobics, sculpting, and toning.

Recreation Swimming, tennis, golf.

Children's Program? Yes. CopperWynd Kids Club.

Accommodations 40 guest rooms and villas.

Dining Not included. Two restaurants: Alchemy (New American with Sonoran flair), Poolside Pavilion Bar and Grille.

Attire/What to Bring Standard yoga/workout attire, sun protection, swimsuit.

Travel Information 30 miles from Phoenix Sky Harbor Airport; transportation is not provided to and from the airport but can be arranged at a cost. Preferred vendor is ExecuCar (602-232-4600).

Protect Your Neck Besides practicing the in-flight yoga stretches in this book (see page 184), you can prevent a stiff neck by using an inflatable neck pillow on the plane. –K.F.M.

I carry around a directory of small luxury hotels in my briefcase, and that's how I found CopperWynd. When I know it is time to take a break, I whip out the book and choose a place. I returned to CopperWynd twice within one month.

When I take any time off, I always go to spa resorts because I like getting treatments. What's great about CopperWynd is it is a short trip from the airport, but it's almost like a secret hideaway. Before CopperWynd I would go to Sedona, which is getting a bit congested. Usually I only stay two or three nights, so I get two treatments a day. I've had massages, facials, body wraps, and deep-tissue massage.

–Kristi Grooms, banker, Cincinnati, Ohio

Rates $99–$950 per night, double occupancy.

Contact 13225 North Eagle Ridge Drive, Fountain Hills, AZ 85268; tel: 877-707-7760, 480-333-1900; fax: 480/333-1901; www.copperwynd.com.

Sanctuary on Camelback Mountain   Scottsdale, Arizona

Sanctuary on Camelback Mountain is a resort and spa providing a mix of Eastern and Western philosophies. Built in 1969 and formerly known as John Gardiner's Tennis Ranch, it was redesigned and reopened in 2001. The casitas and villas are built into the mountain and have their own outdoor steeping tubs. There is also an infinity edge pool, lap pool, five tennis courts, hiking trails, a fitness center, and a spa.

The 12,000-square-foot Sanctuary Spa features a Zen meditation garden, indoor and outdoor treatment rooms, fitness center, yoga studio, a watsu pool, and the Sanctum, a spiral yin/yang walled outdoor treatment room for two. Yoga classes are taught by hatha yoga instructor Angie Rupiper, co-owner of the Anusara yoga studio Arizona Yoga, and Power yoga instructor Gretchen Black.

Guest Yoga Teachers? No.

Types of Yoga Classes Hatha, Power. Tuesday through Saturday, once or twice daily. $15 per class. Private classes are available.

Services Acupuncture, facials, massage, shiatsu, Reiki method, reflexology, body treatments, watsu, nail care.

Other Classes Kickboxing, qigong, Pilates, tai chi, meditation, dance.

Recreation Biking, golf, horseback riding, swimming, tennis, ballooning, hiking, Jacuzzi, biking.

Children's Program? No.

Accommodations 98 mountainside and spa casitas.

Dining Not included. One restaurant: Elements (American/Asian fusion cuisine).

Attire/What to Bring Standard yoga attire, swimsuit, sun/insect protection, hiking boots.

Travel Information Sanctuary is eight miles north of the Phoenix Skyharbor Airport.

Rates $175–$1,010 per night, double occupancy.

I take out-of-town people to Sanctuary every chance I get. The view of Mummy Mountain from the restaurant, Elements, is amazing. There are new casitas, a pool, and a spa. The yoga instructor there, Angie Rupiper, is a fabulous person. She is the top yoga professional in the area. I watch her work with the other students, and she is so gentle and thoughtful. The spa manager has assembled a first-class crew. I travel a lot, mostly on airplanes, and I tend to stiffen up. I see Angie on Thursday mornings, and I feel like a million bucks after a session with her. I started taking classes with her in January 2002. The spa is an indoor/outdoor environment. It's a peaceful, serene setting—like a relaxed retreat. They have a very comprehensive fitness class schedule.

The chef at Elements makes a cold eggplant relish—you can make a meal of it. They also have two or three vegetarian dishes, and they make a hell of a martini. It is a very eclectic menu with a pan-Asian feel to it.

One of the nice things about Sanctuary is the Asian theme. A lot of Arizona resorts tend to go indigenous, so Sanctuary is unique for this area.

—Michael Rappoport, utility company executive, Phoenix, Arizona

Contact 5700 East McDonald Drive, Scottsdale (Paradise Valley), AZ 85253; tel: 800-245-2051, 480-948-2100; fax: 480-948-7314; www.sanctuaryaz.com.

Enchantment Resort   Sedona, Arizona

Enchantment Resort, in Sedona's Boynton Canyon, is two hours north of Phoenix and two and a half hours south of the Grand Canyon. Sedona, at an elevation of 4,500 feet, enjoys moderate weather year-round. The area is thought to be the birthplace of the Yavapai-Apache tribe. In fact, ancient ruins of Native American cliff dwellings are nearby.

The design of the 24,000-square-foot Mii amo Spa was inspired by these dwellings. (Mii amo means "a journey or passage" in the Yuman dialect.) The spa's five adobe brick towers are set into the face of a red rock canyon wall. Communal areas and pools are on the ground level; 24 treatment rooms are in the towers. This is also where yoga classes take place. Yoga weeks and workshops are offered throughout the year. The rest of the resort's adobe buildings also blend in with the surrounding red rocks for which Sedona is famous.

Mii amo Café serves breakfast, lunch, and dinner. The menu combines Asian and Southwestern flavors with organic and macrobiotic options. Fine dining is available in the Yavapai Restaurant, which has 180-degree views of Boynton Canyon. A breakfast buffet is served daily with a jazz brunch on Sundays. And Tii Gavo offers casual dining.

Guest Yoga Teachers? Yes. Including Jane Fryer, Dianne Harman.

Types of Yoga Classes Hatha, flow, restorative. Classes offered twice daily. $18 per day or included in spa packages.

Services Ayurvedic treatments, shirodhara, massage, watsu, shiatsu, reflexology, craniosacral therapy, Reiki method, hydrotherapy baths, body treatments, facials, waxing, nail care.

Other Classes Step aerobics, qigong, meditation, tai chi, hula-hooping, aquaerobics, tennis clinic.

Recreation Water volleyball, tennis, horticulture talks, hiking, stargazing tours, croquet, golf, plane and train tours, horseback tours, bocce ball.

Children's Program? Yes. Camp Coyote for ages 4 to 12.

Accommodations 220 adobe casitas, haciendas, and casa suites.

I went to the Enchantment Resort and Mii amo Spa because I needed to relax after years without a real vacation. The spa and resort, in a gorgeous canyon, blend beautifully into the landscape. The spa is a magical fusion of Asian feng shui concepts and Native American tradition.

I loved the women's lounge. It features a Jacuzzi, steam room, sauna, and a host of products to rub and spray on yourself. You can sit in the lounge in a spa robe and drink tea specific to your Ayurvedic dosha. Hatha yoga is taught in the morning and restorative yoga in the evening. I had a great hot stone massage, which was heavenly, and I also experienced shirodhara, which included a light facial and massage. The treatment rooms have windows, so you can view the sky and red rocks.

The casita I stayed in was secluded and had a gas fireplace, bar and living room area, patio, and a Native American vibe to it. A CD with Native American music was next to the bed as well. Each time I left the casita, I would see wildlife: mule deer, hummingbirds, geckos, butterflies, and pinyon jays.

The food in the spa was great, healthy but not about deprivation. The spa serves such items as organic wine, sushi, salmon, crème brûlée, and sorbets.

I hiked in the canyon several times. It only takes 15 minutes to reach the kachina woman, an energy vortex. I also went on a red rock Jeep tour and took a plane to the Grand Canyon, where we helicoptered down into the canyon and had a pontoon ride.

—Jennifer Worick, freelance writer, Philadelphia, Pennsylvania

Dining Not included. Three restaurants: Mii amo Café (spa cuisine), Yavapai Restaurant (fine dining), Tii Gavo (casual dining).

Attire/What to Bring Standard yoga/workout attire, hiking boots, swimsuit, sun protection.

Travel Information Enchantment Resort is 120 miles from Phoenix Sky Harbor Airport.

Rates $195–$1,045 per night, double occupancy.

Contact 525 Boynton Canyon Road, Sedona, AZ 86336; tel: 800-826-4180 (reservations), 928-282-2900, 888-749-2137 (Mii amo Spa); fax: 928-282-9249; www.enchantmentresort.com.

Canyon Ranch   Tucson, Arizona

Canyon Ranch set the standard for the industry. Not only can you go there and get pampered, hike, bike, and eat healthy food, but you can also get a bone density test, because it's a medical facility with all types of doctors on staff to address guests' mental and physical issues. The special theme weeks are great—I went to one for menopause. At Canyon Ranch they understand that we are more than just a body.

The facility has the most amazing hiking and biking programs in Sabino Canyon. I find it so wonderful to go there and jump into the hiking program. You get to experience both forests and desert terrain. There are more than 60 fitness classes—nobody offers a better variety. You never know who is going to be speaking that night, and it's always someone terrific. The atmosphere is very casual—you can look disorderly all week—and there is no need for makeup.

–Carol Isaak Barden, contributing editor, *Travel & Leisure* magazine, Houston, Texas

Canyon Ranch is, quite simply, an überspa. What else do you call a facility with a 62,000-square-foot spa complex and an 11,000-square-foot indoor aquatic center? The first location, in Tucson, opened in 1979. In 1989, a second location, Canyon Ranch in the Berkshires Health Resort, was built in the woodlands of Lenox, Massachusetts. Spa services, fitness and outdoor sports, medical and behavioral services and consultations, nutrition consultations and workshops, spiritual pursuits, and healthy gourmet cuisine are available at both locations. There are 50 fitness classes daily. You can usually choose from five different yoga classes each day, many of which are taught in the yoga dome.

In fact, it would take you about a month to complete every consultation, service, and workshop offered, so pick your activities mindfully. At the Tucson property, with its adobe cottages, it's typical to see roadrunners by day and hear distant coyotes by night. The casual style and large, knowledgeable staff (three staff members for every guest) put visitors at ease. This is an ideal environment for either an active vacation or a pampered, relaxing getaway.

Guest Yoga Teachers? Yes. Including De De Daniels, Jane Fonda, Carol Kline, Lisa Shremp.

Types of Yoga Classes Basic, intermediate, introduction to sun salutations, Power, restorative. Offered five times daily. No extra charge.

Services Massages, facials, body treatments, Ayurveda, craniosacral therapy, reflexology, Reiki method, shiatsu, shirodhara, hydromassage, Jin Shin Jyutsu, watsu.

Other Classes Tai chi, qigong, meditation, nutrition, movement therapy, exercise physiology, behavioral health, aerobics, Boxercise, Spinning, ballet, kickboxing.

Recreation Biking, hiking, swimming, sauna, Jacuzzi, gym, racquetball, tennis, golf lessons, basketball.

Children's Program? No. Minimum age 14 to participate in regular spa program.

Accommodations Up to 240 guests. Standard, executive, hacienda/casita, or casa grande.

Dining Included. Vegetarian/vegan available.

Attire/What to Bring Standard gym/yoga attire, swimsuit, sun protection, tennis/golf attire.

Travel Information Canyon Ranch is 18 miles from the Tucson International Airport. Shuttle service to and from the airport is provided by Canyon Ranch.

Rates Four-night stay $2,000–$5,000 per person.

Contact 8600 E. Rockcliff Road, Tucson, AZ 85750; tel: 800-742-9000, 520-749-9000; fax: 520-749-7755; www.canyonranch.com.

Loews Ventana Canyon Resort — Tucson, Arizona

The 93-acre Loews Ventana Canyon Resort is located on a plateau above Tucson and surrounded by the Catalina Mountains. Twelve thousand years ago, Tucson was a Native American village called Stukshon. Loosely translated, it means "springs from the foot of the black hill," which aptly describes Tucson.

On the Loews Ventana property you'll find Saguaro cacti, coyote, and horned owls. Two championship golf courses, an on-site spa, two swimming pools with Jacuzzis, hot- and cold-water plunge, eight lighted tennis courts, miles of hiking and running trails, biking, horseback riding, Ping-Pong, and basketball keep guests as busy as they want to be. On cool winter afternoons, traditional English tea is served in the Cascade Lounge.

At the spa, guests can take advantage of the sauna and steam rooms, the fully equipped fitness center with floor-to-ceiling windows, aerobic studio, lap pool, and Jacuzzi.

Yoga classes are taught by, among others, Bonnie Schroeder, who has trained with Priscilla Potter and Lilias Folan. Intermediate classes are

Loews Ventana Canyon Resort feels like it is in the middle of the remote desert. I like it because it is not in the middle of town, but it is only a half-hour drive from the airport. A big cactus greets you as you enter the lobby. The hotel is built into the side of the mountain, and many of the rooms look out onto the desert. During the cooler months there is outdoor dining with views of the desert and golf course. It's a very upscale environment.

—Debbie Richards, associate publisher, *Meetings Magazine*, San Francisco, California

offered for more advanced yogis. Outdoor yoga classes are also available, and private yoga sessions are available in your room.

Nearby attractions include the Arizona-Sonora Desert Museum, Sabino Canyon, Saguaro National Park, Center for Creative Photography, Mission San Xavier Del Bac, Tucson Botanical Gardens, and Biosphere II.

Guest Yoga Teachers? No.

Types of Yoga Classes Hatha. Once daily. $12 per day includes entrance to fitness center.

Services Massage, shiatsu, facials, body treatments, Reiki method, cranio-sacral therapy, reflexology.

Other Classes Aquaerobics, step aerobics, body sculpting, meditation, tai chi.

Recreation Hiking, biking, running, golf, tennis, swimming, basketball, horseback riding, Ping-Pong.

Children's Program? Yes. Coyote Club for ages 4 to 12.

Accommodations 398 rooms, including 31 suites.

Dining Not included. Four restaurants: Flying V Bar & Grill (Southwestern), Ventana Room (New American), Canyon Cafe (casual American), Bill's Grill (poolside dining).

Attire/What to Bring Standard yoga/workout attire, running and hiking gear, golf and tennis wear.

Travel Information Loews Ventana Canyon Resort is 25 minutes from Tucson International Airport.

Rates $120–$390 per night, double occupancy.

Contact 7000 North Resort Drive, Tucson, AZ 85750; tel: 520-299-2020; www.loewshotels.com.

CALIFORNIA

The Claremont Resort and Spa   Berkeley, California

A majestic white vision in the Oakland/Berkeley hills overlooking the San Francisco Bay, this 22-acre historical resort offers guests a spa, a 10-court tennis center, two pools, and remarkable views of San Francisco. The Claremont was built in 1915 and was remodeled in 1937, and a four-year renovation was just completed in 2003. A new spa, opened in 2001 in the historic hotel, offers Ayurvedic beauty therapies as well as traditional skin and body treatments and massage. Yoga, which takes place two to four times a day, is free for hotel guests. This is an ideal place to bring the family, with a pool, tennis courts, nearby hiking and biking trails, and a day camp to amuse those not interested in yoga.

Guest Yoga Teachers? Yes. Including Seane Corn, Rod Stryker.

Types of Yoga Classes Hatha, restorative, active. Two to three times daily. No extra charge.

Services Aromatherapy, deep-tissue massage, flotation tank, pressure point massage, reflexology, facials, manicures, pedicures, Ayurveda.

Other Classes Aerobics, nutritional counseling, personal training, tennis, restorative fitness, Pilates, kickboxing, Feldenkrais, Breema, pranayama.

Recreation Swimming, tennis, hiking.

Children's Program? Yes. Day camp for ages 4 to 10; swimming and tennis clinics for ages 7 to 16.

Accommodations 269 rooms, 10 suites

Dining Not included. Three restaurants: Jordan's Restaurant (fine dining), Paragon Bar & Cafe (California cuisine), Bayview Café (poolside).

Attire/What to Bring Standard gym/yoga/tennis attire.

Travel Information The Claremont is 12 miles from Oakland International Airport and 24 miles from San Francisco International Airport.

Rates $270–$1,000 per night, double occupancy.

Contact 41 Tunnel Road, Berkeley, CA 94705; tel: 800-551-7266, 510-843-3000; fax: 510-843-6239; www.claremontresort.com.

You can see the Claremont from across the bay in San Francisco. People unfamiliar with the area always ask "What is that?" because it is a striking white building surrounded by the trees of the Berkeley/Oakland hills. It's got the grand feel of a historic hotel, a bit like that rambling place in the movie The Shining. Supposedly room 422 is haunted, which adds to the mystique. In contrast, there is a modern spa and fitness facility, so it's really the best of both worlds. And I love the new, hip Paragon Bar & Cafe, which offers live jazz Wednesday through Saturday and great views of San Francisco. It has sleek furniture and a great little menu with items like a roasted beet salad, bruschetta with glazed onions and blue cheese, and fried calamari with chipotle aioli.

—Jeanne Ricci

Post Ranch Inn & Spa   Big Sur, California

Big Sur is a community of fewer than 1,400 residents, set among the ridges of the Ventana Mountains at the edge of the Pacific Ocean. In 1860, William Brainard Post was one of the first to homestead the area. He ran a working ranch with apple orchards and livestock, which later became the Post Ranch Inn & Spa. Today, the inn offers spa treatments, 30 guest rooms in seven unique houses, daily yoga, and hiking trails. The 96-acre property has a variety of trees and animals that have been native to the land for centuries.

Relax in two very different pools on the property. The basking pool, overlooking the ocean, is kept at a constant 104°F and is the perfect place to take in the view. Visit the lap pool if you want to go for a brisk swim.

I've been going to the Post Ranch Inn for a long time. I keep returning because Post Ranch offers the ultimate in what I want when I want to get away: the mountains, sea, pampering for the body and soul, disconnect from the stresses of the outside world, and connection with the inner body. It heals.

Post Ranch has recently added a fitness center. There is a basking pool with mineral water at the edge of a cliff that looks out at the ocean. And they have a wonderful massage program. Some of the masseuses have been with them a long time, and that says a lot.

There are two kinds of accommodations. You can stay in an ocean house built into the cliff with earth and grass growing on top of it and a patio that fronts on the ocean. The view is spectacular. Or you can choose a tree house built on stilts. Some have views of both the ocean and mountains. All have fireplaces.

The chefs at Sierra Mar Restaurant are among the finest in the country. They use organic ingredients and are health-minded in their preparation. The complimentary breakfast is a buffet laden with the freshest fruit of the season, yogurt, three or four quiches, one of which is vegetarian, bacon and eggs, homemade pastries, and vegan food as well. If you hike, do yoga twice a day, swim, eat that food, and drive along that coast, it relieves your stress.

–Jane Wetzel, community volunteer, Dallas, Texas

Each of the 30 rooms has a king-size bed, fireplace, pull-out massage table, and indoor spa tub. The refrigerator is stocked with complimentary snacks and nonalcoholic beverages. There are no televisions to disturb the serenity of the resort. Music is available from an in-room CD and cassette stereo with 45-channel DMX satellite music system. The Sierra Mar Restaurant, with spectacular views of the Pacific, has won multiple awards for its cuisine.

Guest Yoga Teachers? No.

Types of Yoga Classes Hatha with pranayama every day at 8:30 AM, with a second class at 10 AM on Tuesday, Wednesday, and Thursday, and at 12:30 PM on Saturday. No extra charge. Private lessons are available for a fee.

Services Massage, facials, body treatments, reflexology, craniosacral therapy, Reiki method.

Other Classes Meditation, tai chi, qigong.

Recreation Nature walks with Bill Post, great-grandson of the original homesteader of the ranch, herb garden talks, star gazing, swimming, sculpture garden tours.

Children's Program? No. Minimum age 18.

Accommodations 30 rooms with views of ocean or mountains.

Dining Breakfast included. One restaurant: Sierra Mar. Vegetarian available.

Attire/What to Bring Standard yoga/workout attire, hiking boots, swimsuit, sun/insect protection.

Travel Information Post Ranch Inn is about 150 miles from San Francisco International Airport and 30 miles from the Monterey County airport.

Rates $485–$935 per night, double occupancy. Weekend two-night minimum stay.

Contact Highway 1, P.O. Box 219, Big Sur, CA 93920; tel: 800-527-2200; fax: 831-667-2824; www.postranchinn.com.

Ventana Inn & Spa   Big Sur, California

Ventana Inn & Spa is an upscale resort in an upscale location, 1,200 feet above the Pacific Ocean on the Big Sur coast. Sixty rooms and suites are housed in 12 buildings.

Each morning, a continental breakfast that includes fresh bread and pastries from Ventana's own bakery is served in the lobby and sometimes in the oceanview library, both with stone fireplaces. You'll be sure to return again in the afternoon for the complimentary wine, cheese, and fresh fruit.

Ventana is known for its Japanese-style baths, which are open each day from 8 AM to 2 AM. Clothing-optional areas are available. Two heated swimming pools and two saunas round out the facilities.

The fitness room, with a variety of equipment including treadmills, elliptical cross trainers, bicycles, and free weights, is open from 7 AM until 10:30 PM. Guests can also hike, whale watch, and horseback ride nearby along the coast.

The Allegria Spa offers pampering services such as an aromatherapy massage, a sea enzyme facial, and an ocean salt body polish, as well as yoga, tai chi, and meditation classes. Private classes (yoga, Pilates, meditation) are $75 per hour. Each month, a different form of energy work, such as polarity or Reiki, is available. Call in advance for an appointment.

Guest Yoga Teachers? No.

Types of Yoga Classes Hatha, Bikram, Power, Kundalini, Raja. Once daily. No extra charge during high season.

Services Massage, craniosacral therapy, reflexology, shiatsu, Reiki method, body treatments, facials, aromatherapy, astrology readings, color readings.

Other Classes Tai chi, meditation, Pilates.

Recreation Hiking, swimming, saunas, whale watching, horseback riding.

Children's Program? No.

Accommodations 59 rooms and one house.

Dining Breakfast included. One restaurant: Cielo Restaurant (California cuisine, vegetarian available), daily wine and cheese reception.

Attire/What to Bring Standard yoga attire, hiking boots, sun/insect protection, swimsuit.

Travel Information Ventana Inn is about 150 miles from San Francisco International Airport and 30 miles from the Monterey County airport.

Rates $410–$975 per night, double occupancy.

Contact Highway 1, Big Sur, CA 93920; tel: 800-628-6500, 831-667-2331; fax: 831-667-2419; www.ventanainn.com.

Ventana Inn provides upscale lodging and an extraordinarily good restaurant that compares favorably to high-end eateries in San Francisco. Ventana also has lovely Japanese-style baths, lots of nearby hiking trails, and a great massage staff.

—Todd Jones, *Yoga Journal* senior editor

The Fairmont Sonoma Mission Inn & Spa

Boyes Hot Springs, California

Sonoma Mission Inn is right off a main thoroughfare in Northern California, so at first you think "This isn't going to be relaxing." But once you go through the gates and walk through the gardens past gurgling fountains to your room, you know the place will prove you wrong. Couple a massage with a soak in the hot mineral pool, and you're in heaven. And the inn is a short distance from Sonoma Plaza, a green area in the middle of town surrounded by shops and restaurants. Samples of the inn's signature bath and spa products are in the bathroom so you can take a little bit of the place home with you. I especially love the apricot-scented body lotion.

—Jeanne Ricci

The Fairmont Sonoma Mission Inn & Spa, set in the heart of the California Wine Country, has a rich history. Native Americans were the first to visit the natural hot thermal waters on the current inn grounds. This site was considered a sacred healing ground for generations. In 1895, Captain H. E. Boyes bought the property and discovered 135°F spring water while drilling a well. Within five years, he had built the Boyes Hot Springs Hotel. Soon, San Franciscans were arriving to "take the waters." In 1923, a fire destroyed the hotel. The current Sonoma Mission Inn, a replica of a California mission, was completed in 1927. The newly renovated 40,000-square-foot spa revolves, as always, around the property's mineral springs, which flow 1,100 feet beneath the inn.

Guest Yoga Teachers? Yes. Including Leslie Gifford, Leslie Murphy, Suzanne Shonbrun.

Types of Yoga Classes Hatha. Twice daily. No extra charge.

Services Body treatments, facials, aromatherapy, massage, reflexology, shiatsu, watsu, nail care.

Other Classes Ai chi, aerobics, aquaerobics, step aerobics, personal training, Pilates, meditation.

Recreation Mineral springs, swimming, biking, hiking, golf.

Children's Program? No. Minimum age 18 to visit the Spa.

Accommodations 170 rooms, 60 suites.

Dining Not included. Three restaurants: Big 3 Diner; Sante Restaurant; Spa Café.

Attire/What to Bring Standard yoga/workout attire, swimsuit, hiking boots, sun/insect protection.

Travel Information Sonoma Mission Inn & Spa is 60 miles north of the San Francisco International Airport.

Rates $229–$1,000 per room, double occupancy.

Contact 100 Boyes Blvd., Boyes Hot Springs, CA 95416; tel: or 800-862-4945, 707-938-9000; fax: 707-938-4250; www.fairmont.com/sonoma/.

The Ashram   Calabasas, California

The Ashram has been described as a boot camp for health seekers and those who want to lose weight. Either you love it or hate it. Only 12 people can visit the facility at one time, and all guests participate in the same seven-day routine together. A week at the Ashram starts on Sunday at 2 PM and ends the following Saturday at 11 AM. A typical day begins at 6 AM with 60 minutes of yoga followed by breakfast. Then get ready for a 10- to 15-mile hike in the Santa Monica Mountains. You return for lunch and a massage. The afternoon consists of a pool class, free-weight workout, and a long yoga and meditation session. The Ashram, which opened in 1974 in Calabasas, is on six acres in a secluded valley surrounded by mountains and running streams. The city of Calabasas is in northwest Los Angeles County, about 25 miles from downtown Los Angeles and adjacent to Malibu, Topanga, Agoura Hills, Hidden Hills, and Woodland Hills in the San Fernando Valley. Yoga and meditation are practiced in a large dome, and daily massages take place in the surrounding cottages. Famous Ashram "survivors" include Ashley Judd, Dan Aykroyd, Jane Fonda, and Oprah Winfrey.

Guest Yoga Teachers? No.

Types of Yoga Classes Hatha. Twice daily. No extra charge.

Services Massage.

Other Classes Meditation, health and spirituality lectures, nutritional counseling, dance, pool exercise.

Recreation Swimming, hiking.

Children's Program? No.

Accommodations 12 guests double up in six rooms.

Dining Included. Very low-calorie vegetarian.

Attire/What to Bring Hiking boots, standard yoga/fitness attire, swimsuit, sun/insect protection, energy bars.

Travel Information The Burbank Airport is about 25 miles away; the Los Angeles International airport is 32 miles away.

Rates One-week package $3,300 per person.

Contact Box 8009, Calabasas, CA 91372; tel: 818-222-6900; fax: 818-222-7393; www.theashram.com.

I've been to The Ashram at least 20 times since 1973. Life is challenging and we forget how to take care of ourselves. The Ashram helps us remember. You do yoga, you hike, you play volleyball. It's a very physical program, that's why some people refer to it as boot camp, but it has the possibility for transformation because it hits a lot of levels. There is a lot of natural laughter and fun that happens organically in doing this particular program. I call it refreshment for the mind and body.

When people come into situations like this and have goals, part of what shocks them into a new paradigm is changing habits. I think it's good to alter the things that seduce us into not taking care of ourselves. It's like shocking our body.

I like the yoga at the Ashram. You have a mix of 14 people, some who have never done yoga in their life. I think the Ashram does a wonderful job of teaching disparate people. I don't find the yoga compromised, although it is not designed for the person who does yoga four times per week.

It's a big commitment to be healthy and balance all the mental demands of your life. A spiritual focus is essential, and the Ashram provides that experientially through joy and yoga. The week is really an awakening, because you come away peaceful and rejuvenated.

—Leigh Taylor-Young, actress

I wanted to experience a well-known spa and hotel while I was visiting Los Angeles, so I booked a room at the Century Plaza. The first time I visited, it was for a spa treatment with some friends. We were very impressed with the decor of the spa, which has an Asian theme. It was a very relaxing environment, and the staff was very professional. The waiting area of the spa was well lit, with glass windows that gave it a very pleasant feel, and they provide herbal tea while you wait for your treatment.

My second visit was to stay in the hotel on a Friday night. We didn't get in till midnight, so there wasn't a soul in sight when we entered the hotel. The bar at the front of the hotel was very elegant, but there wasn't anyone there. The front desk explained to us that the hotel was mainly used for business during the week. Our room was very cozy, with an amazing bed and plenty of plush pillows. We had a balcony that looked over Century Avenue. The bed was definitely the best part of our stay. On our way out on Saturday, we checked out the pool area. I would describe it as something similar to a hotel pool in Vegas—very elaborate and tropical. We took a hatha yoga class (level one to two) with Heidi. She was very knowledgeable.

—Jennifer Bender, sales executive,
  San Francisco, California

Century Plaza Hotel & Spa   Los Angeles, California

Perhaps Los Angeles isn't the most relaxing yogic destination you can think of. But if you are traveling to Los Angeles for business or you promised the kids a trip to Disneyland, check out the Century Plaza Hotel & Spa. The peaceful, seven-acre resort, landscaped with rare tropical plants and reflecting pools, is a respite from bustling, nearby Beverly Hills and Rodeo Drive.

One of the hotel's most notable features is the 35,000-square-foot, Asian-influenced spa. Spa Mystique has 27 indoor treatment rooms. It was designed using feng shui principles, so you'll notice water, fire, metal, wood, and earth throughout. Try the rejuvenating Japanese furo baths and Vichy showers. Between treatments, guests can enjoy the meditation garden and cafe. The 4,500-square-foot fitness area has a full range of weights and exercise equipment and a yoga studio. Four different styles of yoga plus a basics class are offered daily.

Guest Yoga Teachers? No.

Types of Yoga Classes Hatha, hot, restorative flow. Two to three times a day (not offered on Friday and Sunday). $10 per class plus $12 per day to enter the fitness center.

Services Akasuri (Korean scrub), Vichy shower, body treatments, facials, massage, shiatsu, reflexology, Reiki method, aromatherapy, nail care, enzyme facial.

Other Classes Pilates, stretch, cardio sculpt, aquaerobics, power ball.

Recreation Golf nearby, fitness center.

Children's Program? No.

Accommodations 724 rooms.

Dining Not included. Two restaurants: Breeze Restaurant (California cuisine), Cafe Mystique (spa cuisine).

Attire/What to Bring Standard yoga/workout attire, swimsuit, sun protection.

Travel Information The Century Plaza is 10 miles from the Los Angeles International Airport.

Rates $247–$455 per night, double occupancy.

Contact 2025 Avenue of the Stars, Los Angeles, CA 90067; tel: 310-277-2000; fax: 310-551-3355; www.centuryplazala.com.

Silverado Resort & Spa   Napa, California

Silverado Resort's white-pillared mansion was built in the early 1870s by General John Miller and his wife. Today, the mansion houses the lobby, two restaurants, and several meeting rooms.

Guests stay in cottages bordering courtyards and secluded swimming pools as well as lining the resort's two golf courses. Each unique unit was individually designed and decorated. All have a balcony or patio and private entrance.

Silverado has two 18-hole golf courses, 17 tennis courts, a spa, and eight swimming pools. The main pool complex contains two pools and a Jacuzzi. Guests can also bike, walk, or jog on the resort's 1,200 acres. Bikes are available at the tennis shop, and the concierge has jogging route maps.

The 18,000-square-foot Romanesque-style spa offers a steam room, sauna, whirlpool, Vichy and Swiss showers, juice bar, and yoga studio.

Guest Yoga Teachers? No.

Types of Yoga Classes Hatha. Once daily, on Thursday, Saturday, and Sunday. $10 per class.

Services Massage, tui na, shiatsu, reflexology, aromatherapy, body treatments, hydrotherapy, facials, nail care.

Other Classes Cardio training, step aerobics, strength and flexibility, body sculpting, stretching, aquaerobics.

Recreation Golf, tennis, swimming, fitness room.

Children's Program? No.

Accommodations 290 guest rooms.

Dining Not included. Four restaurants: Vintner's Court (Asian-inspired), Royal Oak (California), Silverado Bar and Grill (casual), Spa Cafe.

Attire/What to Bring Standard yoga/workout attire, tennis/golf attire, swimsuit, insect/sun protection.

Travel Information The Silverado Resort & Spa is 72 miles from San Francisco International Airport.

Rates $285–$555 per night, double occupancy. Two-night weekend minimum stay April–October.

Contact 1600 Atlas Peak Road, Napa, CA 94558; tel: 707-257-0200; fax: 707-257-2867; www.silveradoresort.com.

Silverado Country Club and Resort, right in the heart of the beautiful Napa Valley, is considered one of the most ideal locations in which to live, whether it be in California or the rest of the U.S. There is nothing quite comparable, because of its innate beauty, climate, and location. My husband, Don, and I enjoy living at the club, because everything we love is right here and outside our door. (My favorite area is the spa.) The weather is warm and gorgeous for much of the year, and we love our vegetable gardens and fruit trees in the backyard.

There are various types of yoga classes offered here. Some are beginning and some are more advanced. Judith teaches gentle yoga, which is a type of hatha, and it focuses on deep breathing and releasing. Ann Yates teaches Iyengar (which is a slow stretch and hold) and Integral (which is strong in the fundamentals of hatha yoga). Ann also does some Ashtanga.

My favorite food is from the spa. I work out almost daily, and my husband and I particularly enjoy the spa salads, fresh smoothies, and soups. Everything is natural and freshly made to order. My last name is Winter, and I have them make me "Winter Salad" (my creation) made up of romaine, fresh vegetables in season, Asiago cheese, avocado, onions, and grilled chicken breast.

My husband and I particularly enjoy the massage medley and the sports massage. There is also tui na, an ancient Chinese modality, which is a vigorous energetic massage, combining acupressure and stretching to affect the flow of chi. I particularly love the Jacuzzi, steam room and sauna. The decor and the surroundings are so soothing.

—Dr. Katherine Winter, life coach, Silverado Country Club

The Oaks   Ojai, California

The Oaks at Ojai wants you to lose weight! With the Power yoga, 1,000-calorie-per-day diet, and rigorous exercise program, it's almost impossible not to. But this isn't a boot-camp style spa. You can participate in as many or as few activities as you like. Guests are advised to consult with the Oaks nurse before diving in, especially if you are new to exercise or if you haven't been to a fitness class since Jane Fonda was popular. The complex occupies an entire block in downtown Ojai, one of Ventura County's oldest towns. It's known for its artist community, environmental concerns, and community activism, and it serves as a hub for the Ojai Valley and as a gateway to the Los Padres National Forest.

Guest Yoga Teachers? No.

Types of Yoga Classes Hatha, Iyengar-style, Yoga for Strength, chair. Once daily. No extra charge.

Services Facials, massage, acupuncture, watsu, Reiki method.

Other Classes Aerobics, aquaerobics, step aerobics, strength training, qigong, Pilates.

Recreation Gym, swimming, hiking.

Children's Program? No.

Accommodations 27 rooms, 19 cottages.

Dining Included. No salt, sugar, white flour, or red meat. 1,000 calories per day. Vegetarian available.

Attire/What to Bring Robe or pool coverup; swimsuit; sun/insect protection; standard exercise and yoga wear; footwear for hiking, aerobics, and aquatic exercise; a sweater or jacket and gloves during the winter months.

When I walked into the Oaks' cozy lobby, I immediately felt comfortable. The whole place has a casual and warm atmosphere. The landscaping by the pool is lovely and conducive to relaxing. I had my own room (although some guests request a roommate), and it was in an outside cottage. The room was spacious and tastefully furnished. And the food was terrific. The fish dishes were my favorite, although all of the meals were delicious and satisfying (if only I could take the chef home).

I went to the Oaks for their yoga weekend and found it to be inspiring. I specifically went to the Oaks to get myself started in yoga, and the instructors were outstanding. They offered several levels during this special weekend. I definitely favored the yoga classes, but I also enjoyed the morning walks and hikes, as well as their pool and stretch classes.

—Lena Rivkin, artist and graphologist, Studio City, California

Sip Herbal Tea Anxiety, tension, or sheer excitement from your travels may leave you unable to relax or sleep. Nature has a treasure trove of safe herbal relaxants such as passionflower, kava, chamomile, and linden flowers. Elson Haas, M.D., author of *The Staying Healthy Shopper's Guide: Feed Your Family Safely* (Celestial Arts, 1999), suggests making a nightly travel ritual of drinking tea made with a blend of these herbs. —K.F.M.

Travel Information The Oaks is 83 miles from the Burbank airport.

Rates $159–$295 per person per night.

Contact 122 E. Ojai Avenue, Ojai, CA 93023; tel: 800-753-6257, 805-646-5573; fax: 805-640-1504; www.oaksspa.com.

Ojai Valley Inn & Spa   Ojai, California

Ojai Valley Inn & Spa began as a private country club and golf course in 1923 and was transformed into Camp Oak, a military training center, during World War II. The Ojai Valley Inn reopened in 1947, hosting Hollywood celebrities such as Clark Gable, Irene Dunne, Lana Turner, Loretta Young, Walt Disney, Nancy and Ronald Reagan, Judy Garland, and Paul Newman.

In 1997, guest rooms were renovated and the 31,000-square-foot Spa Ojai opened. All adult guests have complimentary use of the spa facilities during their stay. This includes classes such as yoga and tai chi and use of cardiovascular and resistance equipment, spa pool, wet areas, and locker room facilities. The spa contains 28 treatment areas, six with fireplaces. The kuyam treatment, which combines the use of mud, dry heat, inhalation therapy, and guided meditation, is a spa specialty.

On the inn's grounds, more than 10,000 flowers, herbs, annuals, and perennials are planted each year. In the Sunken Garden alone you'll find aromatic lavender, rosemary and thyme, sweet broom, purple-blooming artichokes, lamb's ears, and society garlic. Next to the Oak Cafe Terrace, the Fragrance Court overflows with thyme, tarragon, sage, chives, sorrel, oregano, cilantro, rosemary, marjoram, basil, mint, lemon balm, exotic perilla, and dozens of roses. The herbs are used daily by the inn's chefs.

Guest Yoga Teachers? No.

Types of Yoga Classes Hatha, restorative, strength, flow, flexibility. At least twice daily. No extra charge.

Services Massage, aromatherapy, shiatsu, reflexology, hydrotherapy, craniosacral therapy, Reiki method, facials, body treatments, Ayurvedic detox wrap.

Other Classes Aerobics, water aerobics, qigong, Spinning, tai chi, meditation, Pilates, boxercise, step aerobics, Feldenkrais, makoto (an interactive machine that tests reflexes), dance, art, writing.

Recreation Bicycling, volleyball, croquet, bocce ball, water volleyball, water basketball, horseshoes, Frisbee, hiking.

I live in Northern California, and I wanted to go abroad but only had five days to relax and get back in touch with my body, so I chose the Ojai Valley Inn & Spa in Ojai, which is a five-hour drive away. It has a sense of quaintness unlike larger spas. I wanted to detox, cleanse, swim, hike, and do yoga. The hydrotherapy, aromatherapy, and Ayurveda treatments were heavenly. I just indulged myself for five days.

I enjoyed yoga with two different teachers. Private instruction is available for those who are newer to yoga, but they always review the fundamentals in class, so if you are a beginner, you won't feel uncomfortable. There are a variety of yoga classes, such as flow, essentials, and restorative.

What I found extremely helpful was the medical health center on property. You can get blood tests and EKGs. It's really wonderful and right next to the spa. For $285 you can have a preventative medicine screening and counseling. I spent an hour talking to a doctor, and I've never spent more than five minutes talking to my own physician. If you're going through menopause, you can talk about what things you need to do to stay healthy. The inn might not be for everyone since it's quiet and there is not much else to do. But I'm planning on returning once a year.

—Deborah Olson, owner of a 100-year-old cherry-growing business, Sunnyvale, California

Children's Program? Yes. Camp Ojai for ages 3 to 12.

Accommodations 206 rooms, including 15 suites.

Dining Not included. Four restaurants: Maravilla (California cuisine), the Oak Cafe (casual dining), Acorn Poolside Cafe (spa cuisine), Splashes (sandwiches, salads).

Attire/What to Bring Standard yoga/workout attire, hiking boots, sun/insect protection, swimsuit.

Travel Information The Ojai Valley Inn and Spa is 73 miles from Los Angeles International Airport.

Rates $279–$2,500 per night.

Contact 905 Country Club Road, Ojai, CA 93023; tel: 800-422-6524, 805-646-1111; fax: 805-646-7969; www.ojairesort.com.

The Palms   Palm Springs, California

The Palms, located in Palm Springs, California, is the sister property to the Oaks in Ojai. Like the Oaks, it offers a 1,000-calorie-per-day diet and fitness activities designed to increase flexibility, burn fat and calories, condition the heart and lungs, and tone the body. Sheila Cluff, a former television fitness show host, has been running both spas since the 1970s. Gentle yoga is offered daily. In the past, yoga weekends have been offered at least twice a year.

Guest Yoga Teachers? No.

Types of Yoga Classes Hatha, gentle, pool, and bedtime yoga. Once daily. No extra charge.

Services Facials, body scrubs, hypnotherapy, massage, reflexology.

Other Classes Aerobics, cardiostep, aquaerobics, strength training.

Recreation Gym, biking, hiking, golf, horseback riding.

Children's Program? No.

Accommodations 43 guest rooms.

Dining Included. No salt, sugar, white flour, or red meat. 1,000 calories per day. Vegetarian available.

Attire/What to Bring Standard yoga/workout attire, swimsuit, hiking boots, sun/insect protection.

Travel Information The Palms is 70 miles from the Ontario airport.

I have been practicing yoga for 25 years and enjoy being exposed to different yoga classes. I have been to the Palms before and love the place. I especially like the friendly, well-trained staff and the relaxed informal atmosphere.

The grounds are well maintained and the older buildings have a friendly and comfortable appearance. I was surprised to find a place like this a block from Palm Springs' main street.

The rooms are large, clean, and comfortable—not as fancy as some of the newer spas. The food is always outstanding and beautifully served. Massages were all I had time for. They were excellent.

I did all the yoga classes, which included regular hatha yoga, bedtime yoga, pool yoga, chair yoga. All were well taught and catered to the wide level of students. The pool was warm—perfect for a pool yoga class, and the yoga room was comfortable and very quiet.

—Elaine Usell, fitness and yoga instructor, Poway, California

Call Desert Valley Shuttle (800-413-3999, 760-251-4020) in advance. Shuttle costs about $45 each way.

Rates $159–$260 per person per night.

Contact 572 N. Indian Canyon Drive, Palm Springs, CA 92262; tel: 800-753-7256, 760-325-1111; www.palmsspa.com.

Meadowood Napa Valley   St. Helena, California

Meadowood was built in the early 1960s as a club for the local wine community. Today, it still has the air of a private country estate yet offers the amenities of a well-run hotel, with golf, tennis, croquet, wine tastings, and fine dining. Guests stay in cottages, suites, and lodges that are surrounded by trees for privacy.

The Meadowood Cultural Affairs Program was created in 1997 to establish a cultural presence on the estate. Guests can attend a classical music series, artist-in-residence series, or a lecture series if they time their visit correctly. The spa offers a host of Ayurveda treatments as well as daily yoga classes, making the variety of activities available at Meadowood quite eclectic.

Area activities, such as winery tours, classic automobile tours, and hot-air ballooning, can be arranged by the staff.

Guest Yoga Teachers? No.

Types of Yoga Classes Hatha, Vinyasa. Once or twice a day. No extra charge.

Services Aromatherapy, massage, body treatments, Ayurveda, shirodhara, abhyanga, facials, nail care.

Other Classes Aerobics, step aerobics, personal training, cooking.

Recreation Biking, croquet, wine tasting, golf, hiking, tennis, swimming.

Children's Program? No.

Accommodations 85 cottages, suites and lodges.

Dining Not included. Two restaurants: the Restaurant at Meadowood (fine dining; four-course vegetarian tasting menu available), the Grill (casual).

Attire/What to Bring Standard yoga/workout attire, swimsuit, hiking boots, golf/tennis attire, sun/insect protection.

Travel Information Meadowood is 75 miles north of San Francisco International Airport.

Rates $500–$750 per night, double occupancy.

When I first came to Meadowood, I was taken by its natural beauty and peacefulness. The grounds are kept as much as possible in their natural state, with landscaping that blends into the native environment. The buildings are unobtrusive and spaced throughout the grounds in a way that also respects the harmony and peacefulness of the forest. In a quiet space in front of the spa is the pool area. A large lap pool is used year-round, as well as a separate Jacuzzi. There is also a kid's pool further away for families to enjoy. Croquet is popular here, and there is a small nine-hole golf course nestled between the hills where rice fields once were. There are plenty of tennis courts for those who love tennis. No matter what your favorite sport, the pros here are the best. Most guest rooms have fireplaces and great views of the surrounding oaks and pines.

I teach what I call a yoga of natural awareness. It is a combination of the different branches of yoga, especially hatha and raja. It is a meditative style with an emphasis on self-awareness, opening the body gently with breath, and strengthening. I trained at the Napa School of Yoga, with Margit Jacob and other excellent teachers. I am still a student there and have been for the last 13 years. Yoga is a lifelong lesson, and it is always fresh. I have also studied with Jean Couch in Palo Alto, California, who is doing some great work with balance and natural posture.

—Dawn Thomas, Meadowood Resort yoga instructor

Contact 900 Meadowood Lane, St. Helena, CA 94574; 800-458-8080, 707-963-3646; fax: 707-963-3532; www.meadowood.com.

Golden Door Resort and Spa   San Marcos, California

The beauty of the Golden Door is that the founder based the design on a Japanese ryokan (inn). The spa feels like Japan, with the Japanese gardens, art, and roofline. You are even greeted upon arrival by someone in a kimono offering tea.

It is very tranquil and peaceful, and with no more than 40 guests at one time, you are assured personal attention. You have your own personal trainer and massage in your room every day. One price includes all spa treatments.

Outside of every room is a beautiful view and the most wonderful fountains and gardens. Much of the food that is served is grown in on-site organic gardens. Your morning orange juice is probably squeezed from fruit grown out back. It is a very healthy diet.

Golden Door is probably the most spiritual of all the spas I've been to. It's about the inner person. I went there after my marriage broke up and after my mother died of breast cancer. It is a very healing place and it has made the biggest difference in my life.

−Carol Isaak Barden, contributing editor, *Travel & Leisure* magazine, Houston, Texas

Golden Door, located five miles north of Escondido and 40 miles northeast of San Diego in a valley surrounded by avocado country, was created in 1958 by Deborah Szekely. The Door was designed to replicate an ancient Japanese inn, and a million-dollar art and antique collection is exhibited throughout the grounds. There are three guest lounges, indoor/outdoor exercise studios, the Dragon Tree Gym, two swimming pools, two tennis courts, and a spacious bathhouse that contains a steam room, sauna, showers, fan-shaped therapy pool, and private rooms for spa treatments.

All guests arrive on Sunday for a seven-day stay. The spa can host 40 women each week. (There are a few coed weeks each year.) After you complete a health and fitness profile, the Door staff will create a personalized schedule for you. If you want to change your program, you can do so at any time during the week. You meet with your fitness guide up to four times to develop a take-home fitness program.

The day begins with a hike balanced by either a massage or beauty treatment. Activities such as meditation, yoga, tai chi, and qigong are scheduled after lunch. In the evenings, guests can enjoy a speaker, movie, workshop, or cooking class.

The organic vegetable garden supplies the kitchen with most of the fresh vegetables it needs. About 75 varieties can be harvested throughout the year.

Guest Yoga Teachers? No.

Types of Yoga Classes Hatha, chair yoga, restorative, yoga Zen, Power, yoga ball. Once daily. No extra charge.

Services Massage, reflexology, facials, body treatments.

Other Classes Archery, Feldenkrais, haiku, fencing. meditation, self-defense, stress management, tai chi, cardio boxing, dance, Spinning, step aerobics, NIA, mindful eating.

Recreation Hiking, walking the labyrinth, tennis, swimming.

Children's Program? No.

Accommodations 39 rooms, one villa.

Dining Included. Low-calorie, low-fat. Vegetarian available.

Attire/What to Bring Standard yoga attire, workout shoes, hiking boots, bathing suits, warm jacket, sun/insect protection, tennis attire. Warm-up suit, robes, and sandals provided.

Travel Information Courtesy transportation is provided between the Golden Door and the San Diego International Airport 40 miles away.

Rates $6,275 per person per week.

Contact 777 Deer Springs Road, San Marcos, CA 92069; tel: 800-424-0777, 760-744-5777; fax: 760-471-2393; www.goldendoor.com.

Bacara   Santa Barbara, California

Bacara, a 78-acre resort, is strategically located on the bluffs between the Pacific Ocean and the Santa Ynes Mountains. Guests stay in one-, three-, and four-story villas, each with a patio or balcony. About 70% of the rooms have either gas or woodburning fireplaces. The resort also operates 1,000 acres of land bordering the Los Padres National Forest for guided hiking and horseback riding; 450 acres of this land is used to grow lemons, avocados, and other organic vegetables and fruits for the resort.

The 42,000-square-foot spa has 36 treatment rooms, semiprivate sunbathing, open-air or indoor massage, a 3,500-square-foot cardiovascular and strength-training center, fitness classes and one-on-one training, a heated negative-edge pool, Swiss showers, personalized wellness programs, a full-service beauty salon, the all-organic Spa Café, and a large menu of pampering treatments. Yoga is offered daily to guests at no extra charge.

Guest Yoga Teachers? No.

Types of Yoga Classes Hatha, partner, restorative. One to two times daily. No extra charge.

Services Body scrubs, hydrotherapy, Ayurveda (shirodhara), massage, facials, reflexology, Reiki method, shiatsu, nail care.

Other Classes Strength training, qigong, Feldenkrais, meditation, tai chi, Pilates.

Recreation Golf, tennis, swimming, whirlpool, ocean kayaking, surfing, sailboat, yacht or catamaran excursions, windsurfing, paragliding, whale watching, horseback riding, biking, deep-sea fishing, scuba, snorkeling, hiking.

Children's Program? Yes. Kid's Club.

Accommodations 311 rooms, 49 suites.

Bacara is beautiful and very peaceful. The gardens are lush and the views of the ocean create a wonderful soothing backdrop. My room had a balcony overlooking the main pool area and Pacific Ocean. Lots of little extras made the room special—slippers, candles, fireplace, and lovely wood window shutters.

I took a yoga class and found it to be enjoyable but not advanced enough for me. The class was more about deep relaxation with a helpful overview of the ancient practice of yoga. The yoga room was beautiful, and the instructor was great. The tai chi was more enjoyable for me, because it was new and different.

I had an antiaging facial that was amazing, with just the right amount of massage. There was no hard product sell yet plenty of helpful information offered.

All the food at the resort was amazing—great yogurt cheesecake in the spa cafe, chopped chicken and avocado salad in the Bistro (the avocado was from Bacara's ranch).

I was surprised by the cool evenings and misty mornings. I expected the climate to be warmer. However, it is ideal for working out and hiking. I would definitely return with friends or family—or even by myself if I needed a couple of days of total pampering.

—Sonia Rendigs, technology sales specialist, New York

Dining Not included. Three restaurants: Miro (mostly organic, French-California cuisine), the Bistro (Mediterranean and Continental cuisine), the Spa Café (organic).

Attire/What to Bring Standard yoga/workout attire, hiking boots, sun/insect protection, swimsuit, clothes for upscale dining.

Travel Information Bacara is six miles from the Santa Barbara airport.

Rates $395–$2,500 per night, double occupancy.

Contact 8301 Hollister Avenue, Santa Barbara, CA 93117; tel: 805-968-0100, 877-422-4245; fax: 805-968-1800; www.bacararesort.com.

Cal-a-Vie Resort   Vista, California

It has been two months since my return from the idyllic experience at Cal-a-Vie during one of their yoga weeks with the esteemed Geo Takoma. Having been to the spa before, I was quite resolved there was little chance of even closely approximating the wonderful experiences I had on my two previous trips. Well, I was wrong. Not only did I get the benefits of the wonderful staff, facilities, food, and procedures provided year-round at Cal-a-Vie, but I completely immersed myself in the wonderful yoga with Geo. Although I am back to my hectic life, I have retained so much from my Cal-a-Vie yoga experience. I have continued and expanded my yoga practice and feel confident that yoga, in some form, will be an essential part of my life forever. I plan to return to Cal-a-Vie next summer for this particular yoga week, now knowing it can only get better.

—Julia Colella Carver, arts advocate, Woodside, California

Cal-a-Vie, on 200 acres in a valley 40 miles north of San Diego, offers European-influenced spa treatments and lodging. Each of the 24 Mediterranean-style villas can accommodate two people, so no more than 48 guests are on-property at any one time.

During a weeklong stay, each guest participates in a personalized fitness program that can focus on stress reduction, relaxation, weight control, or toning. Spa treatments, low-fat meals, accommodations for seven nights, and transportation to and from the San Diego International Airport are part of the all-inclusive package.

The day begins with a hike through the property. After breakfast, guests can participate in activities such as a yoga class, a workout with weights, a private tennis lesson, a Spinning class, or a game of water volleyball. Afternoons are dedicated to spa treatments, including aromatherapy massages, seaweed wraps, and facials. Educational lectures are offered throughout the year.

Guest Yoga Teachers? Yes. Geo Takoma teaches a yoga week each year.

Types of Yoga Classes Hatha or restorative. Daily (frequency varies based on customized guest programs). No extra charge.

Services Massage, facial, hair and scalp treatments, hand and foot treatments, thalassotherapy, hydrotherapy, aromatherapy, reflexology.

Other Classes Abdominals, aerobic dance, beginning mat Pilates, body sculpting, kickboxing, circuit training, fitness evaluation, NIA, personalized training, Spinning, sports conditioning, step aerobics, stretch, tai chi, qigong, aquaerobics.

Recreation Golf, hikes, tennis, water volleyball.

Children's Program? No.

Accommodations 24 cottages.

Dining Included. Low-fat, low-sodium, high in natural complex carbohydrates in the form of whole grains, legumes, fresh vegetables and fruit; modest amounts of lean animal proteins such as dairy, egg whites, poultry, and fish.

Attire/What to Bring Standard yoga/workout attire, swimsuit, sun/insect protection, hiking/walking shoes, golf/tennis attire.

Travel Information Cal-a-Vie is 42 miles from San Diego International Airport.

Rates Regular week sessions begin on Sunday afternoon and end the following Sunday morning. European Plan (three meals a day, accommodations, 16 therapeutic treatments, and all fitness classes) $5,395 plus room tax. California Plan (three meals a day, accommodations, all fitness classes, and six body treatments) $4,995 plus room tax. Three- and four-night programs are offered throughout the year. Visit the website for details.

Contact 29402 Spa Havens Way, Vista, CA 92084; tel: 760-945-2055, 866-772-4283; fax: 760-630-0074; www.cal-a-vie.com.

COLORADO

Park Hyatt Beaver Creek Resort and Spa   Avon, Colorado

The Park Hyatt Regency Beaver Creek Resort is a ski-in/ski-out 1,700-acre mountain resort in the heart of Beaver Creek Village, eight miles west of Vail. Upon entering the hotel, with its vaulted ceilings and sandstone interior, you immediately understand what this resort is all about: Western elegance. In the lobby area, which overlooks the slopes, numerous oversized fireplaces are surrounded by plump couches and chairs, making it a prime après-ski hangout. On winter nights, the Park Hyatt Beaver Creek takes on a European air, with horse-drawn carriages and sleighs. The resort offers on-site ski rentals, ice skating, shopping in the adjacent village, year-round heated indoor/outdoor pool, three indoor and six outdoor whirlpools, a health club, and the Allegria Spa.

The 20,000-square-foot Allegria Spa, with 20 treatment rooms, was designed using feng shui principles. In summer and winter, guests can enjoy the indoor steam room, spa lounge, coed sauna, outdoor spa deck, six outdoor whirlpools, tea and book bar, and individual indoor whirlpool tubs.

At the heart of the complex is the yoga studio, which has a suspended

The Allegria Spa at the Park Hyatt Beaver Creek Resort was my first-ever spa experience. I remember being a little nervous, not knowing what to expect. The staff put me completely at ease. First I had a whole-body scrub. It was an awesome experience: The aesthetician turned the lights down low, put on an Enya CD, and started rubbing a coarse paste all over my skin. Then she wrapped me in warm towels and left me alone for a while. I completely relaxed. Next, I was led into a Swiss shower. (This isn't for self-conscious people, because basically we showered together.) The resort itself has unbeatable views. The skiing was challenging, but I enjoyed the snowshoeing, because it was great to be removed from the sounds of the ski area.

—Carol Cambo, freelance writer and editor, Wilbraham, Massachusetts

wood floor. Guests may choose from a variety of daily group fitness classes, including Spinning, step, body sculpting, tai chi, stretch, strength training, hikes and walks, meditation, yoga, Pilates, biking, and snowshoeing. The schedule varies according to the season.

Guest Yoga Teachers? No.

Types of Yoga Classes Hatha. Once or twice daily. $15 per class.

Services Body treatments, facials, massage, shiatsu, reflexology, aromatherapy, nail care.

Other Classes Spinning, Pilates, Alexander Technique, tai chi, meditation, kickboxing, belly dancing.

Recreation White-water rafting, tennis, golf, swimming, boating, snowmobiling, ice skating, skiing, snowshoeing, hiking, mountain biking, horseback riding, Jeep tours, fly-fishing, sleigh rides.

Children's Program? Yes. Camp Hyatt.

Accommodations 275 rooms.

Dining Not included. Six restaurants: Bivans (family dining), Cafe (deli), McCoys Cafe (skier cafeteria; winter only), Antler Hall (cocktail lounge), Vue (gourmet French), Whiskey Elk (appetizers).

Attire/What to Bring Standard yoga attire, sun/insect protection, swimsuit, ski attire in winter, hiking boots.

Travel Information The Park Hyatt Beaver Creek is 20 miles from the Eagle County Regional Airport.

Rates $115–$930 per night, double occupancy.

Contact P.O. Box 1595, Avon, CO 81620; tel: 970-949-1234; fax: 970-949-4164; www.beavercreek.hyatt.com.

Drink Energy Boosters Caffeine can add to jangled nerves and disrupt sleep patterns. If your body needs a boost, reach for ginseng and other herbal stimulants such as kola nut or yerba maté, according to Elson Haas, M.D., author of *The Staying Healthy Shopper's Guide: Feed Your Family Safely* (Celestial Arts, 1999). He also recommends roasted-root beverages made from chicory or barley, and spirulina, chlorella, and blue-green algae to revitalize the travel-weary. –K.F.M.

Wyndham Peaks Resort & Golden Door Spa   Telluride, Colorado

At the Wyndham Peaks Resort & Golden Door Spa in Telluride, you can choose from a mountainside cabin or an upscale guest room, both with views of the San Juan Mountains. While you sleep, the ski valet warms and tunes your ski gear.

Guests can participate in a variety of cold- and warm-weather activities. Telluride is known for its powder, so outdoor sports enthusiasts flock here in winter for the cross-country and downhill skiing, snowboarding, and snowmobiling. Summer is just as active, with horseback riding, mountain biking, fly-fishing, tennis, swimming, and golf.

For those who prefer to stay indoors—or just need a break from the slopes—there's the Golden Door Spa, which has a workout facility along with pampering spa treatments like facials, massages, and body scrubs. Men's and women's kivas (Native American ceremonial shelters) have steam rooms with aromatic herbs, cedar-filled saunas, and mineral-infused whirlpools.

To help you remain active at high altitude, stop by the oxygen bar, where you can inhale scented oxygen for 20 to 60 minutes.

Guest Yoga Teachers? No.

Types of Yoga Classes Hatha, Vinyasa. Once or twice a day. $10 per day.

Services Massage, facials, hydrotherapy, Ayurveda (including shirodhara), body treatments, shiatsu, Reiki method, aromatherapy, reflexology.

Other Classes Pilates, tai chi, climbing, Spinning.

Recreation Golf, fishing, hiking, jet-skiing, swimming, racquetball, squash, tennis, whirlpool, sauna, mountain biking, white-water rafting, horseback riding, skiing, heli-skiing, cross-country skiing, snowmobiling, snowshoeing, dogsled rides, yoga tone.

Children's Program? Yes. KidSpa for ages 1 month to 11 years.

Accommodations 174 rooms.

Dining Not included. Two restaurants: Appaloosa (American), Legends (American).

Attire/What to Bring Standard workout/yoga attire, skiing attire in winter, hiking boots, sun/insect protection, swimsuit.

Travel Information Telluride airport is 5 miles away; the Montrose airport is 65 miles away.

I have been teaching flow, or Vinyasa-style, classes at the Peaks for about a year. I have regulars and many newcomers and try to cater to all. The grounds here at the Peaks are beautiful. The mountain views are what makes this place so special. I feel like we must be the only spa with views like this. Our spa sits at 9,500 feet and looks out at 14,000-foot peaks—it's majestic.

—Alyssa Gitto, a Wyndham Peaks Resort yoga teacher

Rates $111–$896 per night, double occupancy.

Contact 136 Country Club Drive, Telluride, CO 81435; tel: 800-789-2220, 970-728-6800; www.wyndham.com.

Sonnenalp Resort   Vail, Colorado

When you step inside the Sonnenalp Resort in Vail, you feel as if you've been transported to the Alps: Some of the hotel staff are dressed in dirndls and lederhosen, and a restaurant serves fondue. Of course, mountain activities like downhill and cross-country skiing, snowshoeing, and snow boarding are the norm. You can explore untouched powder-filled bowls and learn the mountain's secrets when you enroll in one of Sonnenalp's guided adventure tours.

Each of the guest suites at the Sonnenalp Resort has a gas fireplace, VCR, and soaking tub with separate shower.

Use of the Sonnenalp Spa and its heated indoor/outdoor pool, indoor and outdoor Jacuzzis, meditation room, Turkish steam rooms, and Finnish sauna is complimentary. Indulge in one of the many massages and body treatments after a day on the slopes. Throughout the day, guests can take yoga classes for free at adjacent Yoga for Athletes.

Guest Yoga Teachers? No.

Types of Yoga Classes Yoga for Athletes. Two to three times daily. No extra charge.

Services Massage, body treatments, aromatherapy, facials, nail care.

Other Classes Aquaerobics, Pilates.

Recreation Tennis, golf, skiing, snowshoeing, hiking, mountain biking, swimming, gym.

Children's Program? Yes. Kidventures for ages 5 to 12 available December–April and June–September.

Accommodations 88 suites, 2 rooms.

Dining Breakfast included. Four restaurants: King's Club (high tea; bar/lounge in winter), Bully Ranch (burgers, barbecue), Swiss Chalet (raclette and fondue), Ludwig's (contemporary continental).

Attire/What to Bring Standard workout/yoga attire, skiing attire in winter, hiking boots, sun/insect protection, swimsuit, golf/tennis attire.

Yoga for Athletes is based on the Iyengar style with Vinyasa flow. We can be considered a Power yoga studio, with meticulous attention to alignment. With correct alignment we help to avoid injury while practicing this vigorous form of yoga. We are located directly across from the Sonnenalp Spa. Yoga creates strength, flexibility, balance, and stamina, which results in improved performance, injury reduction, and quicker recovery rate. In skiing, for example, specific yoga postures will strengthen and stretch the quadriceps. This balance of flexibility and strength will allow a skier to increase performance and can alleviate strain on the knees, a common occurrence in skiing. Also, the development of breath awareness gives one greater body control, which is necessary in the participation in sports. Scanning the different areas mentally reinforces the contact between mind and body, which increases awareness. This translates into quicker reactions to unsuspected situations. For example, if a skier hits unexpected terrain on the hill and one ski is forced out from under them, a tear in the inner groin area can be avoided because you have gained the flexibility to support that abduction of the leg. Awareness also increases coordination, which can improve performance.

—Libby Maio, Yoga for Athletes, Inc. manager and yoga teacher

Travel Information Sonnenalp is 35 miles from the Eagle County Regional Airport.

Rates $240–$2,000 per night, double occupancy.

Contact 20 Vail Road, Vail, CO 81657; tel: 800-654-8312, 970-476-5656; fax: 970-476-1639; www.sonnenalp.com.

Vail Cascade Resort & Spa   Vail, Colorado

Vail has more than 5,000 acres of open bowls and groomed runs. You can ski, snowmobile, snowshoe, ice skate, or just take in the mountain views. Conveniently, Vail Cascade Resort & Spa is a ski-in/ski-out resort, so you'll waste no time getting to the ski lift. The hotel's ski concierge maintains your equipment, and there are ski and snowboard rental and repair shops on site.

After a day on the slopes, you'll want to slip into one of the three outdoor or two indoor hot tubs, or one of the two swimming pools. Then visit one of the resort's two movie theaters.

The Aria Spa & Club is a 78,000-square-foot facility and offers yoga one to two times per day, fitness classes, relaxing massages, and other pampering treatments. Locker rooms are complete with hot tub, steam, sauna, and showers. In case outdoor pursuits weren't enough, the club has exercise equipment, an indoor running track, basketball gymnasium, tennis courts, swimming pool, and more.

Guest Yoga Teachers? No.

Types of Yoga Classes Hatha, Power. Once or twice daily. $12 per class.

Services Massage, facials, body treatments, aromatherapy, shiatsu, reflexology, scalp treatments, nail care, thalassotherapy, hydrotherapy.

Other Classes Pilates, aerobics, aquaerobics, kickboxing, tae kwon do, Spinning, step aerobics, circuit-training.

Recreation Basketball, squash, racquetball, skiing, hiking, snowshoeing, snowmobiling, ice-skating, sleigh rides, dogsledding, white-water rafting, fishing, tennis, golf, horseback riding, mountain biking, kayaking, hot air ballooning.

Children's Program? Yes. Camp Cascade.

Accommodations 292 rooms, 28 suites.

Dining Not included. One restaurant: Chap's Grill & Chophouse (seafood and steak).

I take Ashtanga yoga twice a week at the Vail Cascade Resort as a member of their fitness club. The facilities are tremendous. They also have basketball, racquetball, squash, a kids room, and an indoor running track. And the massages there are great. The resort is right on the mountain and has its own ski lift. It's great to sit in the hot tub or steam room after skiing.

—Andrew Abraham, architect, Edwards, Colorado

Attire/What to Bring Standard yoga/workout attire, hiking boots, ski attire in winter, swimsuit, sun/insect protection, golf/tennis attire.

Travel Information Vail Cascade Resort & Spa is 33 miles from the Eagle County Regional Airport.

Rates $129–$409 per night, double occupancy.

Contact 1300 Westhaven Drive, Cascade Village, Vail, CO 81657; tel: 800-282-4183, 970-476-7111; fax: 970-479-7050; www.vailcascade.com.

Vail Mountain Lodge & Spa   Vail, Colorado

The Vail Mountain Lodge & Spa is an intimate mountain resort with 24 rooms, fireplaces, and views of Vail Mountain and Gore Creek. The 18,000-square-foot fitness center has cardiovascular and strength-training equipment, a 25-foot indoor climbing wall, and a bouldering cave. Locker rooms feature Jacuzzis, sauna, and steam rooms. There is also an exercise studio, a Pilates studio, a movement studio (used primarily for meditation, yoga, stretch and dance classes), and a dojo offering more than six classes weekly in a variety of the martial arts disciplines.

The spa menu includes primarily European treatments plus shirodhara and shiatsu. The spa uses biodynamically grown plant-based and organic products whenever possible.

Guest Yoga Teachers? No.

Types of Yoga Classes Anusara. Two to three times daily. $15 per class.

Services Facials, massage, shiatsu, acupressure, reflexology, body treatments, nail care.

Other Classes Spinning, stability ball, fencing, Pilates, kickboxing, tai chi, meditation.

Recreation Skiing, snowshoeing, climbing, snowmobiling, fishing, mountain biking, hot air ballooning, golf, horseback riding, tubing.

Children's Program? Yes. Climbing Camp.

Accommodations 24 rooms.

Dining Breakfast included. One restaurant: Terra Bistro (seasonal ingredients influenced by Southwest, Mediterranean, and Asian; vegetarian available).

Attire/What to Bring Standard yoga/workout attire, hiking boots, ski attire in winter, swimsuit, sun/insect protection.

I'm a member of the United States Women's White-Water Rafting Team. There are six of us, and we all work out at Vail Athletic Club at the Vail Mountain Lodge & Spa, because they have a great yoga program. Anusara yoga is taught primarily, and there are two days of Power yoga. When you do yoga, your endurance and core strength increases—you have to be able to draw your energy to your core and use that energy for power when rafting. You are firing every muscle in your body during yoga, which you do while rafting as well. Arm balances are also key. I attend yoga class three or four times a week with Geri Bleier, who trained in Anusara with John Friend. The athletic club has added more and more yoga classes, because it is so incredibly popular.

–Katherine Bugby, commercial driver and river guide, Vail, Colorado

Travel Information Vail Mountain Lodge is 45 miles from the Eagle County Regional Airport.

Rates $95–$1,700 per room, double occupancy.

Contact 352 E. Meadow Drive, Vail, CO 81657; tel: 970-476-0700; fax: 970-476-6451; www.vailmountainlodge.com.

CONNECTICUT

The Spa at Grand Lake   Lebanon, Connecticut

Although the Spa at Grand Lake offers yoga twice a day, weight loss is a big focus—900-calorie meal plans and juice fasts are available. Yet yoga practitioners might appreciate this unpretentious spa in rural Connecticut, which was once home to a Jewish summer community, for its Iyengar and Bikram classes and relative affordability.

Packages are all inclusive, with three meals daily, 30-minute massage per night of stay, fitness classes, and unlimited use of the pools, Jacuzzi, sauna, exercise equipment, and weight room. The seven-night package includes a complimentary personal training session. Each day, guests participate in a variety of fitness and wellness classes, walks and hikes on the spa's 75 acres, healthy meals, and evening lectures.

Guest Yoga Teachers? No.

Types of Yoga Classes Iyengar, Bikram, gentle. Twice daily. No extra charge.

Services Massage, facials, reflexology, Ayurveda, aromatherapy, body treatments, Reiki method, craniosacral therapy.

Other Classes Tai chi, qigong, meditation, cardioblast, NIA, kickboxing, step, Pilates, aquaerobics, fit ball.

Recreation Tennis, hiking, swimming, sauna, Jacuzzi.

Children's Program? No.

Accommodations 40 rooms for up to 75 guests.

Dining Included. Low-fat, low-calorie. Juice fast available.

Attire/What to Bring Standard workout/yoga attire, tennis attire, swimsuit, hiking boots, sun/insect protection.

Travel Information The Spa at Grand Lake is 37 miles from the Hartford airport and 128 miles from New York City. Complimentary transfer from the Hartford train station, bus station, or airport.

I've been going to The Spa at Grand Lake for almost 10 years. It attracts people of all ages, sizes, and nationalities. You also see a lot of couples. Now I find I'm going twice a year, because every time I go I drop five to six pounds. And in April there is a special: 10 nights for the price of seven.

The spa is on a lake with woods and gardens surrounding it. I stay in the Constitution building, and I usually share a room. They are not plush hotel rooms, but they're comfortable.

The first yoga class is at 7 AM. It gets your day started. I also take hatha yoga at 5:30 PM—the last half hour is meditation. I do yoga at home as well. I have a massage every day, and I've also tried reflexology and Reiki method.

The food is awesome. There are egg-white omelets in the morning and homemade soups for lunch, followed with salad. Dinner always starts with a salad, followed with chicken or fish or lobster with a vegetable. I select the 900-calorie-a-day plan. They also have vegetarian options, or you can do a juice fast. I always come home feeling much better than when I left. It is a healing experience.

—Liz Davis, receptionist, Boxboro, Massachusetts

Rates Two-night stay $355–$489 per person. Seven-night stay $939–$1,290 per person.

Contact 1667 Exeter Road, Lebanon, CT 06249; tel: 800-843-7721, 860-642-4306; www.thespaatgrandlake.com.

The Spa at Norwich Inn   Norwich, Connecticut

Norwich Inn is an interesting place. There is the creaking, old New England inn with its blazing fireplace we have come to expect in the countryside. Very traditional and Old World. Then there is this jazzy spa, with its state-of-the-art gleaming and modern treatment rooms, and a huge staff of more than 100 spa specialists. All very New Age. In five minutes you go from the 18th century to the 21st. Both very pleasing but both different.

—Michael Carlton, editor, *Yankee Magazine*

The Spa at Norwich Inn combines the atmosphere of a New England inn with a modern spa. Located on the 17th tee of the Norwich Public Golf Course, the inn's 42 acres are landscaped with perennial gardens, ponds, oak trees, a reflecting pool, and an oversized deck.

The spa has 32 treatment rooms and a varied spa menu that includes both European-style and Ayurvedic selections.

On Wednesday evening, you can attend a free wellness presentation by a guest speaker. Topics vary each week and cover nutrition, fitness, weight management, personality profiles, Ayurvedic medicine, and stress reduction. Past speakers have focused on holistic heart health, Native American healing arts, feng shui in the kitchen, acupuncture, and Chinese medicine.

Guest Yoga Teachers? No.

Types of Yoga Classes Hatha. Once daily. $18 per class.

Services Facials, aromatherapy, hydrotherapy, massage, acupressure, shirodhara, polarity therapy, Reiki method, body treatments, Ayurvedic mud wrap, thalassotherapy, nail care.

Other Classes Meditation, cardio sculpt, mindful movement, progressive relaxation, water works.

Recreation Tennis, golf, swimming, hiking, biking.

Children's Program? No.

Accommodations 103 rooms, suites, and villas.

Dining Not included. Two restaurants: Kensington's (continental; vegetarian available), Ascot's (casual pub food; vegetarian available).

Attire/What to Bring Standard yoga/workout attire, clothing for upscale dining, tennis/golf attire, swimsuit, sun/insect protection, hiking boots.

Travel Information The Spa is 55 miles from the Hartford airport and 130 miles from New York City.

Rates $150–$900 per night, double occupancy.

Contact 607 West Thames Street, Norwich, CT 06360; tel: 800-275-4772, 860-886-2401; www.thespaatnorwichinn.com.

FLORIDA

Regency House Natural Health Spa   Hallandale, Florida

Due to its location between Fort Lauderdale and Miami, the Regency House Natural Health Spa attracts both retirees and a younger health-minded clientele. A lot of the Regency's program focuses on weight loss, with a vegetarian diet or a juice fast combined with stress management, behavior modification, and aerobic exercise. A personalized nutrition and exercise program is created for each guest after a consultation with the on-site health director.

A typical day starts at 7 AM with a walk or cross-training. Throughout the day, a variety of fitness classes are offered, including tai chi, yoga, and meditation. First-time guests are encouraged to attend "basic training." The regime consists of fast-paced walking in the sand, abdomen and coordination exercises, and strength training. Hatha yoga is offered once daily.

Guest Yoga Teachers? No.

Types of Yoga Classes Hatha. Once or twice daily. No extra charge.

Services Massage, facials, reflexology, body treatments, aromatherapy.

Other Classes Pilates, basic training, tai chi, meditation, aerobics, step, aquaerobics.

Recreation Swimming, Jacuzzi, sauna.

Children's Program? No.

Accommodations 62 studios and suites.

Dining Included. Vegan. Juice fasting available.

Attire/What to Bring Standard workout/yoga attire, sun/insect protection, swimsuit.

Travel Information The Fort Lauderdale airport is eight miles away.

Rates $995–$1,395 per person per week.

Contact 2000 South Ocean Drive, Hallandale, FL 33009; tel: 800-454-0003, 954-454-2220; www.regencyhealthspa.com.

I think yoga helps you a lot. I've been doing it for years. I'm 78 and I started when I was 40. I always go to the Regency House for the whole month of May, and then I also visit a couple more times a year. The yoga there is just great. I just wouldn't go anyplace else. I like exercising, but you need to have variety. I like classes, but I don't like machines like the treadmill. And I like to go into the ocean and swim. Sometimes we even do water aerobics in the ocean. And I always have the massages.

If I could eat the kind of food they serve at the Regency all the time, I could live to be 100. I just love their meals—they are so healthy. You can do without meat and dairy products if you cook it the way they do. When I go there I feel like I'm coming home. I know I would be unhappy anyplace else. I don't see how anyone couldn't love it. Plus everyone who works there thinks I'm in my fifties. You can't wait until you're old to take care of yourself.

—Teresa Pasawicz, office manager, Miami, Florida

Eden Roc Resort & Spa   Miami Beach, Florida

Overall, the Eden Roc Spa and fitness center has everything that you could want—it's like a mall. The people that work out there are professionals. The clientele, which includes doctors, lawyers, and television personalities, is more demanding and looking for a certain level of service. If doctors go there for a massage, you can bet they have a pretty good person working on them. The staff really has to be up on their services. I get Swedish and sports deep tissue massages there on a regular basis.

—Chris Lagos, attorney, Surf Side, Florida

The Eden Roc looks like somewhere the Rat Pack might have frequented in the '50s. Designed by architect Morris Lapidus, when it opened in 1956 Eden Roc immediately attracted Hollywood celebrities, including Elizabeth Taylor, Lucille Ball, Desi Arnaz, Lena Horne, Jerry Lewis, Milton Berle, Ann-Margret, and others. Today, the restored guests rooms, restaurants, and public rooms retain their art-deco roots. The resort is conveniently located on the beach and just minutes from South Beach attractions.

The Eden Roc Spa features a rock climbing wall and floor-to-ceiling windows so you can watch the ocean waves while you perfect your Down-ward-Facing Dog. A full array of massage therapies and body treatments, plus fitness classes, are also available.

Guest Yoga Teachers? No.

Types of Yoga Classes Hatha, Power, flow. Once or twice daily. $9 per day.

Services Massage, facials, aromatherapy, body treatments, reflexology, shiatsu, Reiki method, nail care.

Other Classes Spinning, step aerobics, aquaerobics, Latin groove, cardio boxing, Pilates.

Recreation Swimming, racquetball, squash, rock climbing wall, WaveRunners, kayaks, Hobie Cat sailboats, aqua bikes, parasailing, scuba instruction.

Children's Program? N/A.

Accommodations 349 guest rooms and suites.

Dining Not included. Two restaurants: Harry's Grille (seafood and steak), Aquatica (casual dining).

Attire/What to Bring Standard workout/yoga attire, swimsuit, sun/insect protection.

Travel Information Eden Roc is 14 miles from the Miami airport.

Rates $210–$439 per night, double occupancy.

Contact 4525 Collins Ave., Miami Beach, FL 33140; tel: 800-327-8337, 305-531-0000; www.edenrocresort.com.

The Breakers   Palm Beach, Florida

The Breakers, a 560-room, Italian Renaissance–style hotel, looks like some-place Jay Gatsby would vacation. The ornate oceanfront property was inspired by the Italian villas of the 1400s.

The newly restored resort features 36 holes of championship golf, 10 ten-nis courts, a 20,000-square-foot spa, a Mediterranean-style beach club, and a variety of water sports. The beach club boasts four pools, including one situ-ated directly on the beach, a children's pool, 10 pool cabanas, 58 beachfront cabanas, a pool deck, and lawn space, and a 6,000-square-foot rooftop terrace.

At the spa and fitness center, yoga classes are held on an ocean terrace 60 feet above the ocean or in the center itself, which has 14-foot-high windows overlooking the Atlantic. The spa also has a lap pool, oceanfront Jacuzzi, 17 private treatment rooms, spa suites, a beauty salon, and ladies' and men's locker rooms with steam and sauna. Massages and a variety of body wraps, scrubs, and Guerlain skin care treatments are available.

Guest Yoga Teachers? No.

Types of Yoga Classes Hatha. Once on Monday, Wednesday, Friday, and Saturday. No extra charge.

Services Massage, aromatherapy, shiatsu, reflexology, facials, body treatments, nail care.

Other Classes Tai chi, water aerobics, kickboxing, snorkeling.

Recreation Golf, tennis, swimming, scuba, bicycling.

Children's Program? Yes. Coconut Crew Camp for ages 3 to 12.

Accommodations 560 guest rooms, including 57 suites.

Dining Not included. Seven restaurants and four bars, including L'Escalier (classic European cuisine; jackets for men), S.S. Reef Bar, the Beach Club, Flagler Steakhouse, the Seafood Bar, the Tapestry Bar, the Circle.

Attire/What to Bring Standard yoga/workout attire, swimsuit, sun/insect protections, golf/tennis attire, clothes for fine dining.

Travel Information The Breakers is located 7 miles from Palm Beach Inter-national Airport, 42 miles from Fort Lauderdale-Hollywood International Airport, and 72 miles from Miami International Airport.

Rates $275–$4,000 per night, double occupancy.

Contact One South County Road, Palm Beach, FL 33480; tel: 561-655-6611, 888-273-2537; fax: 561-655-3577; www.thebreakers.com.

The Breakers has a water aerobics class in the morning and afternoon that is so much fun. You jump around in a pool that looks over the ocean. Then you have 10 minutes to get dressed and get to yoga. They really take care of you at the Breakers. I would rather be there than anyplace else in the world, because the staff makes you feel so special. They just go the extra mile.

Every year we have Thanksgiving at the Breakers—that's how much we love the food. And I have had all the spa treatments. I grew up with Guerlain products, and that is what they use at the spa. Even a simple manicure is something special, because the manicurist massages your hands for five or six minutes. It's like you're in heaven.

—Michele Solange Myers, artist,
 Palm Beach, Florida

GEORGIA

The Cloister & Sea Island Spa   Sea Island, Georgia

I had been wanting to visit the Cloister at Sea Island for some time. I went for the relaxation, the amenities, and the service. The grounds were plush, with blossoms everywhere. Every aspect of the resort had a different element to appreciate: the antiques and decor of the main lobby, the historical markings throughout the grounds, the tranquil atmosphere of the spa, and, of course, the fabulous view from my room.

My room was an oceanfront cottage with a spacious, screened balcony. The food was delicious. I ate mostly in the casual dining Beach Club. I had everything from the seafood buffet to salads and hamburgers. Every meal was a pleasure. On the few occasions I ordered room service, the food and service were just as outstanding.

I took some YogaFit classes. The class took the participants through a dynamic, flowing workout that was well designed and allowed for individuals to experience their own journey.

—Becky Martin, YogaFit master trainer and presenter, Gainesville, Georgia

Perhaps butler service, formal attire for dinner, and ballroom dancing is not the typical yoga practitioner's idea of a retreat. But couple that with an affordable meal plan, tai chi on the beach, and a full menu of spa treatments, and you're bound to attract an eclectic mix of people. Welcome to the Cloister. The Mediterranean-style resort, which opened in 1928, was designed by Addison Mizner. The resort has been attracting political heavy hitters like the Eisenhowers, Churchills, and Bushes since it opened. Whether you're an avid sportsman, a yoga practitioner, or a mother of three, the Cloister appeals because it is a place where modern interests and old traditions converge.

At the Sea Island Spa, individual itineraries are created to meet each guest's goals. For some, this may include peacefully communing with nature by participating in sea turtle walks and marsh kayaking. Others may gravitate toward traditional spa treatments and fitness programs. Meditation, tai chi, aromatherapy, and wellness lectures are other ways guests learn to live a balanced life.

Guest Yoga Teachers? No.

Types of Yoga Classes YogaFit. Once or twice a day. $15 per class.

Services Aromatherapy, body treatments, facials, massage, reflexology, Reiki method, nail care.

Other Classes Meditation, breathing, tai chi, ballet, mindful journaling.

Recreation Golf, tennis, horseback riding, bicycling, clay target shooting, dancing, kayaking, sailing.

Children's Program? Yes. For ages 3 to 11.

Accommodations 269 rooms, 56 ocean house accommodations.

Dining Not included. Meal plan available. In the main dining room (continental), men wear collared shirts at lunch and breakfast; coats and ties are required at dinner. For both men and women, formal attire is preferred on Wednesday, Friday, and Saturday evenings. Other restaurants: the Terrace (refined Southern), Colt & Alison's (steak and seafood), Beach Club (breakfast buffet/steak and seafood), Davis Love Grill (steak, chicken, fish, pasta).

Attire/What to Bring Traditional workout/yoga attire, swimsuit, sun/insect protection, tennis and golf attire, formal dress for dining.

Travel Information The Cloister is 85 miles south of the Savannah, GA, airport and 70 miles north of the Jacksonville, FL, airport.

Rates $194–$1,000 per night, double occupancy. For the three-meals-per-day plan, add $60 per person per day.

Contact First Street, Sea Island, GA 31561; tel: 800-732-4752, 912-638-3611; fax: 912-638-5823; www.seaisland.com.

HAWAII

Mauna Kea Resort Kamuela, Big Island, Hawaii

More than 30 years ago, developer and philanthropist Laurance Rockefeller chose a remote patch of black lava as the site of the Mauna Kea Resort. Today, the 310-room hotel offers amenities such as golf, tennis, and water sports, but it is also home to more than 1,600 pieces of Buddhist art that explore the concept of enlightenment.

The Spa & Fitness Center, located in the Beach Front building of the hotel, features strength training and cardiovascular equipment, workout areas, yoga classes, steam room, sauna, massage rooms, and locker rooms. More than 10 varieties of massage are available, including traditional lomi lomi, aromatherapy, reflexology, and sunburn relief (if you forgot to apply your sunblock). Licensed practitioners are on staff to administer acupuncture.

Guest Yoga Teachers? No.

Types of Yoga Classes Hatha. Once daily. $15 per class.

Services Facials, massage, shiatsu, aromatherapy, lomi lomi, reflexology, body wraps.

Other Classes Aquaerobics, step aerobics, Pilates.

Recreation Swimming, snorkeling, scuba diving, sailing, kayaking, catamaran riding, whale watching, deep-sea fishing, golf, tennis, helicopter flight-seeing.

Children's Program? Yes. For ages 5 to 12.

Accommodations 310 rooms.

Dining Not included. Four restaurants: Batik (fine dining, Euro-Asian), the Pavilion at Manta Ray Point (breakfast buffet, seafood dinner), the Terrace (brunch), Hau Tree/Gazebo (salads, sandwiches, sushi); weekly luau.

Suffice it to say that I fell in love with the Mauna Kea the minute I drove up to the entrance and was totally overtaken when I stepped inside, all without even seeing the beach. As far as the grounds go, the grass bordering the beach adds to its beauty, and the shade provided by all the palm trees makes it a great place to enjoy the day without getting too much sun. And of course, just walking around surrounded by art at every turn is wonderful.

Yoga was not offered until about 1996. And at that time, a big class had five people in it. I've seen the class grow each year that I've been there, which I think is a testament to the growth of yoga in general. The class is Iyengar. It's taught outdoors on the lawn, and you can watch whales breach as you do your postures. The teacher often makes use of the beach lounge chairs but also brings the more traditional aids like straps and blocks. It's basic, but you can take it to your own level.

I took a lei-making class one day. I also took advantage of a couple of golf clinics and, of course, took the art tour that is given by a wonderful woman who is extremely knowledgeable about the collection there as well as the Mauna Kea itself. Snorkeling is always an option, and there's coral close enough in that it's easy and fun just to get in the water and check out the fish whenever you feel like it.

—Patty Bryan, executive director, Capoeira Foundation/DanceBrazil, New York City

Attire/What to Bring Standard yoga attire, sneakers/hiking shoes, swimsuit, sun/insect protection, golf/tennis attire, clothes for fine dining.

Travel Information Mauna Kea Resort is 26 miles from the Kona International Airport.

Rates $360–$1,400 per night, double occupancy.

Contact 62-100 Mauna Kea Beach Drive, Kohala Coast, HI 96743; tel: 800-882-6060, 808-882-7222; fax: 808-880-3112; www.maunakeabeachhotel.com.

Grand Wailea Resort   Wailea, Maui, Hawaii

Make no mistake: Grand Wailea Resort is a *grand* resort, with 780 rooms. A sleepy Hawaiian retreat it is not, with a large offering of sports and sightseeing activities. Kids can enjoy lei making at Camp Grande, while yogi parents dig their toes into the sand during yoga class on the beach.

The 50,000-square-foot Spa Grande offers a mix of Hawaiian, Ayurvedic, European, and Japanese therapies. Spa Grande has 42 treatment rooms, a cedar sauna, marble steam room, Jacuzzi, weight-training room, racquetball/squash court, juice bar, fitness center, and oceanview lounge. In addition, the resort boasts nine pools and seven waterslides.

The hotel houses a $50 million art collection, featuring Fernando Botero, Fernand Leger, Pablo Picasso, and Andy Warhol.

Guest Yoga Teachers? No.

Types of Yoga Classes Hatha. Beach yoga is complimentary. Yoga in the studio is $10.

Services Massage, reflexology, aromatherapy, body treatments, Ayurvedic treatments, facials, hydrotherapy, Reiki method, shiatsu, acupressure, lomi lomi.

Other Classes Aerobics, aquaerobics, Pilates, tai chi, Spinning.

Recreation Golf, tennis, racquetball, squash, swimming, scuba, windsurfing, snorkeling, deep-sea fishing, dinner cruises, hiking, horseback riding, helicopter tours, kayaking, sailing, parasailing, whale watching.

Children's Program? Yes. Camp Grande for ages 5 to 12.

Accommodations 780 rooms.

Dining Not included. Six restaurants: Bistro Molokini (California and Island cuisine), Cafe Kula (breakfast, light meals, dinner), Grand Din-

We decided to go the resort because I was six-and-a-half months pregnant at the time, and we wanted to stay somewhere exclusive and luxurious in the U.S. Our travel agent raved about the Grand Wailea. We were very impressed with the grounds and the resort as a whole. The pools were very nice—there was an area for children and an area strictly for adults. The grounds were neatly manicured and elegant. The beach area was very private and well groomed. The thing we enjoyed the most was the quiet atmosphere.

The spa accommodations and services were outstanding. My husband and I both had facials and massages (mine was a pregnancy massage). Both were wonderful and relaxing.

The snorkeling/diving excursion was very nice, and the tour group hosting the excursion was wonderful. It was a great trip.

—Missy Brown, corporate litigation counsel, Dallas, Texas

ing Room Maui (breakfast), Humuhumunukunukuapua'a (fish and meat entrees with Polynesian or Hawaiian influences), Kincha (Japanese/sushi bar), Volcano Bar (lunch).

Attire/What to Bring Standard yoga attire, sneakers/hiking shoes, swimsuit, sun/insect protection, golf/tennis attire.

Travel Information Grand Wailea is a 35-minute drive from Kahului Airport.

Rates $450–$10,000 per night, double occupancy.

Contact 3850 Wailea Alanui, Wailea, HI 96753; tel: 800-888-6100, 808-875-1234; fax: 808-874-2442; www.grandwailea.com.

Hotel Hana Maui at Hana Ranch   Hana, Maui, Hawaii

The town of Hana hasn't grown much since the 1800s, because the area's infamous and only road is chock-full of hairpin turns. This makes Hotel Hana Maui that much more secluded and unspoiled. The resort consists of a collection of cottages on 67 acres adjacent to the 4,000-acre Hana Ranch.

In the early 1820s, New England missionaries arrived in Hana, and soon the first sugarcane was planted on the site of the present Hotel Hana Maui. Today, many large, old, sugar-boiling pots are used decoratively in the hotel's gardens. The 15,000-acre plantation was purchased in 1944 by a San Francisco entrepreneur, Paul I. Fagan, who developed a ranch and the Hotel Hana Maui. In 2001, the Hotel Hana Maui was purchased and remodeled by the owners of Post Ranch Inn, the resort in Big Sur, California.

Guests have complimentary access to the Wellness Center, which has spa treatments, a fitness room, and daily yoga and aqua exercise classes. Other activities include tennis, croquet, biking, fishing, swimming, and snorkeling. You can even learn how to play the ukulele, make a lei, or hula.

Guest Yoga Teachers? No.

Types of Yoga Classes Hatha partner-assisted yoga. No extra charge.

Services Massage, lomi lomi, shiatsu, reflexology, body treatments, Reiki method, craniosacral therapy, facials.

Other Classes Aquaerobics, hula, ukulele, lei making, tai chi.

Recreation Swimming, tennis, golf, whirlpool, croquet, bicycling, fishing, nature walks, snorkeling, horseback riding, Jeep excursions, kayaking, snorkeling, cave adventure.

Children's Program? No.

I attended yoga class almost every day at Hotel Hana Maui. The yoga room has a lovely wooden floor and plenty of mats. They offer partner yoga twice a week, and my husband, a marathon runner, even participated. It was impressed upon him that yoga would benefit his performance in other sports. It is wonderful doing yoga in weather warm enough to loosen the muscles. The teachers really meet the needs of all student levels.

We also did a lot of hiking, to a red sand beach and to a waterfall area where you can go swimming in one of the pools beneath the falls.

The resort is very much old Hawaii in feeling. All the buildings have green metal roofs and wide porches like the old plantation buildings. All the rooms seem to have a view of the water and mountains. Hana has remained small because the road leading to town has a bunch of hairpin turns. There isn't another resort in sight—it is very secluded and restful.

—Karen Ferlito, homemaker, Carmel, California

Accommodations 66 rooms and suites located in various one-story cottages with private lanais.

Dining Not included. Restaurant serves seafood and Hawaiian-influenced cuisine.

Attire/What to Bring Standard yoga/exercise attire, swimsuit, hiking boots, sun/insect protection, golf/tennis attire, rain pancho.

Travel Information Free transportation to and from Hana Airport.

Rates $295–$917 per night, double occupancy.

Contact PO Box 9, Hana, HI 96713; tel: 800-321-4262, 808-248-8211; www.hotelhanamaui.com.

ILLINOIS

Heartland Spa   Gilman, Illinois

The Heartland is a small, Midwestern health-oriented spa just 90 miles south of Chicago, making it convenient for urban dwellers to attend weekend retreats. Because the spa caters to only 28 guests at a time, each person gets individual attention. The Heartland teaches guests about health, fitness, nutrition, and stress management so they can make appropriate changes to their daily life. Experts of Iroquois Memorial Hospital partner with Heartland Spa staff to create a medical profile for each guest, at an additional charge.

The nutritional program covers healthful cooking techniques, weight loss management, and behavior modification techniques. The stress management program teaches you how to integrate exercise, massage, yoga, tai chi, and relaxation and meditation techniques into your life. During your stay, you can also choose from a wide variety of facials, massages, manicures, pedicures, body treatments, and aromatherapies.

The eclectic mix of activities includes fishing in a stocked, three-acre lake, kickboxing, and cross-country skiing.

Guest Yoga Teachers? No.

Types of Yoga Classes Ashtanga-flow and Iyengar-influenced on Tuesday, Wednesday, Friday, Saturday. No extra charge.

Services Facials, massages, nail care, body treatments, aromatherapy, craniosacral therapy, reflexology.

Other Classes Tai chi, basic training, kickboxing, Spinning, Pilates, meditation.

I've been to Heartland Spa five times. The first time I went, I chose it because it is close to my home, and the setting was comfortable and rural—you're really out there in the cornfields. Heartland Spa is about introducing the notion of balance in your life. For some people it is very transformative. The massages are wonderful, and the food is great—it's not about deprivation. The spa is not into a special regime, but you can request vegetarian, vegan, low sodium, or whatever you want. Many people end up eating in their bathrobes, since you are going to and from treatments all the time. There are very few men, but they are welcome and people go out of their way to make them feel comfortable.

You can participate in a high level or a low level of activity. The morning starts with an optional two-mile walk before breakfast. Every hour, except during mealtimes, there might be two or three classes you can take. There are different types of yoga at different times of the day. There is even nighttime yoga for relaxation. Susan Witz teaches the yoga classes, and now I study with her in Chicago as well.

—Barbara Silk, senior director of a public policy communications firm, Chicago, Illinois

Recreation Cross-country skiing, fishing, tennis, swimming, steam rooms, saunas, whirlpool.

Children's Program? No.

Accommodations 16 rooms.

Dining Included. Mostly vegetarian with some fish and poultry. 1,500 calories per day.

Attire/What to Bring All clothing except shoes, swimsuit, and sleepwear provided.

Travel Information Heartland is 90 miles south of Chicago's O'Hare International Airport.

Rates During the week $350 per person per night ($265 if you share your room). Two-night minimum.

Contact 1237 E. 1600 North Road, Gilman, IL 60938; tel: 800-545-4853; www.heartlandspa.com.

MAINE

Cliff House   Ogunquit, Maine

The Cliff House's yoga studio's full-length windows look out over rocky cliffs to the ocean, making class a relaxing or energizing experience, depending on the weather and size of the waves. Built in 1872 by Elsie Jane Weare, the Cliff House is now owned and operated by Elsie's great-granddaughter, Kathryn M. Weare. Weather permitting, outdoor classes are offered as well as classes in art, guided hikes, and music performances. Yoga, although only available on Fridays, might increase to more days per week.

In May 2002, the Cliff House opened a full-service spa in a new building with indoor and outdoor pools and adult-only guest rooms large enough for in-room spa treatments. Guests staying in other areas of the resort can also reserve spa services. Signature treatments include the Maine Wild Rose Body Wrap and the Cliff House Signature Facial using a blueberry mask.

Guest Yoga Teachers? No.

Types of Yoga Classes Kripalu, Ashtanga. $15 per class.

Services Facials, massage, aromatherapy, body treatments, nail care.

Other Classes Water aerobics, meditation, tai chi, stretching.

Recreation Hiking, swimming.

Children's Program? No.

When I arrived at the Cliff House, I was immediately struck by the powerful force of the ocean washing against the cliffs below the resort. The original building, built in 1872 by the current innkeeper's grandmother, houses the restaurants and older guest rooms and is decorated to reflect the New England coast.

My husband and I were housed in one of the newly opened spa guest rooms, located in the same building as the spa. The room was extra large, designed to accommodate in-room massages on request.

I had a private hatha yoga session in the beautiful yoga studio, overlooking the sea. The instructor was newly hired, though completely experienced, and there were plans to expand the program to include many types of yoga, with classes for varying levels of expertise.

—Debra Bokur, journalist, Nederland, Colorado

Accommodations 194 rooms.

Dining Not included. Meal package available. Breakfast and dinner $47 per person per day. Regional cuisine seafood with some vegetarian options.

Attire/What to Bring Standard yoga/workout attire, swimsuit, sun/insect protection, walking shoes.

Travel Information Portland, Maine, International Jetport is 40 miles away.

Rates $145–$265 per night, double occupancy. Three-night-minimum stay July 1 through September 1 and all holiday weekends. Two-night-minimum stay weekends off-season.

Contact Shore Road, PO Box 2274, Ogunquit, ME 03907; tel: 207-361-1000; fax: 207-361-2122; www.cliffhousemaine.com.

MASSACHUSETTS

Canyon Ranch   Lenox, Massachusetts

Canyon Ranch might be one of the most famous spas in the world. The first location, in Tucson, Arizona, opened in 1979. In 1989, a second location, Canyon Ranch in the Berkshires Health Resort, was built in the woodlands of Lenox. Spa services, fitness and outdoor sports, medical and behavioral services and consultations, nutrition consultations and workshops, spiritual pursuits, and healthy gourmet cuisine are available at both locations. In fact, it would take you about a month to complete every consultation, service, and workshop offered, so pick your activities mindfully.

At the Lenox property, climate-controlled, glass-enclosed walkways connect the buildings of the resort. Even during the New England winter, you can move from one building to the next without bundling up. The 100,000-square-foot spa has six gyms; a 75-foot indoor pool; exercise and weight-training rooms; indoor tennis, racquetball, squash, basketball, and sports courts; men's and women's locker rooms with steam and inhalation rooms, sauna, cold dip, and whirlpools; an indoor running track; and massage and bodywork rooms.

The Bellefontaine Mansion, a replica of the Petite Trianon, Louis XV's Versailles chateau, was built in 1897. Today, it houses the dining room, library, creative arts center, body in balance studio, and the medical, nursing, behavioral health, nutrition, movement therapy, exercise physiology, acupuncture, and neuromuscular therapy departments.

Spa aficionados who have been to both Canyon Ranch locations claim the Lenox spa is less laid-back than the one in Tucson, due in part to the influx of urbanites from Boston and New York.

Guest Yoga Teachers? Yes. Including De De Daniels, Carol Kline, Lisa Shremp.

Types of Yoga Classes Hatha, Power, Yoga Cycle (combines yoga and cycling). Five times daily. No extra charge.

Services Acupuncture, herbal wraps, mud wraps, reflexology, Reiki method, seaweed wraps, shiatsu, thalassotherapy.

Other Classes Weight training, aerobics, aquaerobics, cooking, tai chi, core conditioning.

Recreation Basketball, biking, canoeing, hiking, kayaking, racquetball, skiing, squash, tennis, volleyball.

Children's Program? No. Minimum age 14 to participate in regular spa program.

Accommodations 126 luxury rooms, 24 suites.

Dining Included. Vegetarian/vegan available.

Attire/What to Bring Standard gym/yoga attire, walking shoes, swimsuit, sun/insect protection.

Travel Information Canyon Ranch provides complimentary guest transportation to and from the Albany, NY, and Bradley International (Hartford, CT) airports or the Albany/Rensselaer, NY, Amtrak train station.

Rates Three-night stay $2,165–$3,430 per person, July–October.

Contact 165 Kemble St., Lenox, MA 01240; tel: 800-742-9000, 413-637-4100; www.canyonranch.com.

The grounds of Canyon Ranch are beautiful, serene, quite lush and green. Since it is off a main road, my first thought was how surprising it is that this oasis is right in the middle of a quaint New England town.

The food was very tasty, but portions were small. The good news: You may order double, even triple portions. A great feature is the extensive salad bar at lunch and dinner and the cereal and condiment bar at breakfast. My one issue with the food was its predominance of fiber and roughage. Although I'm sure I lost a pound or two after three days at the ranch, while there I was so bloated, my clothes barely fit.

I took one yoga class at the ranch that was a basic, level-one hatha yoga class. I now practice yoga three to four times a week, but at the time I was a real novice. It was a very thorough introductory class that emphasized breathing and basic postures.

I did morning walks both days, which were lovely ways to start the days. We met in front, stretched, then walked through the surrounding town and back for a total of about three miles. We also did a nature hike through nearby woods where we studied beaver lodges, etc. I fully understood the mission of the ranch by participating in massage, eating extremely healthfully, taking time to rest, and enjoying nature.

—Gwen Flamberg, beauty editor of a national women's magazine, New York City

MINNESOTA

Birdwing Spa   Litchfield, Minnesota

Birdwing Spa—on 300 woodland acres interwoven with ponds, fountains, and 2 1/2 miles of private lakeshore—focuses on fitness, stress reduction, and spiritual rejuvenation in an unassuming atmosphere. Hike 15 miles of trails through prairie grasslands in summer, or cross-country ski or snowshoe in winter. A new outdoor, heated pool hosts a water aerobics class. Indoors, an aerobic studio and yoga room is the site of dozens of year-round classes for all levels. Guests can attend as many or as few classes as they like.

I've been to Birdwing every year for 13 years. They own 300 acres that have trails and ponds. I'm city born and bred, so it's a nice country visit. It's a wonderful break from 1,000 children. It's like bottled calm. They are very laid-back—you don't have to take classes if you don't want to. I feel very pampered when I go there.

A typical day starts with breakfast. Then you can take an exercise class, which could be low-impact aerobics, circuit training, or dance aerobics. They're all held in what was once an airplane hangar. After that, there is stretching for about a half hour, then lunch. In the afternoon you go on a guided hike or canoeing, depending on the weather. You can also have spa treatments or take yoga. The yoga class was lovely and comfortable for a beginner. There were both men and women in the class, which isn't always the case. And the teacher accommodated the different levels of experience.

They use lots of spices but no salt in their cooking and will cater to your dietary needs. There is portion control, but they will serve you more if you want it. I've never had a meal I didn't enjoy.

—Susan Fine, public school librarian,
 Evanston, Illinois

More than 30 pampering spa treatments contribute to guest relaxation. Weekend and weeklong packages are available.

Guest Yoga Teachers? No.

Types of Yoga Classes Hatha. Twice daily. No extra charge.

Services Massage, body treatments, reflexology, scalp treatment, facials, nail care.

Other Classes Low-impact aerobics, aerobic kickboxing, interval fitness, qigong, circuit training, step aerobics, meditation, cardio boxing.

Recreation Canoeing, biking, cross-country skiing, snowshoe, hiking, bocce ball, water volleyball, bird watching, kayaking.

Children's Program? No.

Accommodations Eight rooms, six suites.

Dining Included. Three meals daily. Vegetarian with some fish and poultry.

Attire/What to Bring Toiletries, sun/insect protection, yoga/exercise clothes, water bottle, tennis shoes, hiking shoes/boots, swimsuit, binoculars.

Travel Information Birdwing is 70 miles west of the Minneapolis/St. Paul airport. A shuttle is available for $57.50.

Rates $288–$374 per person per night. Includes two hours of spa services.

Contact 21398 575th Avenue, Litchfield, MN 55355; tel: 320-693-6064; www.birdwingspa.com.

NEVADA

Canyon Ranch SpaClub at the Venetian Resort   Las Vegas, Nevada

In a city known for gambling, smoking, and drinking, the Canyon Ranch SpaClub is a haven of health and serenity. The 65,000-square-foot facility is located in the Venetian Resort Hotel Casino. Like the other Canyon Ranch facilities in Tucson, Arizona, and Lenox, Massachusetts, the spa offers a wide variety of services. In Las Vegas, you can choose from more than 120 spa treatments and activities, including yoga two to four times daily. There's also a 40-foot rock-climbing wall. Breakfast and lunch are served at the Canyon Ranch Café. Or stop by the juice bar for a smoothie after yoga class.

Guest Yoga Teachers? No.

Types of Yoga Classes Hatha. Two to four times daily. Not included in price of accommodations. $30 per day for unlimited use of spa facilities.

Services Nutritional counseling, physical therapy, acupuncture, massage, body treatments, aromatherapy, hydromassage, Ayurvedic treatments including shirodhara, facials, craniosacral therapy, Reiki method, jin shin jyutsu, reflexology, shiatsu.

Other Classes Pilates, aerobics, kickboxing, meditation, Spinning.

Recreation Rock climbing wall, swimming, golf nearby.

Children's Program? No. Minimum age 18 for Canyon Ranch SpaClub.

Accommodations 3,036 suites, including deluxe suites.

Dining Not included. Spa cuisine at Canyon Ranch Café; Venetian has 35 restaurants.

Attire/What to Bring Standard workout/yoga attire, swimsuit, clothing suitable for fine dining.

Travel Information Canyon Ranch SpaClub and the Venetian are 3 1/2 miles from the Las Vegas airport.

Rates $159–$999 per night, double occupancy.

Contact Canyon Ranch SpaClub, 3355 Las Vegas Blvd. South, Suite 1159, Las Vegas, NV 89109; tel: 702-414-3600, 877-220-2688; www.canyon-ranch.com. The Venetian, tel: 888-283-6423; www.venetian.com.

The Canyon Ranch SpaClub at the Venetian is a bit difficult to find. The hotel is huge, and the spa is located at the end of the corridor on the fourth floor, which has guest rooms too, so at first you might think you're not at the right place. The interior of the spa is very clean and high-tech looking. The rock climbing wall is just inside the entrance, and down the hall are the rooms designated for the various classes. Each of the instructors has his or her picture and a brief bio on the wall in the reception area. Like the Canyon Ranch Health Resorts in Massachusetts and Arizona, the overall feeling you get is one of more than just pampering—it's the kind of place that's serious about changing your lifestyle.

—Joy Ricci, marketing executive, Scottsdale, Arizona

NEW YORK

The Sagamore   Bolton Landing, New York

The Sagamore, in the Adirondack Mountains on a 72-acre island in the middle of Lake George, has a rich history. Originally built in 1883, the historic hotel features clapboard siding and classic architecture. Although it was damaged by fire in 1893 and 1914, the Sagamore was fully reconstructed in 1930. Throughout the years, it has served as a social gathering place for the wealthy residents of Green Island and Millionaires Row. Nevertheless, the hotel fell into disrepair and closed its doors in 1981, but was restored in 1983 and reopened in 1985.

Today, the Sagamore has four types of accommodations: the historic hotel, lodges, condominium rentals, and the Wapanak Castle, a historic six-bedroom, four-bath home. Kids can participate in adventure camp while parents take yoga classes in the glass-enclosed fitness center, which has views

The Sagamore is in a beautiful location on Lake George, on the widest part of the lake. It's very relaxing and serene—and even more peaceful during the off-season, in the winter. The staff is very efficient and knowledgeable. I've done a number of yoga classes there. They are more for beginners, but it is what got me started in yoga; now I do privates with one of the Sagamore instructors, Jill Kappesser. I've had quite a few spa treatments too, and they're all good: hot stone therapy, Swedish massage, and facials. The food is very good, too. The restaurants run from elegant to casual dining and are located right in the hotel.

—Amy Wilkinson, investor relations officer, Saratoga Springs, New York

of the surrounding mountains and forests. Or get outside and explore the surrounding mountains by hiking, skiing, or snowshoeing. Or swim, boat, or fish in Lake George. A full menu of European- and Asian-influenced spa treatments is available.

Guest Yoga Teachers? No.

Types of Yoga Classes Kripalu. Once a day in summer, four days a week off-season. $10 per class.

Services Massage, aromatherapy, reflexology, Reiki method, shiatsu, cranio-sacral therapy, jin shin jyutsu, acupuncture, body treatments, facials.

Other Classes Tai chi, aquaerobics, step aerobics.

Recreation Golf, tennis, swimming, sauna, whirlpool, boating, cross-country skiing, downhill skiing, fishing charters, waterskiing, windsurfing, sailing, parasailing, ice-skating, ice fishing, sledding, horseback riding, white-water rafting, scuba, snorkeling.

Children's Program? Yes. Teepee Club for ages 4 to 12.

Accommodations 350 guest rooms: the historic hotel, lodges, condominium rentals, the castle.

Dining Not included. Six restaurants: Trillium (contemporary American), the Sagamore Dining Room (regional American and international selections), Mister Brown's Pub (Adirondack-style with casual menu), the Veranda (afternoon tea, sushi, tapas, and evening cocktails), the Club Grill (New York City–style steakhouse), the Morgan (dining cruises on a 19th-century touring vessel).

Attire/What to Bring Standard yoga/workout attire, hiking boots, swimsuit, sun/insect protection, golf and tennis attire, ski and cold weather attire in winter, clothing appropriate for fine dining.

Travel Information The Albany International Airport is 65 miles away. The Sagamore will provide car service from the airport for a minimal fee.

Rates $149–$669 per night, double occupancy.

Contact 110 Sagamore Road, Bolton Landing, NY 12814; tel: 800-358-3585, 518-644-9400; fax: 518-743-6211; www.thesagamore.com.

New Age Health Spa   Neversink, New York

New Age is a spiritually minded, laid-back spa on the grounds of a former summer community. The 10,000-square-foot Cayuga Yoga & Meditation Center is home to classes in hatha yoga, qigong, ai chi, spirit dance, tai chi, and meditation suitable for both beginners and advanced students. Weekend yoga programs in a variety of disciplines, such as Anusara, Integral, Kripalu, and Sivananda, are offered.

Mornings at New Age Health Spa begin with a 30-minute meditation, followed by a mindful three-mile walk through the surrounding countryside and a 50-minute yoga practice. The afternoon features a selection of yoga and fitness classes and concludes with a predinner meditation that may include pranayama breathing, chanting, and guided visualizations. Periodically throughout the year, Native American sweat lodge ceremonies are offered, designed to purify the body, mind, and spirit. New Age is more rustic and spiritual than other spas, and there are no telephones or televisions in guest rooms. Meals are low in fat, sugar, sodium, and cholesterol. Many ingredients are grown on-site in one of the spa's three organic greenhouses.

Guest Yoga Teachers? Yes. Including Nella Hahn.

Types of Yoga Classes Hatha, Sivananda, Ashtanga, Anusara, Power, Integral, Kripalu.

Services Aromatherapy, body wraps, facials, hydro-colon therapy, massage, reflexology, shiatsu, Vichy shower, Ayurveda.

Other Classes Pranayama, aerobics, dance, boxing, Pilates, muscle conditioning, stretching, tai chi, qigong, ai chi, meditation.

Recreation Swimming, hiking, cross-country skiing, snowshoeing, High Elements athletic course, bird watching, tennis.

Children's Program? No. Minimum age 16.

Accommodations Five cottages with a total of 37 rustic rooms.

Dining Included. Low-fat meals three times daily. Chicken and fish served; vegetarian available. Juice fasting available.

Attire/What to Bring Basic yoga and athletic wear, hiking boots, swimsuit, sun/insect protection, tennis attire.

Travel Information The New Age Health Spa is 115 miles from New York City. Limousine service can be arranged from LaGuardia, Kennedy, and Newark airports, or you can connect with the New Age Health Spa van in Manhattan.

I went to the New Age Health Spa because I had broken my leg and had gained weight. I felt like I needed to check myself in somewhere, and heard New Age was no-frills but spiritually connected. Actually, it's like being at an evolved camp for adults. I did the juice fast program and took yoga every day. Yoga really helped the healing process. Since then I've been to New Age three times. New Age is built on Indian ceremonial grounds, and you really feel the energy. Even though you are only two hours from New York City, you feel like you are in the middle of nowhere. The yoga center is beautiful, and they have teachers young and old, which really appealed to me. And there are great lectures at night and breathtaking scenery and great trails for hiking during the day. The owner will sometimes go on hikes with guests.

—Carolyn Izzo Feldman, business owner, Nyack, New York

Rates $159–$399 per person per night. Two-night minimum.

Contact Rte. 55, Neversink, NY 12765; tel: 800-682-4348, 845-985-7600; fax: 845-985-2467; www.newagehealthspa.com.

NORTH CAROLINA

Grove Park Inn Resort & Spa   Asheville, North Carolina

The spa at the Grove Park Inn Resort is cavernous—it's really like walking into a cave. The spa is underground. There are three different pools. One has piped-in music underwater, so you can hear it while you do laps, and one pool is filled with saltwater. In the South, people are a lot more modest. Even in the women-only side of the spa people are clothed. In the sauna, women will have their swimsuits on.

—Stacy Kunstel, freelance writer, southwestern New Hampshire

The Grove Park Inn Resort & Spa is one of those sprawling Southern resorts with lots of history. It was built in 1913 by Edwin W. Grove, owner of Grove's Pharmacy in St. Louis, Missouri, who began spending summers in Asheville as a cure for his bronchitis.

A lot of guests visit Grove Park for its unusual underground spa, which is like a luxurious . . . cave. Sunlight streams in from a glass skylight above the spa pool, while the stone walls and torches give it a Gothic feel. The sound of waterfalls echoes throughout. The daily fee to use the spa is $50 for guests, $75 for nonguests.

Yoga classes take place in the Sports Complex. There is no daily fee at the Sports Complex, which also has racquetball courts, exercise equipment, fitness classes, an indoor pool, and tennis courts.

As you might expect, you don't visit the Grove Park Inn for healthy, vegetarian food. However, you may want to check out the views of the Blue Ridge Mountains from the glass-enclosed terrace of the Blue Ridge Dining Room, which serves breakfast, lunch, and dinner.

Area attractions include the Biltmore Estate, Chimney Rock Park, white-water rafting, the Cherokee Indian Reservation, Blue Ridge Parkway, Folk Art Center, and the Great Smoky Mountains National Park.

Guest Yoga Teachers? No.

Types of Yoga Classes Hatha. Once or twice a day, no class on Sunday. $8 per class.

Services Aromatherapy, color and light therapy, body treatments, facials, Reiki method, shiatsu, nail care, hydrotherapy.

Other Classes Aerobics, step aerobics, aquaerobics, Spinning, kickboxing, Pilates.

Recreation Golf, tennis, swimming, plunge pool, mineral pool, steam room.

Children's Program? Yes. Ages 3 to 12.

Accommodations 510 rooms, including 12 suites and one cottage.

Dining Not included. Five restaurants: Horizons (formal dining; jackets for men), Chops at Sunset Terrace (beef and seafood), Blue Ridge Dining Room (American-continental), Carolina Cafe, Spa Cafe.

Attire/What to Bring Standard yoga/workout attire, swimsuit, sun/insect protection, hiking boots, clothing for fine dining, golf/tennis attire.

Travel Information The Asheville Regional Airport is nine miles southeast of Asheville.

Rates $119–$709 per night, double occupancy. Cottage $749–$1,199 per night, double occupancy.

Contact 290 Macon Ave., Asheville, NC 28804; tel: 800-438-5800, 828-252-2711; fax: 828-253-7053; www.groveparkinn.com.

OHIO

Kerr House   Grand Rapids, Ohio

From the outside, Kerr House looks more like someone's home than a full-fledged spa. Created by Laurie Hostetler, the spa is in a Victorian house, and a staff of 25 caters to six to eight guests at a time. Five-day, three-day, and weekend programs focus on yoga, nutrition, body treatments, stress management, and self-esteem.

Breakfast is served in bed each morning, followed by a yoga class. Next, white terry robes are donned and body treatments begin. During the week, guests can sample massages, facials, reflexology, raspberry exfoliation, herbal wraps, body wraps, mud baths, hot oil hair treatments, hot paraffin hand and foot waxing, manicures, pedicures, whirlpools, and saunas. After-noon activities vary with the seasons and might include walks along the Maumee River. There is another yoga class before dinner, which is served in the dining room by candlelight, with antique linens, dishes, stemware, and silver. As formal as it sounds, there is no dress code.

Guest Yoga Teachers? No.

Types of Yoga Classes Hatha and Five Tibetan Rites. Twice daily. No extra charge.

Services Massage, reflexology, facials, nail care, body treatments.

Other Classes N/A.

Recreation Walking, hiking.

Children's Program? No.

I started going to the Kerr House in 1986, and I've been there 12 times. It changed my life. In 1986 I didn't know anything about healthy eating or spirituality. They've never had to change their program because they were so advanced and ahead of their time. It is a small place, and Laurie, the owner, is there with you all the time. It's in an old Victorian house in a little town—you feel like it's your family. The day starts with breakfast in bed with a personal schedule on your tray. Then you go to the loft on the third floor for yoga from 8 AM to 10 AM, taught by Laurie. Afterward, you put on your robe and go to the spa area and have two treatments. Lunch, usually soup and salad, is served in the spa. Laurie will talk about herbs and different vitamins over lunch. You have a rest period in the after-noon—you can go for a walk in town or hang out in your room. There is another yoga session from 4 PM to 6 PM. You do gain core strength from the yoga you do during the week, but it is very mild. The clientele is mostly women, but some weekends cater to couples.

—Adelle Morley, retired decorator, Lexington, Ohio

Accommodations Five rooms, some shared.

Dining Included. Spa cuisine.

Attire/What to Bring Standard yoga/workout attire, hiking boots, sun/insect protection.

Travel Information Grand Rapids is located 20 minutes south of Toledo Express Airport. The Kerr House limousine will meet your flight with advance notice.

Rates Weekend $695 each for semiprivate and $795 for a private room. Five-night stay $2,350 each for semiprivate and $2,750 for a private room. Three-night stay $1,275 each for semiprivate and $1,475 for a private room.

Contact 17777 Beaver Street, PO Box 363, Grand Rapids, OH 43522; tel: 419-832-1733; fax: 419-832-4303; www.thekerrhouse.com.

OREGON

Avalon Hotel and Spa   Portland, Oregon

I went to the Avalon Hotel and Spa with a group of friends for a weekend getaway. We have gone to a lot of different spas and tried different services, and this is one of the nicest spas we've been to. I was most impressed with the level of training the people in the spa seem to have. Not only did they seem to know the procedures, they seemed to know why certain things were important, and they could recommend treatments you could do at home.

The hotel rooms are modern and nicely appointed, with great views of the Willamette River and fixtures that are a cut above. We had some wonderful appetizers and champagne brought up to our rooms before we went to dinner in the restaurant, where we had a special five-course feast.

If you want to exercise outdoors, there is a path that goes along the river for walking, biking, and running that leads to nearby boutique shops.

—Kathleen Dotten-Cosgrove, artist, Portland, Oregon

If your travels lead you to Portland, the modern Avalon Hotel and Spa is a good place to have a massage or take a yoga class. As a bonus, many guest rooms offer views of the Willamette River and Mt. Hood.

Located on two levels, the 13,000-square-foot Avalon Spa provides a host of European and Asian spa treatments, including facials and hydrotherapy in the Raindance wet room. Daily use of the spa includes unlimited daily access to all fitness club facilities. Power and restorative yoga are offered on a regular basis.

Guest Yoga Teachers? No.

Types of Yoga Classes Restorative, Power (sometimes combined with Pilates or NIA). Once daily. $10 per class.

Services Body treatments, facials, massage, Ayurvedic treatments, kurs, aromatherapy, shirodhara, shiatsu, reflexology, nail and hair care.

Other Classes Pilates, kickboxing, NIA, body sculpting, step, bath treatments.

Recreation Hiking, tennis, golf, wine country excursions, boating.

Children's Program? No.

Accommodations 99 guest rooms.

Dining Not included. Two restaurants: Rivers Restaurant (American), Spa Cafe.

Attire/What to Bring Standard yoga/workout attire, swimsuit, hiking boots, sun/insect protection.

Travel Information The Avalon Hotel and Spa is 14 miles from the Portland airport.

Rates $155–$650 per night, double occupancy.

Contact 0455 SW Hamilton Court, Portland, OR 97201; tel: 503-802-5800, 888-556-4402; fax: 503-802-5830; www.avalonhotelandspa.com.

TEXAS

The Greenhouse   Arlington, Texas

The Greenhouse was created in 1965 for well-heeled women looking to be pampered. Its reputation for discretion has made it a favorite destination of celebrities in search of privacy, such as American First Ladies, international royalty, actresses, and supermodels. The combination of spa treatments, customized exercise programs, and personalized service has secured a loyal female clientele, who repeatedly return to this Southern-style mansion.

The Greenhouse staff takes care of everything, from picking you up at the airport in a limousine to unpacking for you, if you wish. Forgot something? The Greenhouse provides you with workout attire and a bathing suit. In fact, all you really need to bring is athletic shoes, and dinner attire.

Meals are low in calories (1,200 calories per day) but flavorful enough to please a demanding audience. You can choose to take them all in your room or venture down to the formal dining room, where fine-china table settings are changed each day. (The Greenhouse has nine different china collections for breakfast, seven for lunch, and nine for dinner.) Dressing for dinner is common, so pack something appropriate. Breakfast in bed is offered daily.

A resident exercise physiologist will create a personalized program for you that could include laps in the pool, yoga, tai chi, or sessions with weights and fitness machines. Call to inquire about special yoga weeks, scheduled throughout the year and taught by renowned teachers such as Rodney Yee.

Guest Yoga Teachers? Yes. Including Jenni Fox, Paul Gould, Ellen Heuer, Rodney Yee.

Types of Yoga Classes Hatha. Once or twice daily. No extra charge.

The Greenhouse was originally created in 1965 so rich oil barons could leave their wives there while they did their oil deals. There are no outdoor activities, but it is the most pampering spa in America. A maid knocks on your door and delivers your breakfast to you in bed. It is too wonderful. They have all kinds of treatments, and some of the staff members have been there for decades.

You dine in a formal dining room with finger bowls, but it is not pretentious or uncomfortable. Years ago, you had to dress up, but you really don't have to anymore.

There is a new program called Baby and Me Week, during which a mother can bring her baby to the spa. They have baby massage by the pool and nannies for all the babies so Mom gets a break. Because it is all women, it can be a bit like a college sorority, but in the best way. Women become friends there and continue to return together for decades.

—Carol Isaak Barden, contributing editor, *Travel & Leisure* magazine, Houston, Texas

Services Facials, massage, nail care, Ayurvedic treatments, acupuncture, aromatherapy, craniosacral therapy, reflexology, thalassotherapy, food allergy testing, comprehensive female hormone assessment, neuroregulatory and brain chemistry profile, stress hormone profile.

Other Classes Pilates, tai chi, kickboxing.

Recreation Swimming, tennis, sauna, Jacuzzi, Japanese Hinoki tub.

Children's Program? Baby and Me for ages under one year; Youth Spa Week for ages 16 to 21.

Accommodations 34 rooms and two suites.

Dining Included. Spa cuisine. 1,200 calories per day. Vegetarian available.

Attire/What to Bring Swimsuit, athletic shoes, dinner attire. (Workout clothes provided.)

Travel Information The Greenhouse is nine miles from the Dallas/Fort Worth airport. Airport pickup is provided.

Rates $5,250–$7,225 per person per week.

Contact PO Box 1144, Arlington, TX 76004; tel: 817-640-4000; fax: 817-649-0422; www.thegreenhousespa.net.

Lake Austin Spa Resort   Austin, Texas

Lake Austin Spa Resort hosts special yoga weeks year-round, geared toward every level of experience. A deck resembling a wide pier has been built onto the surface of the lake and is the setting for early morning yoga classes as well as tai chi sessions.

Should the Texas heat dictate, meditation and yoga classes are offered indoors in the Mind/Body Loft, where the sound of a nearby fountain complements meditative practices. Water yoga is taught in the resort's pool. Students first stretch at the wall and then move into the middle of the pool to work on more traditional asanas. And there are more than a dozen other fitness classes to choose from daily, including Pilates, Spinning, and salsa-aerobics. Guests can also use the tennis courts, swimming pools, sauna and steam rooms, mountain bikes, water bikes, kayaks, and canoes.

Organic herbs and vegetables are harvested daily from the resort's gardens for inclusion in healthy gourmet meals. Lake Austin Spa Resort was one of the first spas in the country to shift the focus from rigid diets to balanced meals made from wholesome ingredients.

Lake Austin is a popular recreational site for sculling, boating, water biking, kayaking, and canoeing. Or, if relaxation is the goal, a full menu of spa services is available, including aromatherapy, hydrotherapy, and Ayurveda treatments.

Guest Yoga Teachers? Yes. Including Rodney Yee.

Types of Yoga Classes Hatha, water yoga, Vinyasa. Two or three times per day. No extra charge.

Services Massage, facials, nail care, aromatherapy, craniosacral therapy, Ayurvedic treatments, thalassotherapy, body treatments, reflexology, acupuncture.

Other Classes Meditation, tai chi, Pilates, NIA, boxing aerobics, Spinning, aquaerobics, circuit training.

Recreation Hiking, tennis, swimming, sauna, steam rooms, mountain biking, water biking, kayaking, canoeing, sailing, sculling, bird watching, fly-fishing, golf.

Children's Program? No. Minimum age 14.

Accommodations 40 rooms, 1 suite.

Dining Included. Spa cuisine with Southwestern influences.

Attire/What to Bring Standard yoga/workout attire, swimsuit, sun/insect protection, golf/tennis attire.

Travel Information Lake Austin Resort is 30 miles from the Austin-Bergstrom International Airport.

Rates $420 per person per night, double occupancy.

Contact 1705 South Quinlan Park Road, Austin, TX 78732; tel: 800-847-5637, 512-372-7300; www.lakeaustin.com.

UTAH

Red Mountain   Moab, Utah

Red Mountain, billed as an adventure spa, is surrounded by red rock formations at the entrance to Snow Canyon State Park. Hiking is the focus here. Four different levels of hikes are offered each morning. Since there are more than 40 area trails, it's possible to see a different Utah landscape every morning, so don't forget your camera. Red Mountain also offers a variety of other activities for fitness enthusiasts, plus pampering treatments at the full-service spa, making it an ideal destination for the active couple.

The Red Mountain inclusive program includes daily guided hiking,

The Lake Austin Spa Resort is a wonderful retreat along the lake, 20 miles west of Austin. You feel like you've really escaped to a place and time far away—like a summer camp for adults with these wonderful cabins.

They have a lot of fitness classes—they've always been on the cutting edge. Hiking is always an option, and you can garden or scull for exercise too. They stopped being the food police and starving guests a long time ago. The food is incredible, with Southwestern and Mexican influences. The chef can take almost any recipe and lighten it up. There is a flourless chocolate torte, and you would never guess how few calories that dessert has from the flavor of it.

The yoga is great, because of the complete escape that is afforded by the surroundings. The yoga room is called the Loft and has very dim lighting. The walls are a dark plum color—it is a womblike environment. There is no stimulation from outside sources, so it is easy to escape into the postures. There is also a new yoga deck that juts over the lake. The mist rises over the lake at sunrise, and the ducks quack while you're doing yoga. It is pretty incredible.

—Cyndi Maddox, communications specialist, Austin, Texas

I liked that Red Mountain is labeled an adventure spa where you can do "rough" stuff along with the traditional spa pampering. Red Mountain has many outdoor activities, and the location and scenery are really what sets it apart from other spas. There are organized hikes (geology and archeology) and bike rides, along with rock climbing, horseback riding through the mountain trails, and even kayaking. Of course, you can do the hikes and bikes on your own.

They offered Bikram, active yoga, gentle yoga, and yoga on the ball. They didn't advertise by styles (even the Bikram class was referred to as "hot yoga"). I only took the yoga-ball class, which was fun and different, and I found it especially helpful with my backbends. If you are a hard-core yogi looking for a stimulating yoga class, I don't think you would find it here. The setup seems to be for mostly beginners and intermediates.

I had a hot stone massage, where they use heated smooth stones and implement them into the strokes of typical Swedish massage. I found it much more intense and satisfying than a regular massage.

—Matthew Solan, *Yoga Journal* senior editor

snowshoeing, and cycling; fitness classes such as yoga, kickboxing, Pilates, aquaerobics, hip hop, and Spinning; three healthy meals daily; optional silent dinners that explore mindful eating; cooking demonstrations and nutrition classes; lifestyle lectures; accommodations; and full use of resort facilities, including indoor and outdoor pools, walking trails, and strength-training and cardio equipment. Classes, lectures, and outdoor activities change with the seasons.

Some of the Red Mountain masseuses have been on staff for more than 10 years and know how to soothe muscles aching from hiking and biking. Signature treatments include a massage using warm red rocks and juniper oil, and a native grains body scrub.

Guest Yoga Teachers? Yes. Including Rachel Haines, Lisa Wheeler.

Types of Yoga Classes Gentle, active, and hot yoga. Up to five times daily. No extra charge.

Services Body treatments, facials, massage, reflexology, shiatsu, Reiki method, hair and scalp treatments, nail care.

Other Classes Tai chi, aquaerobics, cardio kickboxing, Spinning, ai chi, hip-hop, salsa, Pilates.

Recreation Hiking, biking, kayaking, rock climbing, horseback riding.

Children's Program? No. Minimum age 18.

Accommodations 98 rooms and villas.

Dining Included. Breakfast and lunch are buffet-style; dinner is served in the dining room. Vegetarian available.

Attire/What to Bring Standard yoga attire/workout gear, hiking boots, swimsuit, sun/insect protection, cold weather gear in winter.

Travel Information Red Mountain is 120 miles northeast of the Las Vegas airport or six miles from the St. George airport.

Rates $225–$385 per person per night. Three-night minimum.

Contact 1275 E. Red Mountain Circle, Ivins, UT 84738; tel: 800-407-3002, 435-673-4905; fax: 435-673-1363; www.redmountainspa.com.

Snowbird Resort   Snowbird, Utah

The 28,000-square-foot Cliff Spa at the famous Snowbird ski resort has 30 individualized treatment areas, a full-service salon, workout facilities, a eucalyptus steam room, saunas, a movement studio, a solarium, a 15-meter rooftop swimming pool, whirlpool, and sundeck. Yoga is offered twice a day at the spa.

Snowbird is known for its ski-in/ski-out facilities and 2,500 acres of terrain. Daily lift tickets are $56, and snowboard and ski clinics for all levels of experience are available. In summer, Snowbird is equally active, with mountain biking, hiking, and swimming and tennis programs.

Guest Yoga Teachers? Yes. Including Jamie Allison, Mishabae Edmond, Maty Ezraty, Chuck Miller, Nancy Ruby.

Types of Yoga Classes Hatha, Vinyasa, Anusara, Iyengar. Daily. $15 per class.

Services Facials, reflexology, massage, body treatments, aromatherapy, shiatsu, craniosacral therapy, Reiki method, polarity therapy, hydrotherapy.

Other Classes Pilates, aerobics.

Recreation Skiing, snowboarding, biking, hiking, tennis, climbing, golf, fishing, swimming.

Children's Program? Yes. For ages six weeks to 15 years.

Accommodations More than 900 rooms.

Dining Not included. 12 restaurants.

Attire/What to Bring Standard yoga/workout attire, swimsuit, hiking boots, cold weather/ski attire in winter, sun/insect protection.

Travel Information The Salt Lake City International Airport is 29 miles from Snowbird Ski Resort.

Rates $109–$359 per night, double occupancy.

Contact Little Cottonwood Canyon Road, Snowbird, UT 84092; tel: 800-232-9542, 800-453-3000; fax: 801-933-2283; www.snowbird.com.

Snowbird Resort overall is breathtaking. The eyes constantly travel up to the sky, following all of the massive vertical reaches of metal, glass, and cement, as well as the enormous reach of mountains. Everything is clean, modern, tasteful, and artistic—chosen to please the eye. I believe the building is constructed in such a way that most rooms afford a view. They have a full-service spa, providing a range of massage and body treatments. The fitness center is perched up on the roof, enclosed by windowed walls, causing you to feel as if you are going to jog from the treadmill right out toward the mountaintops. There is a heated outdoor pool on the roof as well as an adjacent hot Jacuzzi.

The workshop I taught followed a typical three-day schedule, which included a Friday night, a full day Saturday, and a half day on Sunday. The program was An Introduction to Balance Arts, the Art of Partnered Yoga. A number of short, partner Vinyasas were demonstrated and then taught, broken down posture by posture until the participants were able to put it all back together again and experience the Vinyasa as a cohealing dance.

I took a great deal of pleasure in hiking many vertical feet on numerous trails. Mountain biking is also very popular as a nonskiing activity here.

—Mishabae Edmond, yoga instructor, writer, and massage therapist, Bainbridge Island, Washington

Sundance Resort   Sundance, Utah

In 1969, Robert Redford started Sundance with the intention of creating an alliance between the arts and outdoor recreation while preserving the land. Sundance is a year-round mountain resort and community on 6,000 acres at the base of 12,000-foot Mount Timpanogos in the north fork of Provo Canyon.

The heart of Sundance is the Sundance Village, with 95 guest cottage rooms, mountain homes, restaurants, an artisan center, and conference facilities. As you would expect, outdoor activities are lauded here. You can

I moved to Sundance from Salt Lake City when I got married. I'm an avid skier, hiker, and mountain biker. I started practicing yoga when I broke my ankle skiing, and it changed my life. I initially got interested in yoga when one of my neighbors bought me a yoga mat and a few yoga videos after my accident. My yoga practice deepened, and I was certified to teach by both Nancy Ruby, who runs Yoga Motion in Montana, and Ganga White and Tracey Rich of the White Lotus Foundation in California.

I teach a combination of disciplines, because on any given day I might have a student who has studied with Mr. Iyengar in India standing next to someone who has never taken yoga before. It is mixed level and I try to accommodate everyone.

The cottages that are part of the resort are absolutely gorgeous. There are not a lot of people who live at Sundance full-time, so guests can also rent a private mountain home through the resort.

Yoga complements all the outdoor sports available at Sundance. It is also nice for people who are traveling with avid skiers and don't want to ski every day. I welcome parents to bring their kids with them to yoga class. It is something everyone can learn, practice, and take home with them.

—Julie Hooker, fourth grade schoolteacher and a Sundance yoga teacher

enjoy a variety of sports, before or after yoga class, including downhill and cross-country skiing, snowboarding, hiking, horseback riding, mountain biking, and fly-fishing. The Sundance Art Shack Studios offer a wide range of art classes. In addition to the arts program, weekend film screenings and professional summer theater can be enjoyed by guests.

The guest cottages are rustic yet upscale and have stone fireplaces or woodstoves, handcrafted furnishings, Native American art, and warm down bedding.

The 1,900-square-foot Spa at Sundance has six treatment rooms. Spa treatments blend traditional Native American healing methods with all-natural products. The Screening Room Yurt has a fitness studio, where yoga classes take place daily.

Guest Yoga Teachers? Yes. Including Tracey Rich, Mark Schlenz, Ganga White.

Types of Yoga Classes Hatha. Daily at 8 AM and 5 PM. $10 per class.

Services Aromatherapy, massage, facials, body treatments.

Other Classes Pottery, jewelry, painting, photography.

Recreation Skiing, snowboarding, hiking, fishing, biking, horseback riding, fly-fishing, snowmobiling.

Children's Program? Yes. Sundances Kids Camp for ages 3 to 12.

Accommodations 95 rooms.

Dining Not included. Two restaurants: Tree Room (seasonal mountain cuisine), Foundry Grill (hearty, down-home seasonal cooking).

Attire/What to Bring Standard yoga/workout attire, skiing attire, hiking boots, sun/insect protection.

Travel Information Sundance is 50 miles from the Salt Lake City airport.

Rates $205–$1,300 per night, double occupancy.

Take Immunity Boosters Elson Haas, M.D., author of *The Staying Healthy Shopper's Guide: Feed Your Family Safely* (Celestial Arts, 1999), recommends vitamin C to fend off free radical damage brought on by travel stressors. Vitamin E and the mineral selenium counteract chemical exposure, and acidophilus tablets can help protect against intestinal predators. —K.F.M.

Contact North Fork Provo Canyon, Sundance, UT 84604; tel: 801-225-4107; fax: 801-226-1937; www.sundanceresort.com.

VERMONT

New Life Hiking Spa   Killington, Vermont

It's true: Yoga is not the star at Jimmy LeSage's New Life Hiking Spa. Hiking is. But yoga is offered daily and is part of a healthy regimen that takes place here in the Green Mountains of Vermont.

New Life offers a wide range of activities in addition to hiking. A typical day begins at 7:30 AM with a walk and qigong before breakfast. Then there is a three- to eight-mile hike before lunch. Afternoon activities include aquaerobics, Pilates, and yoga. Meals are low in calories, as many guests have weight-loss goals. New Life is open from the first weekend in May until the third weekend in October.

Guest Yoga Teachers? No.

Types of Yoga Classes Hatha or gentle (for beginners). Each taught once daily. No extra charge.

Services Massage, reflexology, facials.

Other Classes Meditation, qigong, aquaerobics, art therapy, teng shui, cooking.

Recreation Hiking, swimming, golf, tennis, lake kayaking, horseback riding, mountain biking.

Children's Program? No.

Accommodations 103 rooms.

Dining Included. Low-calorie. Vegetarian available.

Attire/What to Bring Standard yoga/workout attire, hiking boots, rain gear, sun/insect protection, swimsuit, swim goggles, tennis/golf attire.

Travel Information New Life is 82 miles from the Burlington airport.

Rates $130 for room and meals per person per day. Add $115 per person per day for hiking and spa program.

Contact PO Box 395, Killington, VT 05751; tel: 800-228-4676, 802-422-4302; fax: 802-422-4321; www.newlifehikingspa.com.

The first time I went to New Life Hiking Spa was in 1981. I've been back five or six times because I love the fact that you don't have to get dressed up and worry about makeup and hair. This time I felt like it was time to do something for me and relax and get in shape again. I go for a whole week if I can, because it takes me three or four days to calm down and get used to the change in food. The food is very vegetarian, low in fat, high in complex carbohydrates, with lots of soy—very clean and light. It helps your body to clean itself out.

The yoga is fabulous. The first day, I was reminded of how out of balance I was. I couldn't believe how one side was much stronger than the other. I used to do yoga all the time. Jimmy's reminded me how much I really need it.

You can have a massage every day. They are great—all different depending on which practitioner you get. You can request a more gentle or vigorous masseuse.

Before the hiking begins, everyone is split into groups based on your level of ability. The great thing is that you hike a different trail every day. I went on the intermediate hikes because I wanted to focus more on taking care of myself than pushing myself.

—Jane Strong, market research executive, Weston, Connecticut

I've been to Topnotch about 10 times. I just love it there. I met my husband in Stowe, and we've gone there for skiing quite a bit. Topnotch is very close to the ski area—you can see the mountain from the property. There are also bike paths that start on the property and go into town. There's a barn across the street where you can rent bikes. Hiking is also great in summer, and the staff tennis pros have a big following.

Topnotch is up a hill and in the woods. You feel pretty secluded once you are inside. I've taken the stretch, water aerobics, and yoga classes. I have only done breathing, stretches, and relaxation classes in the past, and this yoga class required more upper body strength. It was a little more rigorous than I'm used to. The massages are phenomenal—Swedish, aromatherapy, hot stone. The deep-tissue massage helped relieve my sciatica.

The food is really good. The Buttertub has a light spa menu. The bar area, with couches and a fireplace, is a really nice place to have a hot drink in the winter. Sometimes they have live music. Topnotch is really a cross between a relaxing vacation and an active one with hiking, biking, or skiing.

—Elise Johnson, Filene's area sales manager, Goffstown, New Hampshire

Topnotch at Stowe   Stowe, Vermont

Topnotch at Stowe attracts well-heeled skiers and hikers year-round. The 120-acre luxury resort and spa is located between the town of Stowe and Mount Mansfield, making it one of the closest hotels to the slopes. You can get your lift ticket at the front desk and rent equipment (skis, skates, bikes, snowshoes, in-line skates, etc.) right on site. You can also ride the resort's complimentary shuttle service to the mountain. Topnotch even has its own trails for cross-country skiing, mountain biking, hiking, and snowshoeing.

The 23,000-square-foot spa allows guests to design a personalized program or enjoy a variety of services and treatments individually. One of the more bizarre offerings is Reiki method and massage for your pooch, should it be traveling with you.

Guest Yoga Teachers? No.

Types of Yoga Classes Alternates between Iyengar ($5 per class) and Bikram ($10 per class). Once daily.

Services Body treatments, massage, facials, craniosacral therapy, Reiki method, scalp treatments, aromatherapy, nail care, acupuncture, reflexology, shirodhara, shiatsu.

Other Classes Meditation, aerobics, aquaerobics.

Recreation Tennis, swimming, saunas, steam rooms, whirlpools, hydromassage waterfall, horseback riding, fishing, white-water rafting, skiing, canoeing, snowshoeing.

Children's Program? Yes. Children's tennis programs and Mud City Adventures. Minimum age 16 for use of the fitness facilities. Guests under age 16 are permitted in the indoor pool area only and must be accompanied by an adult.

Accommodations 90 rooms.

Dining Not included. Two restaurants: Maxwell's at Topnotch (American cuisine and spa menu), the Buttertub Bistro (lighter menu). Full American Plan (breakfast, lunch, and dinner) $65 per person per day. Modified American Plan (breakfast and dinner) $50 per person per day. Breakfast plan $12 per person per day.

Attire/What to Bring Standard yoga/workout attire, sun/insect protection, cold weather/ski attire in winter, hiking boots, swimsuit.

Travel Information The Burlington airport is 40 minutes away.

Rates $345–$485 per night, double occupancy.

Contact 4000 Mountain Road, Stowe, VT 05672; tel: 800-451-8686, 802-253-8585; www.topnotch-resort.com.

WASHINGTON

Rosario Resort & Spa   Eastsound, Washington

Part of Rosario Resort & Spa's appeal is that it is only accessible via ferry or seaplane. Rosario, originally a shipping mogul's mansion, is on Orcas Island, and outdoor activities naturally revolve around the water and include boating, swimming, sailing, scuba diving, and sea kayaking. Golf, tennis, and horseback riding are also available. The Avanyu Spa has two pools, a fitness room, sauna, Jacuzzi, and a host of spa treatments and services. Hatha yoga is taught on the weekend and is free to hotel guests.

The original mansion boasts 6,000 square feet of teak parquet floors and a music room that features a Tiffany chandelier and a working 1,972-pipe Aeolian organ. It's one of nine buildings spread out over eight acres.

Guest Yoga Teachers? No.

Types of Yoga Classes Hatha. Two days a week. No extra charge.

Services Aromatherapy, reflexology, body treatments, facials, nail care.

Other Classes Aerobics, aquaerobics, power walking.

Recreation Jacuzzi, sauna, boating, swimming, golf, horseback riding, fishing, sailing, scuba diving, sea kayaking, whale watching.

Children's Program? Yes.

Accommodations 127 rooms and suites.

Dining Not included. Five restaurants: Compass Room (Northwest- and French-inspired cuisine), Mansionside Dining Room (seafood and Northwest cuisine), Dockside Grille, Moran Lounge & Veranda, Mansion Pool Bar.

Attire/What to Bring Standard yoga/workout attire, swimsuit, sun/insect protection, golf/tennis attire.

Travel Information Kenmore floatplanes fly directly to Rosario Harbor from Lake Union, Seattle. Call 800-543-9595 or 206-486-1257. Washington State ferries sail from Anacortes, WA (80 miles from the Seattle airport), to Orcas Island in about one hour and 15 minutes. Call 800-843-3779.

In the summer at Rosario Resort & Spa we do yoga on the bluffs. There can be as many as 18 people in class. I've been teaching yoga for 15 years and doing bodywork for 30 years. I combine self-massage and hatha yoga positions. First I ask people what is going on with them. It is very important for people to acknowledge their past injuries, because they need to learn how to nurture themselves in order to find inner peace.

I've been at Rosario seven or eight years. It is a very beautiful place, with good energy. I initially was attracted to Rosario because I heard their massage program was great. Plus there is an expansive state park and a 2,000-foot mountain for hiking or biking.

—Sukima Hampton, Rosario Resort yoga teacher

Rates $279 per night, double occupancy.

Contact 1400 Rosario Road, Eastsound, WA 98245; tel: 800-562-8820, 360-376-2222; fax: 360-376-2289; www.rosarioresort.com.

WEST VIRGINIA

Coolfont Resort and Health Spa   Berkeley Springs, West Virginia

The 1,300-acre Coolfont Resort, named for the cool springs that bubble up beneath it, has a full range of year-round activities, including swimming, tennis, hiking, boating, golf, horseback riding. The resort, just 90 miles west of Washington, D.C., sits between two mountain ridges and borders the 5,600-acre Cacapon State Park. For more than two centuries, people have traveled to the mountain town of Berkeley Springs to soak up warm mineral waters.

Coolfont, which opened in 1965, is family-owned and operated. Yoga is taught every afternoon at 4 PM in the spa, and several wellness programs are offered throughout the year, including smoking cessation, couples weekends, and Wild Women weekends.

Guest Yoga Teachers? No.

Types of Yoga Classes Hatha, Kripalu, Ashtanga. Once per day, twice on Saturdays. $12 per class.

Services Shiatsu, aromatherapy, reflexology, craniosacral therapy, Reiki method, polarity therapy, acupuncture, facials, body treatments, scalp massage, nail care.

Other Classes Aerobics, step, aquaerobics, NIA, tai chi, qigong, meditation, nutrition and goal setting.

Recreation Swimming, hot tubs, sauna, tennis, hiking, boating, golf, horseback riding, snow-tubing.

Children's Program? Camp Coolfont, weekend activities for ages 5 to 13.

Accommodations Alpine or ridge chalet, mountainside homes, log cabins, the Woodland House Lodge, the Manor House. 250 maximum occupancy.

Dining Breakfast and dinner included. Vegetarian available.

Attire/What to Bring Leotards, tights, T-shirts, shorts and/or sweat suits, comfortable, athletic shoes for hiking and aerobics, swimsuit, aqua shoes, seasonal clothing, flashlights, rain gear, hiking boots, day pack, sun/insect protection, golf/tennis attire.

My sister and I went to Coolfont for four nights for a special yoga retreat. It is a mountain property not far from a small town. We had our own chalet in the woods. It was a bit rustic but nicely kept.

The classes were not intimidating. Each teacher expertly took you through the asanas. We did yoga for several hours a day and learned a lot of yoga techniques. There were three different instructors: We had one basic yoga instructor most of the time, and then we did Kripalu and Integral yoga with two other teachers. They also incorporated chanting into the last morning. It was a package deal for lodging, spa treatments (I had an herbal wrap, two facials, and a massage), and three meals per day. You could choose spa cuisine, but they also offered filet mignon. We got to meet with other people who were staying at Coolfont but not doing the yoga intensive. We also took tai chi, reflexology, and meditation classes. It was a nice little community.

—Michelle Clark, sales executive, Sterling, Virginia

Travel Information Coolfont is 90 miles from Washington, D.C.–area airports.

Rates $79–$139 per person per day.

Contact 3621 Cold Run Valley Road, Berkeley Springs, WV 25411; tel: 800-888-8768, 304-258-4500; www.coolfont.com.

The Greenbrier — White Sulphur Springs, West Virginia

The Greenbrier may be best known for its military bunker, built under the hotel during the Cold War and designed to protect the members of Congress in the event of a national emergency on Washington, D.C., which is 250 miles away. The hotel also served as an army hospital in the 1940s.

Today, the Greenbrier is a 6,500-acre resort with more than 50 activities, including three 18-hole championship golf courses, swimming, biking, bowling, croquet, fishing, hiking, horseback riding, tennis, skeet shooting, volleyball, badminton, kayaking, canoeing, and soaking in the sulfur waters of White Sulphur Springs. Yoga is taught twice daily and costs $15 per class.

Complimentary first-run movies are shown every evening in the Greenbrier Theatre. Guests can take one of the regularly scheduled guided tours of the hotel (rebuilt in 1913), estate grounds, or former bunker.

Guest Yoga Teachers? No.

Types of Yoga Classes Hatha. Twice daily. $15 per class.

Services Massage, hydrotherapy, body treatments, nail care, aromatherapy, facials.

Other Classes Aerobics, Spinning, step aerobics, body sculpting, circuit-training, kickboxing, cooking.

Recreation Golf, swimming, biking, bowling, croquet, fishing, hiking, horseback riding, tennis, skeet shooting, volleyball, badminton, kayaking, canoeing, soak in the sulfur waters of White Sulphur Springs, steam room, sauna, Swiss shower, falconry, Land Rover driving school.

Children's Program? Yes. For ages 3 to 12.

Accommodations 803 rooms, 96 guest houses, 46 suites.

Dining Breakfast and dinner included. Six restaurants: the Main Dining Room, Sam Snead's at The Golf Club, Slammin' Sammy's, Tavern Room, Draper's Cafe, Rhododendron Spa Cafe. Men must wear jacket and tie in the Main Dining Room and the Tavern Room.

Attire/What to Bring Standard workout/yoga attire, golf/tennis attire, swimsuit, sun/insect protection, formal dress for dinner.

My husband and I go to the Greenbrier every year for an association meeting. The resort is very Southern and historic—you take interior and exterior tours—with old style, formal decor, and a lot of crystal. They really stayed true to the interior design style of Dorothy Draper. The whole history of the Greenbrier is very interesting. The Greenbrier is very rural and remote—you feel like you're away from it all. And cell phones don't work, so you can really relax.

The building itself is very beautiful and ornate. There is a lower level arcade with wonderful shops. I love the gourmet cooking shop—they have every upscale gizmo and tureen. They even have a cooking class.

Service is very important there—they are very accommodating. The food is continental/American—nothing too exotic but good.

I thought the yoga was good. The instructor was very relaxing and instructive and played good music. I also love jogging on the trails and relaxing around the outdoor pool.

The area's sulfur springs are supposed to be good for arthritis, skin conditions, and other ailments. It feels good—it is very warm—but it does smell bad!

—Darlene Bartos, registered nurse, Pittsburgh, Pennsylvania

Travel Information The Greenbrier is 13 miles from the Lewisburg airport.

Rates $219–$390 per person per night, double occupancy; suites: $336–$503; guest houses: $310–$503.

Contact 300 West Main St., White Sulphur Springs, WV 24986; tel: 800-624-6070, 304-536-1110; fax: 304-536-7854; www.greenbrier.com.

MEXICO

Mision del Sol   Cuernavaca, Mexico

I heard Mision del Sol was one of the best spas in Mexico. A friend of mine went there a few months ago. He was delighted with it. I never thought it would be so big and beautiful. It is so big employees use golf carts to transport guests from one place to another. The Jacuzzi is incredible—I spent most of my time in it. The whole hotel is surrounded by streams and fountains. There's no point in the hotel where you can't hear water falling or running.

I stayed in a double occupancy room. There's no air-conditioning system (the hotel says it pollutes), but the adobe structure keeps the temperature acceptable. One of the things that did surprise me is that there are no TV sets in the rooms, only in the library. But there are so many different activities at the resort, TV was the last thing I thought of.

I had a Temazcal (an ancient sweat bath). It's guided by a shaman (a spiritual leader)—very nice and very relaxing. I also had hot stone therapy, one of the wisest things I have ever done. Around 40 or 50 stones are placed on specific body parts (energy points) and then hot oil is poured on your body while being massaged. It is extremely relaxing, comforting, and calming.

—Billy Crosby, architect and designer, Cuernavaca, Mexico

Mision del Sol prides itself on its therapeutic treatments, organic food, workshops, and conferences. Crystals are found throughout the resort; guest room mattresses have magnets for promoting proper energy flow; and Deepak Chopra is a featured guest, so you know this is going to be a "New Age" experience. Day trips include excursions to Xochicalco, an outstanding archeological zone; the mystical town of Tepoztlán; a 16th-century convent; or Tepozteco mountain to see the pre-Hispanic temple at the top. In nearby Taxco, visit the Temple of Santa Prisca, the museums, and artisan shops.

Guest Yoga Teachers? Yes. Including Deepak Chopra.

Types of Yoga Classes Hatha. Once daily. No extra charge.

Services Massage, facials, aromatherapy, reflexology, body treatments, craniosacral, Reiki method, shiatsu, Janzu.

Other Classes Tai chi, meditation, aerobics, aquaerobics.

Recreation Tennis, paddle tennis, kayaking, swimming, volleyball, hiking, biking, Jacuzzi.

Children's Program? No. Minimum age 13.

Accommodations 40 rooms, 12 villas.

Dining Included. Vegetarian.

Attire/What to Bring Standard yoga/workout, swimsuit, sun/insect protection, hiking boots, tennis attire.

Travel Information Fly into Mexico City. Mision del Sol is a 90-minute drive from the airport. Airport transfers are available; call in advance to arrange.

Rates Two-night package $650 per person per night.

Contact Av. Gral. Diego Díaz González 31, Col. Parres, Cuernavaca,

Morelos CP62550 México; tel: 011-52-732-10-999; fax: 011-52-732-11-195; www.misiondelsol.com.mx.

Hotel Spa Ixtapan   Ixtapan de la Sal, Mexico

Hotel Spa Ixtapan, which opened in 1942, is on 14 acres filled with tropical gardens, pools, and tennis courts. The spa features five different programs: classic, relax, sport, golf, and vibrance. All include nutritional guidance, daily exercise, tennis or golf instruction, health and beauty treatments, and alternative medicine options; 4-, 7-, 21-, and 28-day packages are available. Spa facilities include whirlpools, sauna, steam, Swiss showers, solarium, beauty salon, and gym. Yoga practitioners will want to consider the seven-day relax package, which includes six reflexology or shiatsu sessions, six yoga classes, four acupuncture sessions, and six golf or tennis lessons.

Popular nearby attractions include the colonial city of Cuernavaca, the town of Taxco, the caves of Cacahuamilpa, the archeological ruins of Teotenango, and the crafts market in Toluca.

Guest Yoga Teachers? No.

Types of Yoga Classes Hatha. At least once daily. No extra charge.

Services Acupuncture, body treatments, massage, facials, reflexology, nail care.

Other Classes Aerobics, aquaerobics, golf, tennis.

Recreation Golf, paddle tennis, tennis, swimming, mountain biking.

Children's Program? No.

Accommodations 220 rooms and villas.

Dining Included. Vegetarian available.

Attire/What to Bring Standard yoga/workout attire, swimsuit, sun/insect protection, hiking boots/walking shoes, golf/tennis attire.

Travel Information Hotel Spa Ixtapan is 65 miles southwest of Mexico City. Roundtrip airport transfer is $260 per car (for up to four people).

Rates $120 per night without spa privileges. Seven-day relax spa package $1,087 single occupancy or $926 double occupancy.

Contact Ixtapan de la Sal, Mexico, CP51900; tel: 800-638-7950, 210-495-2477, 011-52-721-143-2440; fax: 210-499-0702; www.spamexico.com.

Hotel Spa Ixtapan is lushly landscaped and framed by the Sierra Madres mountains. The feeling was a laid-back approach rather the stiff formality of other spa resorts. The two pools (one is a 100°F thermal mineral pool and the other a swimming pool) were very inviting. The spa is 61 years old and located in Ixtapan de la Sal. I shared a room with a friend. It was no-frills but adequate. You actually spend so little time in your room, it really becomes very secondary to the experience itself. The food was superb. They offer a daily diet of 900 calories in addition to a heavier Continental menu with some Mexican touches in the hotel's main dining room. Fish and an abundance of fresh vegetables were available every day. Crunchy jicama sticks and Red Zinger iced tea are always plentiful.

The yoga classes are held at the convention center at the Hotel Spa Ixtapan. The seven-day spa package I bought included six massages, six facials, one body treatment, a manicure, a pedicure, and final-day hairstyle. Each morning you had the option of taking a short or a more intense hike. Water aquatics and aerobics are also part of the package. I liked the low-key aspect of the spa, with no one running around in designer clothes. For me the other attraction was having the afternoons free, making excursions to nearby towns and markets possible.

—Joy Ricci, marketing executive, Scottsdale, Arizona

Everything about Las Ventanas is subtle yet tasteful. What is so nice about the property is the very calm and tranquil environment. At the same time it is a very high-end experience.

In the spa I had the two-hour Ayurvedic bliss treatment, which combined a bindi body treatment with chanting, shirodhara, and a mini facial. You become so relaxed, you are sort of mesmerized throughout the whole process.

There are a number of pools, but the ocean is too rough for swimming. Yachts owned by the property can take you out on a cruise or to use a WaveRunner.

The food is fabulous, more seafood and grilled meat than heavy Mexican—everything is really fresh. Nightlife is available in nearby Los Cabos—about a 10- or 15-minute drive. But once you're at Las Ventanas, you really end up wanting to lounge.

—Brooks Baldwin, freelance writer, Seattle, Washington

Las Ventanas al Paraíso   Los Cabos, Mexico

Las Ventanas al Paraíso is in Los Cabos on the Baja Peninsula, facing the Sea of Cortés. This luxury resort features Mediterranean-Mexican-style architecture, a serpentine network of swimming pools, a swim-up bar, patios overlooking the sea, and suites with individual relaxation pools and Jacuzzis, rooftop patios, and in-room telescopes for stargazing.

Complimentary services include a tequila welcome, access to the spa, fitness center, and video library, and tennis. Special poolside amenities include CD players (and a choice of CDs), books, sorbets served in chocolate cups, chilled mineral water, spritzers, and cold towels. The place is so swanky, even Fido gets the royal treatment: The resort offers special food menus and massages to pamper pets. And furry friends can find relief from the sun in specially made mini cabanas. Guests are entitled to preferred tee times at six nearby courses, plus two tennis courts on site.

The spa offers a full range of treatments, as well as sauna, steam, and whirlpool. There are separate facilities for men and women and a full range of cardiovascular machines and resistance equipment in the fitness room. Personal trainers and yoga instructors are available, as well as group exercise and fitness activities.

Guest Yoga Teachers? No.

Types of Yoga Classes Hatha. Individual yoga instruction $75. Yoga class (four people) $20 per person.

Services Massage, aromatherapy, reflexology, hydrotherapy, balneotherapy, thalassotherapy, body treatments, facials, Ayurvedic treatments including shirodhara, nail care.

Other Classes Personal training, tennis, qigong.

Recreation Swimming, tennis, golf, horseback riding, sailing, sport fishing, scuba, snorkeling, kayaking, windsurfing.

Children's Program? No.

Accommodations 61 suites.

Dining Not included. Three restaurants: the Restaurant (Baja-Mediterranean), the Sea Grill (modern Mexican), Tequila and Ceviche Bar. The Wine Room ("La Cava") is available by special arrangement. Full American Plan (breakfast, lunch, and dinner) $120 per person per day. Modified American Plan (breakfast and dinner) $100 per person per day.

Attire/What to Bring Standard yoga/workout attire, swimsuit, sun/insect protection, golf/tennis attire, clothing for fine dining.

Travel Information Las Ventanas al Paraíso is located 15 minutes southwest of Los Cabos International Airport.

Rates $375–$3,800 per room per night, double occupancy. Three-night minimum stay for weekend bookings (four-night minimum January–March).

Contact KM 19.5 Carretera Transpeninsular, San Jose del Cabo, Baja California Sur 23400 Mexico; tel: 011-52-624-144-0300; fax: 011-52-624-144-0301; www.lasventanas.com.

Rio Caliente Hot Springs Spa   Primavera, Mexico

Rio Caliente is an unpretentious and affordable spa 45 minutes from Guadalajara. Water from an underground volcanic lake flows into springs and waterfalls along the river that borders the spa on three sides. The water often reaches 157°F and feeds into the spa's four pools, steam room, and all guest bathrooms. The water contains a beneficial (and odorless) combination of salts and minerals, including lithium. Clothing is optional in the private plunge pools.

Guests can explore the region and the more than 100 bird varieties, hike, horseback ride, or visit nearby arts and crafts markets. Stop by the spa for a clay detox foot bath or Swedish massage.

The food at the resort, served buffet-style three times daily, is grain-based, high in complex carbohydrates, low in fat and salt, and includes fresh fruits and vegetables and optional dairy products. Vegetables are grown in the property's organic gardens or come from nearby markets. Bread and pastries are baked on site.

Guest Yoga Teachers? No.

Types of Yoga Classes Hatha. At least once daily. No extra charge.

Services Massage, facials, acupuncture, reflexology, homeopathy, Reiki method, nail care, body treatments.

Other Classes Tai chi, qigong, pool aerobics, meditation, Pilates.

Recreation Swimming, hiking, horseback riding, eco-exploring.

Children's Program? No.

Accommodations 50 rooms.

Rio Caliente has been around since the '50s but has been maintained well and is a great value. The cottages are larger than the typical hotel room, so there is plenty of space to practice yoga on your own in the morning. The river and hot springs that feed the pools are heated by underground volcanic activity. The food is simple and vegetarian, with a Mexican theme but light.

—Todd Jones, *Yoga Journal* senior editor

Dining Included. Three meals daily. Vegetarian buffet.

Attire/What to Bring Standard yoga attire, hiking boots, rain slicker, flashlight, swimsuit, sun/insect protection.

Travel Information Fly into Guadalajara airport and take a 45-minute taxi ride to Rio Caliente. You must arrive at the spa before 10 PM.

Rates $144–$166 per person per night. Seven- to ten-day packages: $1,058–$1,530 per person. No credit cards.

Contact PO Box 897, Millbrae, CA 94030; tel: 800-200-2927, 650-615-9543; fax: 650-615-0601; www.riocaliente.com.

Rancho La Puerta   Tecate, Mexico

Rancho LaPuerta, in a valley at the foot of the sacred 3,885-foot Mount Kuchumaa, was founded in 1940 by Edmond Szekely, a Hungarian scholar, philosopher, and natural living experimenter, and his Brooklyn-born wife Deborah (who later established the Golden Door Spa near Escondido, California). On hikes, guests are likely to see cottontail rabbits, foxes, ravens, golden eagles, red-tailed hawks, wren, and quail.

On arrival day (Saturday), you are encouraged to design your own fitness schedule based on the ranch's signature Six Facets of Fitness, which promotes both vigorous physical activity and relaxation. Guests also receive descriptions of each class, a question-and-answer period, and a tour of the ranch. There are 60 different classes and activities, many scheduled every day. Each is 45 minutes long. Forty miles of trails provide for both meditative meadow walks and challenging, steep hikes. Yoga weeks are scheduled throughout the year.

Pulitzer prize–winning poet Galway Kinnell, author Dan Wakefield, and other writers are among those who have given evening lectures at the ranch. Other evening choices include workshops on health, science, the arts, aromatherapy, stargazing, crafts, and more.

An on-site, six-acre organic farm, Rancho Tres Estrellas, provides a large portion of the kitchen's vegetables and fruits. Olives are grown for oil, and bees are kept for honey. The food is primarily vegetarian, with fish at some dinners and eggs at breakfast. All ranch cottages and casitas are set amongst lush gardens and have patios. No more than 160 guests are hosted each week.

Guest Yoga Teachers? Yes. Including Mara Carrico, Jenni Fox, Paul Gould, Michele Herbert, Aman Keays, Alison Lewis, Eddy Marks, Tim Miller,

Mehrad Nazari, Mary Obendorfer, Larry Payne, Phyllis Pilgrim.

Types of Yoga Classes Hatha, Iyengar, Ashtanga, restorative. Three or more times daily. No extra charge.

Services Facials, aromatherapy, massage, wraps, body scrubs, nail care, reflexology, scalp treatment.

Other Classes African dance, circuit-training, aquaerobics, NIA, aerobics, Spinning, step aerobics, cardio boxing, Pilates, tai chi, self-defense, meditation.

Recreation Basketball, hiking, Ping-Pong, tennis, volleyball, swimming, hot tub, sauna, steamroom.

Children's Program? No. Minimum age 15.

Accommodations Studios, suites, haciendas. 160 guests maximum.

Dining Included. Lacto-ovo vegetarian; fish twice a week.

Attire/What to Bring Standard exercise and yoga attire, hiking boots, swimsuit, hat and gloves in winter, tennis attire, sun/insect protection.

Travel Information Rancho La Puerta is located 40 miles southeast of San Diego. Scheduled complimentary ground transportation is provided for Saturday arrival and departure to and from the San Diego International Airport.

Rates Seven-night package $1,970–$3,501 per person. One-week minimum stay.

Contact Rancho La Puerta Reservations, PO Box 463057, Escondido, CA 92046; tel: 800-443-7565, 760-744-4222; fax: 760-744-5007; www.rancholapuerta.com.

ASIA

Park Hyatt Goa Resort and Spa   Goa, India

The 45-acre Park Hyatt Goa Resort and Spa opened in March 2003. The philosophy of the resort's 28,000-square-foot Sereno Spa is based on the ancient sciences of Ayurveda and yoga. The Integrated Wellness Program combines lifestyle advice on natural self-care techniques, nutrition, and fitness to foster calmness, well-being, and balance. Treatments include abhyanga (synchronized massage performed by two masseurs), pizhichil (two Ayurvedic therapists apply warm herbal oils all over the body in a rhythmic way), shirodhara (medicated oil is poured in an even stream on the forehead),

I went to Rancho La Puerta with my mom, sister, and sister-in-law, and we stayed in a two-bedroom cottage. There is nothing on the grounds that doesn't blend with the mountains and desert environment. It is definitely a Birkenstock crowd. You can take about four classes a day. I loved the African dance and took it whenever it was offered on the schedule. I did that four or five times. Every morning they had different two- to six-mile hikes before breakfast. Yoga is also a big focus there. I loved being able to try a bunch of different activities, like Pilates, kickboxing, and water aerobics. All of the instructors balanced fun with a workout that was vigorous but not so tough that you were pooped. I felt like staff was interested in me and meeting me.

The breakfast and lunch buffets were amazing. They had a lot of good options to satisfy any diet. Dinner was a sit-down affair, and there were always vegetarian and vegan offerings.

The evening programs are great, with creative writing, poetry workshops, movies, and arts and crafts.

—Sarah Guck, social worker, Easton, Maryland

Holistic wellness is the essence of Sereno Spa philosophy and therapies. The unique wellness program integrates yoga, Ayurveda, and contemporary spa healing principles like thalassotherapy, aromatherapy, and energy healing.

Ayurveda, a truly profound and holistic science of life, forms the backbone of our spa therapies to redefine and transform the modern spa approach to an all-encompassing and fulfilling experience. The Sereno Spa delivers customized and transformative holistic health care therapies in a compassionate healing environment to help guests achieve their mind, body, and spiritual goals.

The approach is not clinical but holistic and based on preventive medicine principles geared toward maintaining wellness and promoting vitality and health. We would not accept medical patients, but we would want guests to come to us to learn ways of healthful living. Guests would come for a transformational experience on all levels of mind, body, and soul, and not just a massage.

—Dr. Sanjay Khanzode, Sereno Spa director

Indian head massage, crystal energy healing, and yoga massage (deep tissue and includes gently assisted yoga postures). The yoga program focuses on postures, meditation, and breathing (sudarshan kriya) based on raja yoga. Classes are offered at different levels: beginning, intermediate, and advanced, three to four times a day.

Guest Yoga Teachers? No.

Types of Yoga Classes Hatha, Power. Three to four times per day. No extra charge.

Services Ayurvedic treatments (abhyanga, pizhichil, shirodhara, panchakarma), ancient Indian head massage, crystal energy healing, massage, body treatments, facials, aromatherapy, shiatsu, hydrotherapy, reflexology, nail care.

Other Classes Meditation, aerobics.

Recreation Swimming, volleyball, tennis, lawn bowling, croquet, windsurfing, biking, inland river tours, architectural tours of Goa.

Children's Program? Yes. Camp Hyatt for ages 3 to 12.

Accommodations 251 rooms.

Dining Not included. Nine restaurants and bars, including Juice Bar, Sambar (vegetarian restaurant).

Attire/What to Bring Standard yoga attire, swimsuit, sun/insect protection, trousers/long sleeve shirt for the evenings to protect against mosquitoes, golf/tennis attire.

Travel Information Dabolim Airport is 15 minutes away. Shuttle service is available for a fee. Call in advance to arrange.

Rates $160–$1,750 per night, double occupancy.

Contact 73/2 Arrossim Beach, Cansaulim, South Goa 403712 India; tel: 011-91-832-272-1234; fax: 011-91-832-272-1235; www.goa.park.hyatt.com.

Ananda in the Himalayas   Tehri Garhwal, India

Once the residence of the Maharaja of Tehri Garhwal, Viceregal Palace now serves as the reception area for Ananda in the Himalayas. The resort has a 21,000-square-foot spa, which offers more than 79 body and beauty treatments, integrating traditional Ayurveda with a contemporary Western spa approach. Each of the 70 rooms and five suites has views of the Ganges

River, the town of Rishikesh, or the palace. Ananda spreads over 100 acres of wooded forest next to the town of Rishikesh, which is known for a number of ashrams. Ananda's yoga instructors can lead personalized visits to some of them, including Swami Rama Ashram, International Himalayan Vishaguru Yoga Institute, Parmarth Niketan, and Maharishi Mahesh Yogi.

Look into Ananda's three-night yoga package, which includes one customized massage; two personalized yoga sessions; one personalized yoga consultation; one personalized pranayama and meditation session; two-way transfer to the local train station at Haridwar or the Jolly Grant Airport (New Delhi transfer at extra cost); morning wake-up signature tea and daily fresh fruit bowl; three meals per day; introductory spa and fitness orientation sessions with an initial spa consultation; daily use of the hydrotherapy facilities; yoga, pranayama, meditation, fitness, cooking demonstrations; lectures and workshops; excursions; daily use of the nutritional, wellness, and lifestyle library; and lifestyle consultation.

Guest Yoga Teachers? No.

Types of Yoga Classes Ananda included in yoga package. No extra charge.

Services Massage, 16 Ayurvedic treatments, facials, aromatherapy, reflexology, hydrotherapy, body treatments.

Other Classes Aerobics, cooking, meditation, pranayama, Indian dance, aquaerobics, step aerobics.

Recreation Squash, tennis, golf, billiards, trekking, swimming, river rafting, mountain biking, fishing, bird watching, kayaking, hiking, sauna, steam room, cold plunge bath.

Children's Program? No.

Accommodations 70 deluxe room and five suites.

Dining Included in yoga package. Three meals daily. Organic. Vegetarian available. One restaurant and a tea lounge.

Attire/What to Bring Standard yoga attire, hiking boots, sun/insect protection, swimsuit.

Travel Information 260 kilometers north of New Delhi (six-hour drive).

Rates From $270 per night, single occupancy. Three-night yoga package from $1,100 per person, single occupancy.

Contact The Palace Estate, Narendra Nagar, Tehri - Garhwal, Uttaranchal - 249175, India; tel: 011-91-1378-227500; fax: 011-91-1378-227550; www.anandaspa.com.

Ananda is palatial, gorgeous, dramatic, and magical. I believe the beauty of the Ananda Spa would hold up to most any other luxury retreat in the world. The Ananda Spa is an Indian "Western" retreat high in the mountains—the air is clean and clear there are no sounds other than the hushed tones of nature.

The accommodations are of a generous size, each with its own patio and view of Rishikesh and the Ganges in the distance. There isn't a detail forgotten, from the beautifully starched white yoga pajamas hanging in the closet with the straw yoga mat folded next to it to the plethora of Aveda products to sample.

The food is attractive and beautifully served but was somewhat of a disappointment. A bit on the oily side and not really up to the standard of the rest of the facility.

I took a sunrise yoga class. It was a lovely way to greet the day.

—Sydney Rice, president and owner, Boston Coaching Company, Inc., West Newbury, Massachusetts

Begawan Giri Estate   Ubud, Bali, Indonesia

I was at Begawan Giri for a week and got the chance to stay in all of the villas. The architecture is extremely sophisticated. It is on quite a large estate, so everything is very spread out. A river runs through a gorge on the property, and you can see monkeys playing in the trees by the river. It's like staying in a wonderful wild location. It is a bit remote and away from everything—you're really out in the country. To get to Begawan Giri, you drive through real traditional unmanicured village ambience until you get to the resort itself. The resort landscaping is very attractive. Each villa has its own theme. The water villa is very Japanese, with lots of reflecting pools. There is another villa [Sound of Fire] that is very tribal with a lot of rock—that's the one I like the most, actually.

It is a large hike to get to the spa, which is at the bottom of a 300-foot ravine. It is quite idyllic, with this wonderful stone pathway that leads you down toward the river past waterfalls. You can plunge into these rock pools surrounding the spa. It is an energetic hike to get back up, especially when it is hot.

When Begawan Giri was constructed, it upped the ante for the area. It is grander in scope than staying in the other hotels. Unless you can go to the huge expense of taking over an entire villa, you have to share a terrace and a pool, which might be slightly awkward, although not unlike the situation at other hotels.

—Tim Street-Porter, photographer,
  Los Angeles, California

Begawan Giri Estate, built over a nine-year period by Bradley and Debbie Gardner, has 22 suites housed in five unique residences and seven villas. Named after the natural elements of fire, wind, water, and earth, the residences have interior designs that reflect both European and Asian influences. Each residence comes with a private pool and butler. The villas have been named Golden Space, Seventh Cloud, Bamboo Whispering, Spirit Tree, Pure Moon, Golden Stone, and Distant Mountain. The Gardners personally designed and decorated the interiors of the villas with furniture from the region, including Thailand, Burma, and China.

The Source, Begawan Giri's health spa, offers holistic treatments based on ancient healing methods that use natural ingredients such as volcanic clays, sea salts, flowers, and indigenous plants, such as loofah and aloe vera. All bodywork and massages are performed in a guest's suite or villa, or in garden huts, called "bales." Each 36-square-meter bale has a massage or treatment area, lounge daybed, bathroom, shower, and changing room. The deck space offers an outdoor bath and shower, and sunbeds. Each bale accommodates two people.

Begawan Giri offers customized yoga sessions, which are scheduled at the request of guests. The cost of a private yoga session (one guest) is $80; the cost of a semiprivate session (a couple) is $140. All yoga sessions take place in the yoga pavilion overlooking the river valley with Jane Robinson, Begawan Giri's yoga master. Robinson began her yoga practice 15 years ago in India and has continued to study the teachings of various yoga masters, including B. K. S. Iyengar, T. K. V. Desikachar, Swami Sivananda, and K. Pattabhi Jois. Classes also include discussions about the principles of yoga as well as nutrition and chakra balancing.

Guest Yoga Teachers? Yes.

Types of Yoga Classes Hatha. Private yoga session (one guest) $80. Semiprivate session (a couple) $140.

Services Facials, massage, nail care, body treatments, reflexology, Reiki method.

Other Classes Pilates, meditation.

Recreation Hiking, swimming, biking, rafting, cultural tours.

Children's Program? Yes. Dance lessons.

Accommodations 22 suites in five residences, seven private villas.

Dining Breakfast included. Two restaurants: Biji (New World with Asian accents), Kudus House (Indonesian).

Attire/What to Bring Standard yoga attire, swimsuit, sun/insect protection, hiking/walking shoes.

Travel Information Ubud is a one-hour-and-fifteen-minute drive from Bali's international airport. Chauffeured airport transfers are included.

Rates Suites $495–$2,950 per night, double occupancy. Residences $2,550–$4,400 per night. Villas $1,495–$1,995 per night.

Contact PO Box 54, Ubud 80571, Bali - Indonesia; tel: 800-225-4266, 011-62-361-978-888; fax: 011-62-361-978-889; www.begawan.com.

Chiva-Som Health Resort   Hua Hin, Thailand

Chiva-Som, meaning Haven of Life, is located on the beach and surrounded by seven acres of tropical gardens. The resort combines ancient Eastern healing therapies with the latest Western spa techniques, focusing on weight loss, stress reduction, and relaxation.

A variety of pools keep guests in the water, including a bathing pavilion for aquaerobics, an outdoor pool for swimming laps, plunge pools, hydro pools, a watsu pool, and more. Medical and complementary therapies like acupuncture are also offered. Tai chi, qi gong, and yoga classes are held each morning.

The food served at the resort is a low-calorie fusion of Asian and Western cuisine. Meals are prepared with produce grown in Chiva-Som's organic garden. Champagne and wine are available in the evening. Cleansing diets are also offered. Guests may want to avoid the rainy season, from July through October.

Guest Yoga Teachers? No.

Types of Yoga Classes Hatha. Twice daily. No extra charge. Private lesson $56 per guest per hour.

Services Shiatsu, watsu, Reiki method, hydrotherapy, facials, aromatherapy, body treatments, massage, nail care, acupuncture, acupressure, reflexology, chi nei tsang.

Other Classes Tai chi, qigong, Pilates.

Recreation Sauna, steam room, Jacuzzi, swimming, sea kayaking, beach biking, tennis, thai boxing.

Children's Program? No. Minimum age 16.

The city of Hua Hin was a lot more populous than I had anticipated. But once you go through the gates of Chiva-Som, you officially enter an oasis.

The food was extraordinary; not only was it fantastic spa cuisine, but I would put it up against any top big-city restaurant. Portion control most definitely rules, but I always ended every meal sated, not stuffed. They do offer a captain's table for single guests wishing to mingle.

I had private one-on-one yoga because I am very new to the practice. I had sessions with two teachers, who were both wonderfully versatile and supportive. I noticed classes being taught throughout the day in various locations on the property. They were open to everyone. I spent many hours at the spa. My first Thai massage was very mild, and I mentioned this to the spa consultant. I was told I might prefer a session with Geng (whom I called Master Geng) who offered a more aggressive massage. I also spent some time in the flotation chamber, which was a new experience and very relaxing. I had an acupuncture session the first day, and I haven't had a cigarette since.

Quite often I would think, "Who knew it was possible to feel this relaxed?"

—Greg Minch, account executive, New York City

Accommodations 57 rooms.

Dining Included. Low-calorie. Vegetarian available.

Attire/What to Bring Standard yoga/exercise attire, swimsuit, sun/insect protection.

Travel Information Bangkok Airways flies daily, leaving Bangkok at 8:40 AM and arriving in Huahin at 9:15 AM. Driving from the Bangkok airport to Chiva-Som takes less than three hours.

Rates Seven-night stay $2,415–$6,930 per person, double occupancy.

Contact 011-66-2711-6905-10, 011-66-3253 6536; fax: 011-66-2381-5852; www.chivasom.net/main.asp.

CARIBBEAN

Wyndham El Conquistador Resort   Fajardo, Puerto Rico

I love infinity pools, and El Conquistador has a gorgeous pool with dramatic views over the cliff. My hotel room had breathtaking views of the ocean. There was a beautiful marble bathroom and oversized tub.

I love lobster and I ate it for breakfast, lunch, and dinner. The sushi was also very good. They have a spa menu if one is into that sort of thing, but I prefer oversized meals on vacation. I tried a few spa items, and I was hungry a few hours later.

I am a high-strung New Yorker who enjoys running, but I decided to try yoga. Full moon yoga was an amazing experience. I tried two classes, and the instructors were cognizant of each student's level and taught the class appropriately.

I had a hot stone massage and a Swedish massage. Both were excellent. In the spa, I enjoyed relaxing in the huge Jacuzzi before heading to the women-only waiting room.

I went horseback riding, which turned out to also be a history lesson about the island. I recommend a sail on the catamaran.

—Kellie Pelletier, public relations executive, New York City

Wyndham El Conquistador Resort is on a cliff overlooking the Atlantic Ocean and Caribbean Sea. The resort is divided into four "villages": the Grand Hotel; the Spanish-style Las Casitas Village, with its own check-in, pool, and personal butler; Las Olas Village, with villas built into the side of a cliff; and La Marina Village, with rooms facing the sea.

The Golden Door Spa is located in Las Casitas Village, which is modeled after the city of San Juan, with cobblestone streets, white stucco and terra-cotta buildings, and open-air plazas.

The three-level, 26,000-square-foot spa is housed in a plantation-style building. You enter the Welcome Level, which echoes with the sound of flowing water. Yoga, tai chi, and aerobics classes are offered on the Vitality Level, which also features a fitness room, juice bar, and wellness center where guests can receive fitness appraisals and individual consultations on health, nutrition, and stress management. The Treatment Level, with ocean views, has 25 rooms for massages and skin and body care.

Daily spa membership, which costs $20, includes use of the Vitality Level, unlimited classes, and use of the niwa facilities (Japanese furo bath, steam room, showers, and lockers).

Guests can also attend full moon yoga, held monthly on each night of the full moon, on the tai chi lawn overlooking the Caribbean sea.

Guest Yoga Teachers? No.

Types of Yoga Classes Hatha. Once daily. $20 per day.

Services Massage, aromatherapy, reflexology, shiatsu, Reiki method, craniosacral, Ayurvedic treatments including shirodhara, body treatments, facials, hydrotherapy.

Other Classes Spinning, aerobics, tai chi, Pilates.

Recreation Boating, fishing, golf, hiking, Jacuzzi, jet-skiing, mountain climbing, racquetball, sauna, snorkeling, tennis, whirlpool.

Children's Program? Yes. Ages 3 to 12.

Accommodations 750 rooms.

Dining Not included. 16 restaurants.

Attire/What to Bring Standard yoga attire, swimsuit, sun/insect protection, clothes suitable for formal dining.

Travel Information Wyndham El Conquistador Resort is 35 miles from the Luis Munoz Marin Airport. Shuttle provided for a fee.

Rates $175–$485 per night, double occupancy.

Contact 1000 Conquistador Avenue, Fajardo, 00738, Puerto Rico; tel: 787-863-1000; fax: 787-863-6500; www.wyndham.com.

Parrot Cay   Providenciales, Turks and Caicos Islands

Parrot Cay is a 50-acre resort on a Caribbean island of the same name. Parrot Cay, believed to have originally been named "Pirate Cay," was once frequented by pirates. Today, its secluded beaches are often frequented by such celebrities as Donatella Versace, Bruce Willis, and Jerry Seinfeld.

Keith Hobbs, who styled London's Nobu restaurant, designed the guest accommodations. All rooms have four-poster beds with mosquito nets and verandas with hammocks.

At Shambhala, Parrot Cay resort's healing center, yoga, meditation, and Asian-inspired spa treatments are offered. Yoga retreat weeks are led by a host of renowned yoga teachers from around the world. Retreat fees include six nights' accommodations, three meals daily, five hours of yoga per day, and roundtrip airport transfers.

Guest Yoga Teachers? Yes. Including Donna Farhi, Sharon Gannon, David Life, Shiva Rea, Shandor Remete, Erich Schiffmann, Rodney Yee.

Types of Yoga Classes Hatha. Once daily (except Wednesday). No extra charge.

Services Massage, shiatsu, Reiki method, reflexology, body treatments, facials, nail care.

We love this retreat because it is so serene. Parrot Cay is on its own little island. It's an oasis of peacefulness, with beautiful water and sand, wonderful food, and amazing spa treatments such as the Thai massage.

—David Life and Sharon Gannon, Jivamukti Yoga Center founders, New York

Other Classes Pilates, meditation, pranayama, tai chi.

Recreation Tennis, golf, scuba diving, deep-sea fishing, snorkeling, waterskiing, windsurfing, sailing, eco-kayaking, walking tours, jogging trail, Jacuzzi, swimming, sauna/steam room.

Children's Program? No. Baby-sitting available.

Accommodations 60 luxury rooms, including six beach houses and eight beach villas.

Dining Breakfast included. Other meals: Lotus Restaurant (Mediterranean-style cuisine with an Asian flavor), Terrace Restaurant, Shambhala Spa menu.

Attire/What to Bring Standard yoga attire, swimsuit, sun/insect protection, golf/tennis attire, walking shoes.

Travel Information Fly into Providenciales. Take a 20-minute minibus ride to the Leeward Marina, then a 35-minute boat ride to Parrot Cay.

Rates $380–$3,660 per night, double occupancy. Includes roundtrip airport transfers, full English breakfast, and use of nonmotorized watersports, tennis courts, gym. Six-night yoga retreats $3,420 per person, single occupancy or $2,655 per person, double occupancy.

Contact PO Box 164, Providenciales Turks and Caicos Islands, British West Indies; tel: 649-946-7788; fax: 649-946-7789; www.parrot-cay.com or www.shambhalaretreat.com.

Caneel Bay   St. John, U.S. Virgin Islands

Caneel Bay prides itself on its "alternative" offerings. At the Self Centre, yoga is offered once or twice daily. Other classes include aqua-chi, breath-walk, drumming, journaling, meditation, breathing techniques, Ayurveda, Pilates, partner yoga, YogaPlay for kids and parents, and chakra meditation, plus astrology consultations. There are no phones or televisions in rooms, so guests can further relax and reconnect with nature.

The resort was created by Laurance Rockefeller in 1955 and is in the middle of the 5,000-acre Virgin Islands National Park. Seven beaches border the resort's 170 acres. In addition to yoga, you can sample a different beach every day for a week, enjoy a watercolor lesson, experience marine life up close with the resident "snorkologist," take nature walks with the staff horticulturist amidst 2,000 different varieties of plants, hike resort trails or those of the national park system, or sail on a 65-foot schooner.

Guest Yoga Teachers? No.

Types of Yoga Classes Hatha, partner, kids, restorative, Vinyasa. Once or twice daily. $35 per class.

Services Massage.

Other Classes Meditation, breathing techniques, Ayurveda, Pilates, chakra meditation, aqua chi, drumming circles.

Recreation Swimming, fishing, scuba, snorkeling, tennis, windsurfing, sailing, kayaking.

Children's Program? Yes. Turtle Town for ages 3 to 12, with a nominal charge.

Accommodations 166 guest rooms and cottages.

Dining Not included. Four restaurants: Turtle Bay Estate House (American), the Wine Room at Turtle Bay (prix fixe, seven-course menu), Equator Restaurant (seafood and meat), Caneel Beach Terrace (spa lunch buffet). Meal plans: breakfast and dinner $80 per person per day; breakfast, lunch, and dinner $100 per person per day.

Attire/What to Bring Standard yoga attire, swimsuit, sun/insect protection. Shorts or dry bathing suits with shirts or cover-ups and footwear are acceptable during the day in the dining rooms and public areas. Swimwear, shorts, jeans, and tennis shoes are not permitted after sunset. Men: collared shirts, slacks or Bermuda shorts, and close-toed shoes are required for dining at the Equator and Caneel Terrace. Slacks are required for men in the Turtle Bay restaurant. During winter season only, jackets are customary for men in the Turtle Bay restaurant.

Travel Information Flights are available directly to St. Thomas. Hotel will pick you up at Cyril King Airport, St. Thomas. You will be escorted to a private ferry for the 35-minute journey to Caneel Bay ($65 per person).

Rates $300–$1,100 per night, double occupancy.

Contact PO Box 720, St. John, U.S.V.I. 00831-0720; tel: 340-776-6111; fax: 340-693-8280; www.caneelbay.com.

My girlfriend and I stayed at Caneel Bay. Caneel Bay was basically an upscale campground with 170 acres of beautiful scenery and beaches. The rooms were nice, with a good bed and a really cool stone shower, but beware of the mosquitoes in the late afternoon. There was no phone or television in the room. They did have a free movie showing every night, but we were too tired to go at 9 PM.

I would suggest the tennis garden rooms. They were not the most expensive but were close to the front desk. You will need to use their shuttle that goes around the resort; remember, this place is huge. You don't need to pay extra for the ocean-front rooms, because all seven beaches are accessible. I thought Honeymoon Beach was the best. It wasn't crowded at all.

If you visit St. John, you will probably want to visit Trunk Bay, but be aware that these tourist traps are really, really crowded. I honestly enjoyed just using the Caneel Bay beaches. They were all private except for one. There were two computers with free Internet access. You will need this, since long distance was very expensive. Email was my primary way of communication with the outside world.

I recommend asking for a refrigerator before you arrive. It will be in your room before you check in. There is a market in Cruz Bay. You should buy some snacks and drinks. Food can get expensive.

—Julian Romero, sales and marketing executive, Belle Mead, New Jersey

Yoga Inns and B&Bs

Pearson's Pond Luxury Inn and Adventure Spa   Juneau, Alaska

Pearson's Pond calls itself a bed and breakfast inn, a mini resort, and an adventure spa—all in one. The inn is on a private pond. You'll find trails, wildlife, garden fountains, and two hot tubs right outside your suite door. An unstructured yoga retreat program is integral to the inn. Rebecca Garcia teaches Iyengar yoga most summer mornings outdoors on the pond pier. On her days off, Rebecca's former student, innkeeper Diane Mayer Pearson, takes over, while husband Steve bakes bread for breakfast. Suites are private and well equipped with two phone lines and efficiency kitchens. Just in case you're snowed in with a loved one: The bathrooms are stocked with condoms!

Pearson's is within walking or biking distance to Mendenhall Glacier and many hiking trails and the historic downtown. Guests can flight-see, take glacier helicopter trips, kayak, raft, and canoe.

Guest Yoga Teachers? No.

Types of Yoga Classes Iyengar. Once daily. No extra charge.

Services Massage, aromatherapy.

Other Classes Dance and tai chi at participating health club.

Recreation Hiking, biking, kayaking, rafting, canoeing, glacier trekking, dogsledding, wildlife viewing (whales, bears, eagles), fishing, exploring, skiing, hot tub.

Children's Program? No.

Pearson's is located at the edge of a neighborhood, but set apart by the pond and forest. The pond has a dock with a rowboat and paddleboat for guests. Each room has a four-poster bed, sitting area, fireplace, kitchenette, and full bathroom. There was enough space in my room for a yoga mat and stretching in front of the fire.

The food at Pearson's is all self-serve. In the shared kitchen and dining area is a fully stocked refrigerator and pantry. Each day, the innkeeper bakes fresh bread for the guests.

I recently returned to a yoga practice and was delighted that it would be available. It was just Diane (the owner) and I for yoga the day I arrived. My sense was that Diane enjoys a very regular yoga practice herself that she wants to share with her guests and contribute to the positive experience of the inn as a retreat and spalike atmosphere. I had a full massage, with some deep-tissue work. I had traveled all the way from Vermont and needed it.

—Susan Maslack, higher education administrator and faculty member, Burlington, Vermont

Accommodations Seven suites with efficiency kitchens; off-site condominiums.

Dining Breakfast included.

Attire/What to Bring Standard yoga attire, warm and cold weather clothing, hiking and rain gear, workout wear, sun/insect protection.

Travel Information Pearson's is seven minutes from the Juneau airport. Shuttles are available.

Rates $119–$299 per night, double occupancy.

Contact 4541 Sawa Circle, Juneau, AK 99801; tel: 888-658-6328, 907-789-3772; fax: 907-789-6722; www.pearsonspond.com.

HAWAII

Dragonfly Ranch   Honaunau-Kona, Big Island, Hawaii

Did you ever want a tree house while you were growing up? Dragonfly Ranch satisfies that desire. More than a bed and breakfast, Dragonfly is a getaway for the kid in all of us—unique indoor/outdoor suites brush the tops of monkeypod trees. Near the spiritual Pu'uhonua O Honaunau (Place of Refuge) on the Big Island's sunny Kona Coast, Dragonfly periodically hosts workshops that can include yoga, lomi lomi massage, sacred dance, and flower essences. Five nearby beaches give you plenty of opportunities to snorkel, scuba dive, sail, kayak, whale watch, and swim with dolphins. The temperature is almost always 72°F with very little wind and limited rain, so you can get in the water year-round.

The Dragonfly Ranch has three suites. Each has a private entrance, secluded outdoor shower, and "light food preparation facilities" (a bar sink, toaster oven, small refrigerator, electric tea kettle, coffee maker, and utensils). A complimentary continental-style breakfast includes pastries, fresh homegrown organic fruit, granola, fruit juices, tea, and coffee.

Guest Yoga Teachers? Yes. Including Joyce Anue, Cheri Clampett.

Types of Yoga Classes Various styles. Daily. $10 per class (Five Tibetan Rites complimentary). Call in advance to arrange private yoga sessions.

Services Lomi lomi, shiatsu, massage, flower essence therapy.

Other Classes Tai chi, qigong.

Recreation Swimming, boat rides, whale watching, sailing, snorkeling, swimming with dolphins.

I went to Dragonfly in 1984, and I've been back there once or twice a year ever since. It is an amazing place. Four days at the Dragonfly is like a week or two somewhere else for relaxing and getting out of the rat race. The owner, Barbara (Moore), is such a unique individual and has such an artistic eye that everywhere you look you see beauty. When you're there, it's like you're living outdoors, because the rooms are really these screened-in areas. It's like being in a tree house.

Barbara does wonderful lomi lomi, which includes being bathed in fragrant water. And I swam with 50 dolphins in a bay that is five minutes away. Breakfast at the Dragonfly is always fun because the property attracts such an eclectic group of people. Sometimes there are spontaneous community dinners, but you are always welcome to the greens in the organic garden for a salad or to pick papaya. And there are lots of cute little restaurants in the area for dinner.

For yoga there is a wonderful wood platform above the house that has a labyrinth painted on it. You can join Barbara in the morning for the Five Tibetan Rites.

—Susan Lawton, graphic designer, Sacramento, California

Children's Program? No.

Accommodations Three suites and two rooms.

Dining Breakfast included.

Attire/What to Bring Standard yoga attire, yoga mat, swimsuit, sun/insect protection, rain poncho.

Travel Information The Keahole-Kona airport is 26 miles away.

Rates $85–$200 per night, double occupancy.

Contact Box 675, Honaunau-Kona, HI 96726; tel: 800-487-2159, 808-328-7412; fax: 425-795-0631; www.dragonflyranch.com.

IDAHO

Hidden Creek Ranch & Spa   Harrison, Idaho

If you've been longing for a yoga retreat but your kids want an active vacation, then Hidden Creek Ranch may be for you. It combines the activities common on a dude ranch, such as riding, hiking, fishing, archery, trap shooting, and horseshoes, with a well-being slant. The holistic education program, comprising meditation, pranayama, and visualization, makes this retreat unique. In fact, you can take a yoga class before a two-hour horseback ride.

The ranch, open year-round, is in a private valley surrounded by 350 square miles of national forest. If you plan on riding, your stay begins with a horse orientation, during which you will be assigned a horse and saddle for the duration of your stay.

Guest Yoga Teachers? No.

Types of Yoga Classes Hatha. Once daily. No extra charge.

Services Massage, lymphatic drainage, reflexology, Reiki method, shiatsu, Jin Shin Jyutsu.

Other Classes Meditation, horseback riding, horse grooming and saddling, roping, ropes course.

Recreation Horseback riding, hiking, hot tubs, swimming, wagon rides, cow herding, pipe and sweat lodge ceremony, nature walks, fly-fishing, archery, boat tours, volleyball, climbing wall, snowshoeing, cross-country skiing, snowmobile tours, downhill skiing, snowboarding nearby.

Children's Program? Yes.

I took my dad to Hidden Creek to celebrate his 60th birthday. We're both into horseback riding. We thought the place was fabulous—the staff, facility, and food were wonderful. We went on a two-and-a-half-hour ride each morning throughout the ranch and in the mountains. It was beautiful.

The yoga was good—it is one of many amenities they offer. We did basic hatha yoga in a sunrise class before riding. They also had a great masseuse who was very popular after the morning ride.

They have a children's camp that my kids attended and loved. The kids put on a little show and rodeo at the end of the week. It's a real family place.

The meals were mostly sit-down, with an occasional lunch buffet. I told them ahead of time I was vegetarian, and they fully accommodated me.

There is so much to do—hiking, ropes course, fishing, and a whole array of outdoor experiences. There is barely time to do it all.

—Jennifer Monness, yoga instructor, New York City

Accommodations Six log cabins with 16 units.

Dining Included. Vegetarian available.

Attire/What to Bring Standard yoga/workout attire, riding boots, skiing/snow attire, sun/insect protection.

Travel Information The ranch is 71 miles from the Spokane (WA) airport. The ranch shuttle will meet you at 1 PM at the Spokane airport on your arrival day. Following your stay at the ranch, the shuttle leaves the ranch at 10 AM to return you to the airport. Transportation is available on Saturday and Sunday ($75 per person roundtrip).

Rates In winter, $762 per person, double occupancy (two-night minimum stay). In summer, $2,165 per person, double occupancy (six-night minimum stay).

Contact 11077 East Blue Lake Road, Harrison, ID 83833; tel: 800-446-3833, 208-689-3209; fax: 208-689-9115; www.hiddencreek.com.

MAINE

Sewall House   Island Falls, Maine

Every summer, Donna Davidge (Amrita) teaches yoga at Sewall House, built in 1865 by her great-grandfather, William Sewall. In the winter, you can take classes with her at various locations around New York City, where she has been teaching since 1985.

The day begins at 8:30 AM with over an hour of Ashtanga yoga. After breakfast, you are free to hike, bike, kayak, or relax on your own until the 4:30 PM Kundalini yoga class. A vegetarian dinner is served at 6:30 PM.

Island Falls is close to Canada and near Mt. Katahdin, forests, lakes, state parks, and wildlife. Guests can choose to practice karma yoga (selfless service) by volunteering some time every day to the upkeep of the house. This could include kitchen duties, gardening, cleaning, etc.

Guest Yoga Teachers? Occasionally. Lisa Rosof.

Types of Yoga Classes Kundalini, Ashtanga. Twice daily. No extra charge.

Services Massage.

Other Classes Meditation.

Recreation Sauna, Jacuzzi, hiking, fishing, swimming, biking, golfing.

Children's Program? No.

Accommodations Five private bedrooms, each with double beds.

Sewall House is a lovely B&B situated in northern Maine, only minutes from exquisite lakes. I loved the staff—they were so warm and friendly. It's a real family feel—small and intimate. I had my own room and a huge four-poster bed in the historic house that was built at the turn of the century. I don't always eat vegetarian food, but the chef knows how to throw a feast. I can't say I lost weight there, however. I couldn't wait to wake up in the morning to do yoga. The yoga practiced was Kundalini, which I had never done before. But Donna Davidge is a great teacher with the sweetest spirit. Kundalini is more energy-based and is quite vigorous. I now integrate it with my other yoga practice, which is more Kripalu-based. I had a massage that was heaven on Earth. We went on a lake tour, and later I went kayaking, which was a thrill. I also went for a bike ride and was able to see the mountains in the distance.

—Karen Friedman, retirement income advocate, Washington, D.C.

Dining Included. Two meals daily. Vegetarian.

Attire/What to Bring Swimsuit, flashlight, fleece or sweater, loose comfortable clothes for yoga, rain jacket, hiking boots, water shoes (for lake swimming), sun/insect protection, water bottle.

Travel Information Sewall House is 90 miles north of Bangor.

Rates $125 per person per day, single occupancy. $102 per person per day, double occupancy.

Contact 1027 Crystal Road, PO Box 254, Island Falls, ME 04747; tel: 888-235-2395; www.sewallhouse.com.

MICHIGAN

Neahtawanta Inn   **Traverse City, Michigan**

The Neahtawanta Inn may look like a typical B&B from the outside, with its large porch and clapboard siding. But inside you'll find an oak floor yoga studio and vegetarian kitchen. Innkeeper Sally Van Vleck, a certified yoga teacher with 25 years of experience, teaches yoga class when workshops are not in session.

The inn, on Grand Traverse Bay, was built in the early 20th century and opened in 1906 as the Sunrise Inn. It became the Neahtawanta Inn Bed and Breakfast in 1985. The inn houses the Neahtawanta Research and Education Center, which sponsors events on peace, the environment, and inner peace. Upon entering, you'll notice a large living/dining room with a sunken fieldstone firepit and a library filled with books and periodicals. Guests can enjoy a wood-burning sauna as well as a complimentary vegetarian breakfast made by Sally's husband and co-innkeeper, Bob Russell.

Guest Yoga Teachers? Yes. Including Roger Eischens.

Types of Yoga Classes Hatha. Weekly (morning classes for guests). $10.

Call to reserve a space (800-220-1415) or email (sally@nrec.org).

Services Massage.

Other Classes N/A.

Recreation Hiking, swimming, fishing, boating, golf, wineries.

Children's Program? No.

Accommodations Four rooms, one suite.

Dining Breakfast included.

The setting of Neahtawanta Inn on Old Mission Peninsula is lovely, with Grand Traverse Bay in front and a small woods behind. The water is visible from the front rooms, porch, and yard, which borders the beach. The water is often warmer than in Lake Michigan, which makes for good swimming and kayaking. They've added handicapped access, a large country kitchen, and a yoga room, and managed to maintain the historic look.

I've been there many times for yoga workshops with Roger Eischens and High Energy Yoga. Some have been teacher trainings; others are designed for all levels. At the workshops, the food is fabulous low-dairy, vegetarian fare. The cooks are able to accommodate special dietary needs. Massage from qualified, competent practitioners is always available.

During workshops, innkeeper Sally Van Vleck schedules optional evening events. These range from a guided walk through the woods to singing and dancing, campfires, and sunset beach gatherings. These are typically low-key events, to enjoy after a day of yoga. It's a very relaxed atmosphere, with yoga, good food, conversation, reading, walking, and time on the beach.

—Chris Smith, yoga teacher and garden shop manager, Grand Rapids, Michigan

Attire/What to Bring Standard yoga attire, cold weather gear, swimsuit, sun/insect protection, walking shoes.

Travel Information Four airlines provide air service to Cherry Capital Airport (three miles from downtown) from the hub cities of Detroit, Chicago, Minneapolis, and Milwaukee.

Rates $95–$125 per night, single occupancy. Two-night minimum stay weekends, June 1–November 1.

Contact 1308 Neahtawanta Road, Traverse City, MI 49686; tel: 800-220-1415; www.oldmission.com/inn/.

NEW HAMPSHIRE

The Darby Field Inn   Albany, New Hampshire

The Darby Field Inn overlooks the Mt. Washington Valley and White Mountains of New Hampshire, making it a popular place during fall foliage season. It's a country inn with a full-service restaurant and a good place if you are athletic, since the area is prime for cross-country skiing, snowshoeing, mountain biking, and hiking. Or just relax by the fireplace in the living room, on the mountain-view patio, in the sunny tavern, the extensive gardens, or in the heated swimming pool.

The inn also offers yoga weekends, which include two nights' accommodations for two, two yoga classes, a class on aromatherapy, one dinner for two, two breakfasts, and a massage or reflexology treatment. Private yoga sessions are always available for one to six people and require one week advanced reservation.

Guest Yoga Teachers? Yes. Including Heather Giles, Beverly Hammond.

Types of Yoga Classes Hatha. Once daily during yoga weekends. No extra charge. Private sessions $75 per class (reserve one week in advance).

Services Massage, reflexology, aromatherapy.

Other Classes Aromatherapy.

Recreation Swimming, sleigh rides, skiing, cross-country skiing, snowshoeing, snowmobiling, ice skating, mountain biking, hiking, fishing, golfing, tennis.

Children's Program? No. Minimum age eight years old.

Accommodations 13 rooms.

Dining Breakfast included. Add $70 for dinner for two.

My sister and I were planning to go to Kripalu one weekend, but when we called they were booked up. I searched on the Internet for a yoga retreat, and found Darby Field Inn. The inn has scheduled retreats but nothing on our dates. However, they arranged 90-minute, semi-private yoga sessions for us each morning. The instructor was trained in Kripalu yoga (just so happens). We had wanted to enhance our practice and make sure we were doing postures correctly, and the instructor really helped us a lot. Her peaceful demeanor was also very inspiring.

They made a special breakfast time for us because of the yoga, with vegan choices for my sister's dietary needs.

The rooms are sweet and each one different. The grounds are beautifully landscaped, and there are bird feeders everywhere with lots of winged visitors. You could borrow binoculars at your breakfast table for sighting many varieties or watch the hummingbirds through the windows in the pub.

Awesome hiking! We filled all three days with climbs to the tops of mountains. It was breathtaking being right in the middle of the White Mountains.

—Joey Jablonski, sculptor/potter/teacher, Ashford, Connecticut

Attire/What to Bring Standard yoga attire, hiking boots, ski gear/attire, sun/insect protection, tennis/golf attire.

Travel Information The Darby Field Inn is 92 miles from the Manchester airport, 127 miles from Boston, and 337 miles from New York City. The Portland jetport is 60 miles away.

Rates $100–$280 per night, double occupancy. Minimum stay requirements apply when your visit includes a Saturday night or a holiday and during the fall foliage and Christmas week.

Contact 185 Chase Hill Rd., Albany, NH 03818; tel: 800-426-4147, 603-447-2181; fax: 603-447-5726; www.darbyfield.com.

NEW MEXICO

Riverdancer Retreat and Inn   Jemez Springs, New Mexico

Once you step foot on the Riverdancer property, you'll see why the locals believe that ancestral Pueblons still inhabit the area. The center is located at the base of the 2,000-foot Virgin Mesa, the home of ancient pueblos. Nearby is the centuries-old village of Jemez Springs, in a valley that was created by prehistoric volcanoes. People have been coming to the area for centuries to take the hot mineral spring water.

Riverdancer is a five-acre, Southwestern-style retreat facility on the Jemez River that accommodates 14 to 19 overnight guests. Its healing arts program combines spa treatments with yoga, meditation, tai chi, art therapy, pranayama, visualization, altar building, and more. The healing arts center and spa is housed in a refurbished adobe casita. Here, you can choose from such treatments as aromatherapy, sea algae body treatments, and therapeutic healing massages.

A basic retreat package includes accommodations, two meals daily, one massage, and one class. Special workshops in papermaking, meditation, art therapy, and hiking are offered throughout the year.

Guest Yoga Teachers? No.

Types of Yoga Classes Hatha. Once daily. Donation requested but not required for class.

Services Acupressure, aromatherapy, craniosacral therapy, massage, polarity therapy, reflexology, Reiki method, body wraps, shiatsu.

Other Classes Qigong, tai chi.

We toured northern New Mexico for seven days on bicycles, logging 50 miles per day, and stopped at the Riverdancer during the trip. The Riverdancer has that New Mexican feel, with tile floors, adobe walls, and desert colors. The common areas are exceedingly restful, and the people running the place are very welcoming. I got to see a number of the rooms, and they are all beautiful. Each is named for different groups of Native Americans. The artwork reflects that heritage, and there is a book about each tribe in the rooms.

A river flows behind the property, and they've created a series of gravel paths that lead to the water. When you head toward the river and look back toward the hotel, you see this immense red mesa.

The yoga was fantastic—as good as any yoga class I've taken anyplace else. Brittany is a very good teacher; she's calm and encouraging. The class began before dawn. I was facing a window and watched the sun rise over the mesa. Brittany geared the whole session toward preparing our legs for our ride that day.

—Megan Ballard, bike guide, Calgary, Canada

Recreation Hiking, nearby natural hot springs, cross-country skiing, mountain biking, fishing, bird watching.

Children's Program? No. Minimum age 10.

Accommodations Six guest rooms, one apartment.

Dining Vegetarian breakfast included.

Attire/What to Bring Standard yoga attire, hiking boots, swimsuit, ski/cold weather attire in winter, sun/insect protection.

Travel Information Riverdancer is 60 miles from the Albuquerque airport.

Rates $109–$160 per night, double occupancy.

Contact 16445 Scenic Hwy. 4, Jemez Springs, NM 87025; tel: 800-809-3262, 505-829-3262; www.riverdancer.com.

Sunrise Springs Inn & Resort — Santa Fe, New Mexico

I was attracted to Sunrise Springs because of its variety of classes and healing rituals and the opportunity for meditation. I participated in clay firing classes, massage, yoga, and a Japanese tea ceremony. There were people of all abilities in the yoga class. It was gentle yoga, but more experienced people took it to their own level.

The food is Southwestern in theme and delicious, and the presentation is impressive. They grow their own vegetables, spices, and herbs.

The buildings are sophisticated adobe—they really blend with the earth. The decor is Southwestern and very native—upscale but not ostentatious.

I like Sunrise Springs because the service is superb. They are casual yet accommodating.

—Anna Lloyd, president and executive director of a professional organization of women entrepreneurs and corporate leaders, Chicago, Illinois

Most activities at Sunrise Springs take place at the Living Center, which offers a wide range of meditative and creative programs designed to help you design a more balanced life. Classes include cooking, pottery, gardening, massage, yoga, poetry, and more. Personal and group retreats are available. A Meditative Arts package includes mindful arts classes, twice-daily yoga, spa treatments, sweat lodge, astrology, three meals per day, and accommodations.

The adobe, stone, and wood inn is on 69 acres of desert valley with views of the Sangre de Cristo and Sandia Mountains. Guests stay in casitas or garden- or pond-view rooms.

In addition to taking advantage of the Living Center offerings, guests can soak in outdoor hot tubs, participate in Japanese tea or sweat lodge ceremonies, or receive a full range of spa treatments.

Guest Yoga Teachers? No.

Types of Yoga Classes Hatha. Saturday and Sunday. Included in spa package or $15 per class.

Services Massage, facials, aromatherapy, ko bi do (Japanese facial massage), shiatsu, Reiki method, craniosacral therapy, polarity, healing touch, sacred oil anointing.

Other Classes Meditation, cooking, pottery, gardening, poetry.

Recreation Hiking, sauna, hot tub, Japanese tea ceremony, sweat lodge.

Children's Program? No.

Accommodations 60 rooms.

Dining Not included. Blue Heron Restaurant (organic cuisine).

Attire/What to Bring Standard yoga/workout attire, swimsuit, sun protection, walking shoes.

Travel Information Sunrise Springs Inn & Resort is 55 miles from the Albuquerque airport.

Rates Overnight retreat package $198–$243 includes lodging, 50-minute spa treatment, and yoga.

Contact 242 Los Pinos Road, Santa Fe, NM 87507; tel: 800-955-0028, 505-471-3600; fax: 505-471-7365; www.sunrisesprings.com.

NORTH CAROLINA

Westglow Spa   Blowing Rock, North Carolina

Westglow is the former summer home of impressionist artist and writer Elliott Daingerfield. He named the estate Westglow because of the views, which he described as "never glaring, always glowing throughout the shadows, clouds, or mist." The surrounding landscape also inspired much of his work.

In 1978, Glynda Valentine purchased Westglow. She eventually converted the estate into a European-style destination spa in 1991. Valentine has more than 25 years of experience running fitness centers in the South. Under her supervision, Westglow focuses on health rather than weight loss.

The mansion was built in 1916, and nearly 85% of Daingerfield's furnishings are still in place, including a collection of 2,200 books in the library. The house has seven guest rooms furnished with period antiques. Two cottages and the Cedar Lodge across the street can lodge additional guests.

The Life Enhancement Center, erected on the same spot where Daingerfield maintained his studio, is where fitness and therapeutic programs take place. It contains an indoor pool for lap swimming and aquaerobics, fitness center, whirlpools, saunas, body treatment rooms, hair and nail salon, yoga studio, and poolside cafe. A tennis court and croquet court are also available outdoors.

Guest Yoga Teachers? No.

Types of Yoga Classes Hatha. Once or twice daily. No extra charge.

Services Massage, craniosacral therapy, aromatherapy, body treatments, reflexology, facials, nail care, hair services.

I take yoga classes at Westglow because we live so close. We've been members of their spa for seven or eight years. Classes are offered every day, and they've even increased their frequency. I also have facials regularly and massages every few months. The newer Life Enhancement building houses the spa and yoga classes.

This year, the restaurant began to offer both spa-sized and regular-sized portions. It's all very fresh, healthy food. We eat there on a regular basis, and the chef works around my dairy allergy. They always offer vegetarian entrees.

The setting is absolutely spectacular. The Westglow is a beautiful, white, imposing structure overlooking Grandfather Mountain and facing west. It is a beacon in the valley. You can sit on the porch and watch the sun set in the evening, and the view is beautiful—you can see for miles.

—Nancy Brittelle, artist, Blowing Rock, North Carolina

Other Classes Stretch and tone, aquaerobics, circuit training, fit ball, step aerobics, Spinning, cooking.

Recreation Hiking, tennis, swimming, croquet.

Children's Program? No. Minimum age 16.

Accommodations Seven rooms, two cottages, three lodge rooms.

Dining Included. Three meals daily. Spa cuisine. Vegetarian available.

Attire/What to Bring Standard yoga/workout attire, swimsuit, tennis attire, hiking boots, sun/insect protection.

Travel Information Westglow is 38 miles from the Hickory airport and 120 miles from the Charlotte airport.

Rates $356–$560 per person per night. Six-night package $1,875–$2,333.

Contact 2845 Highway 221 South, Blowing Rock, NC 28605; tel: 800-562-0807, 828-295-4463; www.westglow.com.

WASHINGTON

The Yoga Lodge on Whidbey Island — Greenbank, Washington

Yoga teacher Gail Malizia has opened up her home to create the Yoga Lodge. Midweek guests may join one of Gail's ongoing small group classes, Tuesday to Friday, for $14 per person. (The yoga studio accommodates 16 people.) Classes are usually taught twice daily. Workshops are held throughout the year. Check the website for details.

The Yoga Lodge is on five acres with two small orchards, an organic vegetable and flower garden, a small pond, and a wood-fired sauna in the woods. Guests can hike in nearby South Whidbey State Park and bicycle to Ebby's Landing, the Port Townsend ferry, and Beachcomber's Beach.

A percentage of the Yoga Lodge's annual proceeds is donated to nonprofit organizations. The Yoga Lodge also has a work/study program. Participants receive an overnight stay, yoga lesson, and breakfast in exchange for four to five hours of labor, which can involve helping in the garden, doing chores around the property, or cleaning the guest bedrooms, bath, or sauna. Work/study participants are expected to make a monetary contribution toward meals and bring their own sleeping bag or bed linens and towels.

Guest Yoga Teachers? Yes. Including Lee Atwell.

Types of Yoga Classes Hatha/Iyengar. Once or twice on weekdays. $14 per session. On weekends, private session $40 per person or $50 per couple.

I originally went to The Yoga Lodge to attend a workshop with Sheila Belanger, who does shamanic work. The facility is so nice, and the grounds are beautiful, with a large vegetable garden. Gail Malizia, the owner, did all the cooking, and it was excellent—primarily vegetarian. Three sleeping rooms can accommodate 12 people, and there are separate bathrooms for men and women. Gail lives upstairs. I now take Iyengar yoga with her once a week. She has been teaching for more than 20 years. The yoga room has beautiful hardwood floors that are heated and big windows that look out onto the garden. There are tons of props and equipment. It is the nicest yoga facility I've ever been to.

—Marcia David, birthing doula and massage practitioner, Brier, Washington

Services N/A.

Other Classes Yoga teacher training.

Recreation Hiking, biking, kayaking.

Children's Program? No.

Accommodations Three rooms for 11 people; shared bath.

Dining Breakfast included.

Attire/What to Bring Standard yoga attire, hiking boots, rain gear.

Travel Information The Yoga Lodge is a two-hour drive plus ferry from the Seattle airport. Whidbey Island is accessed by ferry from Mukilteo (30-minute drive north of Seattle), or via Deception Pass from Bellingham and points north.

Rates $55–$65 per person per night. No credit cards.

Contact 3475 Christie Road, Greenbank, WA 98253; tel: 360-678-2120; www.yogalodge.com.

WEST VIRGINIA

Sleepy Creek Retreat   Berkeley Springs, West Virginia

The 20-acre Sleepy Creek Retreat calls itself an "alternative bed and breakfast." Each of the three guest rooms has a private bath with Jacuzzi tub. A self-serve continental breakfast is served each morning. The workshop space accommodates up to 12 people.

A stone pillar circle facing Cacapon Mountain is a place for meditation, prayer, and contemplation. Three yoga teachers in the area offer custom-designed wellness retreats that include bodywork, aromatherapy, qigong, vegetarian cooking classes, training in meditation, and guided visual imagery as well as yoga. The retreat is open from mid-March through mid-December.

Nearby Cacapon State Park has a Robert Trent Jones championship golf course, full-service restaurant, horseback riding, swimming, paddleboats, 6,000 wild acres for hiking trails, and nature tours.

Guest Yoga Teachers? Yes. Including Suzen (Sharda) Segall. Check website for workshop options.

Types of Yoga Classes Call to arrange yoga classes. Private sessions start at $55.

Services Massage, Reiki method, reflexology, aromatherapy.

The hallmark of my work is customizing and personalizing workshops for small groups, couples, families, and individuals when they book at Sleepy Creek, which has only three guest rooms. Additional rooms are rented in Berkeley Springs when we have larger groups to accommodate. My programs can include services and products beyond yoga and meditation training components, such as dance of the five elements, introduction to self-acupressure, aromatherapy, whole food (vegan and vegetarian) cuisine, anti-aging skin care systems, and bodywork, including integral massage, reflexology, and body-mind acupressure.

—Suzen (Sharda) Segall, certified massage therapist and integrated health and wellness practitioner who teaches at Sleepy Creek

Other Classes Stress reduction, meditation, life counseling.

Recreation Horseshoe pit, badminton, volleyball, croquet, golf.

Children's Program? No. No small children.

Accommodations Three rooms.

Dining Breakfast included.

Attire/What to Bring Standard yoga attire, walking shoes, sun/insect protection, golf attire.

Travel Information Sleepy Creek is 100 miles from Baltimore, MD.

Rates $85 per night, double occupancy. No credit cards.

Contact 394 Covey Run Rd., Berkeley Springs, WV 25411; tel: 304-258-8430; www.sleepycreekretreat.com.

WISCONSIN

Woodwind Health Spa and Wellness Center   Rhinelander, Wisconsin

Woodwind Health Spa and Wellness Center is a holistic oasis in northern Wisconsin, on the Wisconsin River with its own launch for boats and kayaks. This 10,000-square-foot facility on 40 acres of forest offers therapeutic pools, massages, sauna, body treatments, an aromatherapy whirlpool, facials, and yoga classes. In addition to frequent Native American workshops, educational seminars and presentations on holistic health are available. Certification in Integrative Floatation Discovery and Reiki method is offered. Yoga with Betsy Schussler is on Tuesday nights at 4:30 and 6. Weekends guests can request more frequent yoga classes.

Guest Yoga Teachers? No.

Types of Yoga Classes Hatha yoga with Betsy Schussler. Tuesday nights. $15 per session. Kundalini available daily $15. Weekend guests can request additional yoga classes: $50–$100 for a private session, depending on length of session.

Services Massage, facials, body treatments, Reiki method, hypnotherapy.

Other Classes N/A.

Recreation Swimming, hiking, snowshoeing, cross-country skiing, kayaking, canoeing, biking, sauna.

Children's Program? No.

Betsy, the yoga instructor at Woodwind, is a wonderful, gentle, well-qualified instructor, who goes to several conferences and workshops per year to update her teaching abilities and methods. She has a genuine concern for all the students in the class, regardless of their individual capabilities or length of time they've been taking yoga. The first-time student is every bit as welcome as those of us who have been with her for years. She says that we have two teachers: the one in front of the class and our own bodies. We should pay just as much attention to what our bodies are telling us as we do to the teacher leading the class.

I have had a hydrotherapy session, which was wonderful. And the meals are delicious. The owner brings in guest lecturers and practitioners and provides a restful atmosphere for those who stay for a weekend or extended period. The spa is close to town while being tucked away in the woods very close to the Wisconsin River.

—Torrey Youngstrum, potter and clergy person, Rhinelander, Wisconsin

Accommodations Four bedrooms upstairs and two baths, one duplex, camping.

Dining Breakfast included.

Attire/What to Bring Standard yoga attire, swimsuit, cold weather attire.

Travel Information Woodwind is two miles from Oneida County Airport. Shuttle service is available.

Rates $85 per night, single occupancy or $110 per night, double occupancy; $65 single or $85 double if a client uses three or more major spa services while staying at the spa.

Contact 3033 Woodwind Way, Rhinelander, WI 54501; tel: 715-362-8902; fax: 715-362-4316; www.woodwindspa.com.

MEXICO

Hotel Na Balam   Isla Mujeres, Mexico

Hotel Na Balam is located on the small island of Isla Mujeres, just across a patch of Caribbean sea from Cancún. The island is only five miles long and a half mile wide and boasts white sand beaches and turquoise waters. Guests stay in small cottages surrounded by lush gardens; all 31 rooms have air-conditioning, ceiling fans, and a terrace. In the town you will find restaurants and gift shops.

Yoga retreats, held by teachers from around the world, take place throughout the year. Retreats usually include two classes per day, two meals per day, and lodging. Feathered Pipe Ranch in Montana (see page 28) holds winter events here each year.

Guest Yoga Teachers? Yes. Including Kathryn Beet, Baxter Bell, David Cousins, Mary Dunn, Jane Fryer, Rachel Carole Gluckstein, Dean Learner, Susan Lothner, Ceci McDonell, Shelley McTamaney, Victoria Miller, Lucy O'Brien, Jillian Pranski, Karen Rosenberg, Katherine Smith.

Types of Yoga Classes Hatha. Once daily. No extra charge.

Services Massage.

Other Classes N/A.

Recreation Bicycle riding, hiking, scuba diving, snorkeling, kayaking, fishing.

Children's Program? No.

Accommodations 31 rooms.

I sponsor an annual women's mind/body/ spirit retreat with my colleague, Ceci McDonnell, LISW, called Portals to the Self, A Celebration of Women's Stories by the Sea. We chose to stay at Hotel Na Balam for many reasons: It is exquisite, but informal; the staff is outstanding; it's walking distance from town but far enough away from its hustle and bustle; and they have two palapas to do yoga, movement, circle time, etc.

My first impression of Hotel Na Balam was that it was the perfect setting for a retreat—not one of those high-rise resorts. It is on a sandy beach where you can choose to be near the palapa bar or by the water, and the tropical gardens are meticulously maintained. The food is absolutely delicious— gourmet regional Yucatán cuisine.

The hotel offers yoga to guests each morning in a palapa overlooking the ocean. Our workshop begins each day with either yoga, a moving meditation, or a contemplative practice followed by the morning session. There is a massage therapist at the hotel who is quite good.

—Karen Rosenberg, LISW, clinical social worker, Cleveland Heights, Ohio

Dining Not included. Zazil Ha Restaurant (Mayan and vegetarian fusion cuisine).

Attire/What to Bring Standard yoga attire, swimsuit, walking shoes, sun/insect protection.

Travel Information Arriving at Cancún airport, take a taxi to the ferry landing at Puerto Juarez, located 15 minutes north of downtown Cancún. Arrange the fare beforehand with the driver to get a good price. The ferry crossing takes 25 minutes.

Rates $121–$270 per night, double occupancy.

Contact Calle Zazil - Ha No. 118 Playa Norte, Isla Mujeres, Quintana Roo, Mexico 77400; tel: 011-52-998-877-0279, 011-52-998-877-0058; fax: 011-52-998-877-0446; www.nabalam.com.

Rancho Encantado   Laguna Bacalar, Mexico

The grounds at Rancho Encantado are lovely, and local gardeners keep everything thriving. The retreat is on Lake Bacalar, a huge clear, warm lake. All the living, dining, and meeting quarters are thatched palapas of varying sizes and shapes.

I did practice yoga every day in a large, open-air palapa that overlooked the beautiful Laguna Bacalar. I also had a full-body massage one afternoon and a Reiki method treatment on another day in the privacy of my palapa. We took advantage of the side trips to Mayan ruins, many of which were not open to the public, and to the rain forests to see exotic animals and birds. I really enjoyed the lunch we had at a small, sustainable farm on the way to see Mayan ruins. The farm was run by a Mayan family who grew everything they needed to survive—they had livestock, vegetables, fruit, rice, corn. Two palapas stood side-by-side on the property. One housed the kitchen, and the other had several hammocks hung on the walls for family members to sleep in. The women cooked us the most amazing lunch I've ever eaten and served it with such love that it remains forever etched in my memory.

—Linda Sparrowe, editorial consultant and writer, Fairfax, California

Rancho Encantado, located on Laguna Bacalar in Quintana Roo, Mexico, near the border of Belize, attracts ecologically minded travelers. The resort is also popular with guests interested in archeology and birding.

After a day of trekking through the jungle, visiting Mayan ruins, or swimming and kayaking on the lake, you can soak in the Jacuzzi or receive a massage in a thatched hut over the water. Satchidananda Ashram (Yogaville), based in Buckingham, Virginia (see page XX), often holds teacher training workshops here.

Rancho Encantado doesn't normally hold yoga classes unless they're specifically scheduled by a group, in which case the charge is included in the package. If others were specifically interested in a daily yoga session, it can be arranged for an extra charge.

Guest Yoga Teachers? Yes. Including Satya Greenstone, Swami Poornananda.

Types of Yoga Classes Hatha. Included in price during workshops. Fee for private sessions. Request daily classes when making reservation.

Services Massage, lomi lomi, mud wraps, salt glows, papaya peels, facials, acupuncture, acupressure, herbal wraps.

Other Classes Workshops change yearly. Check the website.

Recreation Adventure tours, Mayan ruin treks, birding, swimming, kayaking, Jacuzzi.

Children's Program? No.

Accommodations 12 private cottages; up to 40 people.

Dining Breakfast and dinner included. Vegetarian available.

Attire/What to Bring Standard yoga attire, swimsuit, sun/insect protection, walking shoes.

Travel Information The closest large airport is in Belize City, about 100 miles south. Transportation from Belize City airport is $42.50. Flights are also available into Chetumal airport (30 minutes from the Rancho). Transportation from Chetumal is $20.

Rates $85–$140 per night per person. Children ages 3 to 12 are half price.

Contact 800-505-MAYA (505-6292), 505-758-9790; www.encantado.com.

CENTRAL AMERICA

La Paloma Blanca   Playa de Jaco, Costa Rica

La Paloma Blanca is a small, Mediterranean-style villa on Playa de Jaco. Yoga Costa Rica classes take place in the hotel, overlooking the Pacific. La Paloma Blanca is within easy walking distance of the town of Jaco but far enough away to ensure tranquillity. Each room has a private bathroom with hot water and access to the swimming pool and on-site garden.

Daily yoga classes incorporate a variety of poses, meditation, and breathing practices according to Patanjali's eightfold path. All levels of practitioners are welcome, including novices. A typical day begins with a gentle yoga class, followed by breakfast. There is plenty of free time until the next yoga class in the late afternoon, which tends to be more vigorous. Restorative poses at the end of class help alleviate fatigue. While not in yoga class, guests can bird watch, horseback ride, kayak, swim, take Spanish lessons, receive massages, or visit nearby national parks and reserves.

All yoga classes are led by Anne Jackson, a certified hatha yoga teacher, reflexologist, and environmental educator. Anne has been studying yoga since 1985 and teaching in Costa Rica since 1998. Groups and individuals are welcome.

Guest Yoga Teachers? No.

Types of Yoga Classes Hatha. Twice daily. No extra charge with yoga retreat.

Services Massage, reflexology.

Other Classes N/A.

Recreation Bird watching, horseback riding, sea kayaking, canoeing, forest canopy tours, garden tours, tours to national parks, hot springs, swimming.

For the past several years, I have been offering community yoga classes in the town of Jaco. At one stage, I was looking for another location to use for classes, and the owner of La Paloma Blanca, who is a dedicated yoga student, offered the use of her hotel. We hold the class on the third floor, which overlooks the ocean and is open to the ocean breezes. I teach most of the year, generally excluding October and November, which are rainy season months. In addition to what I consider the community classes, I also offer weeklong yoga vacations, under the name Yoga Costa Rica. This program offers guests twice-daily yoga classes combined with other activities, including horse tours, sea kayaking, snorkeling, canopy tours, rafting, hiking, sport fishing, surfing, sailing, guided ecology tours, or beach trips. Nonyoga spouses and friends are welcome, and we will assist them in organizing their tours and activities.

Massage services are available by an outside provider. The massage therapists are trained in relaxation massage and also do a variety of body treatments, such as mud therapy, seaweed wrap, and salt body scrubs.

—Anne Jackson, yoga teacher, Jaco, Costa Rica

Children's Program? No.

Accommodations Three rooms can accommodate seven people.

Dining Breakfast and lunch included in yoga retreat.

Attire/What to Bring Standard yoga attire, swimsuit, sun/insect protection, hiking boots.

Travel Information Playa de Jaco is a 1^1/2-hour drive from the San Jose international airport.

Rates $45–$75 per night, double occupancy. Yoga retreat $850–$1,100 per person per week. No credit cards.

Contact Playa Jacó, Puntarenas, Costa Rica; tel: 011-506-643-1893; fax: 011-506-643-1892; http://home.austin.rr.com/flaco/lapaloma/; www.yogacostarica.ca.

CARIBBEAN

The Villas at Fort Recovery Estate   Tortola, British Virgin Islands

I always return to the Villas at Fort Recovery . . . and I've sent a lot of people there over the years. It is like paradise on Earth. It is the most soothing, idyllic spot I've ever visited. I'm a spiritual person, but I live a hectic life in New York. The resort is really a place you can go to "recover" from a high-stress life. I take the yoga classes with my three kids and my husband. Yoga is taught on a dock that hangs over the Caribbean, and often you can see a rainbow while you're practicing. You can browse through the spiritual book collection, swim with dolphins, take a 20-minute boat ride to another island, or just enjoy the property's private beach. The complimentary continental breakfast includes home-baked breads, and you can hang out and be social with the other guests or bring it back to your room. The dinners that are brought to your villa are great. You decide your menu in the morning, and they set up a formal table in your villa with tablecloths and china. It is served course by course.

—Lisa Sharkey, senior producer, *Good Morning America*, New York

The Villas of Fort Recovery Estate on Tortola, British Virgin Islands, are on the Caribbean. The villas, built around a 17th-century Dutch fort, have air-conditioning, televisions, fully equipped kitchens, living rooms, libraries, bedrooms, and private baths. Housekeeping services are provided daily.

Area activities naturally revolve around the water. Charter boats for scuba diving and fishing are available for hire. Swimming with dolphins, windsurfing, kayaking, parasailing, tennis, horseback riding, and snorkeling can all be arranged by the hotel. You can also visit an 18th-century rum distillery, the botanical gardens, and Mt. Sage rain forest. Yoga is done each evening at sunset near the water's edge. Specific requests for additional sunrise yoga can be accommodated. Dinners, served in your villa, are $30 per person and include French bread, homemade vegetable soup, entree with all the trimmings, and dessert.

Guest Yoga Teachers? No.

Types of Yoga Classes Hatha at sunset. No extra charge.

Services Massage, shiatsu, reflexology, nail and hare care.

Other Classes Chanting, meditation, Pilates.

Recreation Snorkeling, scuba diving, sailing, sport fishing, windsurfing, kayaking, swimming, parasailing, horseback riding, tennis, gym.

Children's Program? No. Baby-sitting available.

Accommodations 17 one- to four-bedroom beachfront villas.

Dining Continental breakfast included.

Attire/What to Bring Standard yoga attire, swimsuit, sun/insect protection, walking shoes, tennis attire.

Travel Information The Villas at Fort Recovery are a 45-minute ferry ride from St. Thomas, U.S. Virgin Islands. From San Juan, Puerto Rico, take a 35-minute plane ride to Tortola's Beef Island Airport, then a 40-minute taxi ride to the resort.

Rates $145–$475 per night. Additional person in any villa is $50 per night, under age 12 is $35.

Contact Box 239 Road Town, Tortola, British Virgin Islands; tel: 800-367-8455, 284-495-4354; fax: 284/495-4036; www.fortrecovery.com.

Natura Cabanas   Cabarete, Dominican Republic

At this spa getaway, there are no phones or TVs in the simple, thatched-roof bungalows, though the largest cabana has a fully equipped kitchen and can accommodate as many as six people. The secluded swimming pool is separated from the private beach by vegetation. After a yoga lesson, visit the spa for aromatherapy vapor baths, deep massages, mud baths, salt scrubs, facial and body peels, and the sauna. The economical room rates include airport transfers, breakfast, and maid service. You can rent mountain bikes or go on horseback rides or surf. Afterward, refresh yourself at the juice bar and head to the alfresco dining room for a candlelight dinner.

Guest Yoga Teachers? No.

Types of Yoga Classes Hatha. Twice weekly. No extra charge.

Services Massage, aromatherapy, mud baths, body treatments, facials.

Other Classes N/A.

Recreation Surfing, mountain biking, horseback riding, golf, tennis, windsurfing, swimming, scuba diving, snorkeling, whale watching, sauna.

Children's Program? No.

Accommodations Six cabanas.

Dining Breakfast included.

Attire/What to Bring Standard yoga attire, swimsuit, sun/insect protection, hiking boots.

Natura Cabanas was recommended by a friend, so I looked it up on the Internet. I like unique places and thought this could be one, and it was. It is an amazing place—we felt like we were in paradise. I went with my husband, and it was like a second honeymoon. Our room was perfect. It was constructed with stones and wood—even the bathtub was made out of stone. The best thing about this place is the personalized service they offer. And the chef there is great. The food is delicious. We had a shiatsu massage on the beach that lasted two hours. We have already reserved a room for next month.

—Judith Jose, business administrator, Santo Domingo, Dominican Republic

Travel Information Natura Cabanas is 15 minutes from the Puerto Plata international airport. Shuttle service is provided.

Rates $40–$95 per person per night.

Contact Perla Marina, Paseo del sol #5, Sosua-Cabarete, Puerto Plata, Dominican Republic; tel/fax: 809-571-1507; www.naturacabana.com.

Jackie's on the Reef   Negril, Jamaica

I had read about Jackie's in *Essence* and *Oprah* magazines. I had always heard Jackie's was spiritual and healthy, so I went. In the main stone house is a very long hallway that is dark, and then you are faced with this incredible view of the ocean—a brilliant turquoise view that is framed by a window.

Every morning there is yoga. I hadn't done a lot of yoga. I'm a runner, and I thought yoga was for wimps. I didn't want to be antisocial, so I took the class. There is no wake-up call, but Jackie starts playing music a half hour before class. Different teachers from the local area come to teach yoga. One teacher was in her sixties, and I couldn't keep up with her. I learned something new every day. Now I do yoga as part of my regular exercise routine.

Jackie has tons of metaphysical books, and I did a lot of reading while I was there. And you can get some pampering if that's what you want. The best thing was the herbal salt scrub. First you soak in a warm tidal pool. Then Jackie walks you to a thatched-roof room. She heats up fresh herbs and salts and rubs your body with them. Then she encourages you to do a little nude sunbathing. It was beyond relaxing—it was cleansing.

After Jackie bought the land and was getting the house built, she camped on the grounds and built a fire each night, which she still does. Guests would sit around the campfire and tell their stories, and Jackie would tell her tales too.

—Jenine Holmes, advertising copywriter, New York City

Jackie's on the Reef is a small holistic spa retreat located on a secluded coral reef two miles past the oldest lighthouse in Jamaica. Owner Jackie Lewis, a former clothing designer from New York, encourages you to relax with yoga, massage, reflexology, and herbal scrubs. The cottage, perfect for couples, has a double bed and private bathroom, or you can stay in one of four rooms in the stone house, each with a private bathroom and two handmade beds. A yoga, tai chi, or meditation class is held each morning.

Guest Yoga Teachers? No.

Types of Yoga Classes Hatha. Every morning. No additional charge.

Services Massage, aromatherapy, hot stone massage, body treatments, Reiki method, reflexology, facials, nail care.

Other Classes Meditation, tai chi, drum making, drumming, African dance.

Recreation Swimming, snorkeling, bird watching, hiking, horseback riding.

Children's Program? No.

Accommodations One cottage, four rooms.

Dining Breakfast and dinner included. Jamaican, Indian, Chinese, and Creole cuisine. Vegetarian available.

Attire/What to Bring Standard yoga attire, swimsuit, sun/insect protection, walking shoes.

Travel Information Fly into Donald Sangster Airport, Montego Bay. Jackie's is about 1 1/2 hours from the airport.

Rates $125–$150 per person per night. Four-day stay requires purchase of two spa services ($58–$80 each). Seven-day stay requires purchase of four spa services. No credit cards.

Contact General Delivery, Negril PO Box, Negril, Jamaica, West Indies; tel: 718-469-2785 (New York), 876-957-4997 (Jamaica); www.jackiesonthereef.com.

Tensing Pen Hotel   Negril, Jamaica

If sleeping in a thatched hut, dining in an open-air kitchen, and practicing yoga in a bungalow overlooking the Caribbean Ocean is your idea of the ideal vacation, you are in for a treat. Tensing Pen Hotel, located on the western tip of Jamaica in Negril, is in a cove amidst tropical jungle foliage. If you feel like getting out of your hammock, you can scuba, snorkel, get a massage, or visit Negril's famous seven-mile white sand beach before going back to rest in your guest bungalow, with interiors handcrafted by local artisans from indigenous materials.

More than two years ago, the hotel built a special hut just for yoga, called SeaSong, and ran its first yoga retreat with Amrit Desai. Hotel manager Nancy Beckham is a yoga instructor who teaches at least three classes a week at Tensing Pen.

Guest Yoga Teachers? Yes. Including Amrit Desai, Ken Scott-Nateshvar.

Types of Yoga Classes Hatha, Ashtanga. Three times per week. $10 per class.

Services Massage.

Other Classes N/A.

Recreation Swimming, snorkeling, scuba, biking, hiking, parasailing.

Children's Program? No.

Accommodations 15 rooms.

Dining Breakfast included. Dinner served several times per week.

Attire/What to Bring Standard yoga attire, swimsuit, sun/insect protection.

Travel Information Negril is a 90-minute drive from the Montego Bay airport.

Rates $105–$430 per night per bungalow.

Contact PO Box 3013, Negril, Jamaica, West Indies; tel: 876-957-0387; www.tensingpen.com.

I have held a number of yoga retreats at Tensing Pen, because you can combine yoga with swimming in the beautiful Caribbean, amazing accommodations, and some of the best gourmet vegetarian food. Tensing Pen is comprised of individual huts and cabanas, all facing the sea. You can do yoga to the sounds of birds as you watch dolphins pass by. Each cottage is different, but all have the same wide windows and no phones or TV. I hold two yoga sessions per day and evening satsang. Guests can also snorkel, swim, hike, or get a massage.

—Sharon McConnell, yoga teacher, Kingston, Jamaica

Casa Grande Mountain Retreat   Utuado, Puerto Rico

The 20-room Casa Grande Mountain Retreat is on 107 acres of tropical mountainside. Each room has a private bath, balcony, and hammock. Jungle Jane's Restaurant, located in a 19th-century coffee plantation hacienda, uses grapefruits, oranges, lemons, mangos, avocados, bananas, papayas, plantains, peppers, herbs, and spices from the property's gardens. There is

Casa Grande Mountain Retreat was listed in the brochure as "off the beaten track," and the picture of a parador developed from an old coffee plantation attracted us. It was an oasis of peace and tranquillity. The main house is of modest size with a beautiful porch. The guest houses with two units each are built on the mountainside, with views into the green slopes. The structures and stairs connecting them are treated wood, which blends well into the surroundings. The rooms are simple and rustic, but clean; they have small porches with hammocks, ideal for reading or snoozing, surrounded by sounds of mountain streams and birds. The restaurant offers simple local dishes. It could be improved with more nutritious or vegetarian options.

I took yoga classes every day with the owner, a patient teacher, in an old renovated barn where open doors give a view of the jungle. Perfect for meditation. Nearby are beautiful valleys accessible by narrow winding roads, including a mountain lake, Dos Bocas, with boating, etc. This whole area of Puerto Rico is the most scenic.

—Heide Kruse, homemaker, Palmas del Mar, Puerto Rico

a fresh water swimming pool, bar, and a 1,000-square-foot yoga center. Start the day with the owner's one-hour yoga class. Afterward, you can horseback ride, kayak, fish, hike, or make good use of your hammock.

In the 19th century, the site of the hotel was a 5,000-acre farm called La Finca de Santa María, which grew sugar, tobacco, and coffee. It was made into a hotel in the 1970s. In 1996, Steven Weingarten, a New York attorney-turned-yogi/hotelier, bought the place after visiting it while on vacation.

Guest Yoga Teachers? Yes. Including Lizette Arzuaga, Joyce Cossett, Mary Flynn.

Types of Yoga Classes Hatha. Twice daily. $10 per class.

Services N/A.

Other Classes N/A.

Recreation Horseback riding, kayaking, fishing, cave tours, hiking.

Children's Program? No.

Accommodations 20 rooms can accommodate 30 people.

Dining Not included. Jungle Jane's Restaurant. Vegetarian available.

Attire/What to Bring Standard yoga attire, swimsuit, hiking boots, sun/insect protection.

Travel Information Casa Grande is two hours from San Juan.

Rates $80–$90 per night, double occupancy.

Contact Carr. 612, Km. 0.3, PO Box 1499, Utuado, Puerto Rico 00641-1499; tel: 787-894-3939, 787-894-3900, 888-343-2272; fax: 787-894-3900; www.hotelcasagrande.com.

EUROPE

Villa Isis, Holistic Holidays   Lanzarote, Canary Islands

Purported by some historians to be the legendary continent of Atlantis, Lanzarote is one of seven islands belonging to Spain off the coast of Africa. The expansive, Mediterranean-style Villa Isis hosts morning yoga outdoors (bring warm clothes), aquaerobics, walks, and vegetarian meals.

The staff encourages guests to relax, and a host of therapies, such as massage, Reiki, and reflexology, help you leave stress behind. If you must keep active, you can swim, scuba dive, horseback ride, play tennis, or golf.

The villa is located in a quiet cul-de-sac within walking distance of the village and a 10-minute drive to the beach. Accommodations are based on a shared room, so it is ideal if you book with a friend or partner because there is a limited number of single rooms. If you are prepared to share, the villa staff will try to match you with a suitable same-sex roommate.

Guest Yoga Teachers? No.

Types of Yoga Classes Hatha. Once daily. No extra charge.

Services Massage, Reiki method, reflexology, kinesiology, NEI (promotes release of negative emotions from body), shiatsu, facials, nail care.

Other Classes Aquaerobics.

Recreation Diving, swimming, tennis, horseback riding, golf, biking.

Children's Program? No.

Accommodations Five rooms, one suite. Some with private baths.

Dining Breakfast and three dinners included. Vegetarian and vegan.

Attire/What to Bring Standard yoga attire, swimsuit, sun/insect protection, clothing for cool evenings.

Travel Information Fly into Arrecife airport, where a complimentary roundtrip airport shuttle is available.

Rates $700–$1,496 per person per week.

Contact 011-44-207-692-0633 (UK), 011-34-928-524-216 (CI); www.hoho.co.uk.

I was attracted to Villa Isis for its combination of yoga, beach holiday, and spa treatments without the earnest overtones of an ashram or similar retreat. The villa's interior is like your best friend's mum has just bought a thumping great big villa in the sun and filled it with squashy sofas, interesting objects, great beds, and beautiful bathrooms.

Lynne's yoga derives from the hatha school, but she has had many years teaching experience, and her own style has evolved over time. She adapts her classes to the individuals she is teaching. She is a generous and patient teacher with a strong background, which is worthy of trust. I have been practicing yoga seriously for about six years and have been taught by some highly skilled and inspired people in U.K., Canada, and U.S. Lynne Oliver is one of the very best.

—Sarah Dodd, director of a public relations company, Cambridgeshire, England

La Buissière   Duravel, France

La Buissière, open June through September, is a center for yoga and walking in southern France. Guided walks exploring the local valley, hillsides, and vineyards are held each morning. Afternoons at La Buissière are often spent lounging around the saltwater pool or in shaded hammocks.

Yoga takes place in a newly constructed stone building that stays cool in the hot French summers. The yoga room is fully equipped and has floor-to-ceiling glass windows with views of the garden. Pierrette, the resident teacher, normally holds three hatha yoga classes per week. Visiting teachers offer week-long intensive programs throughout the summer. During these workshops, yoga is held twice per day.

Each guest studio has its own kitchenette and private bathroom. Rooms are generally shared, so it is ideal if you come with someone you know. Breakfast is provided each morning.

This part of France is known for its regional cuisine, but eating out can

La Buissière gave me the ideal mix of walking in the countryside with the spiritual lift of yoga. The fact that La Buissière was partly self-catering appealed. It meant I could have my own space when I wanted it, although the six of us there that week tended to eat out together. The guided walks were also a huge attraction, as I do love walking.

La Buissière is a lovely, old French farmhouse on large grounds, with the guest accommodations and yoga room in a converted barn just a little way from the main house. The large pool was a major attraction, and we all spent a lot of the week relaxing there after a morning's walking.

The yoga was quite basic, as I was the only one in the group who had done yoga before. It was gentle hatha yoga, and the teacher was able to spend time with each member of the small group, making sure they were understanding the practice. We did yoga on alternate evenings and ended each session with a relaxation session.

We did two- to three-hour guided walks on alternate mornings, usually taking in historic landmarks and ending with lunch.

—Meg Davis-Berry runs a residential therapy center in Gloucestershire, England

be difficult if you are vegetarian or vegan. Many guests make use of their in-room kitchens and shop at the mini supermarket and bakery in the village, 10 minutes away.

Guest Yoga Teachers? Yes. Including Krishna Lodh, Sara Rossi.

Types of Yoga Classes Hatha. Three classes per week. No extra charge.

Services N/A.

Other Classes N/A.

Recreation Swimming, biking, canoeing, hiking.

Children's Program? No. Not suitable for children.

Accommodations Maximum 10 guests.

Dining Breakfast included.

Attire/What to Bring Standard yoga attire, hiking boots, sun/insect protection, swimsuit.

Travel Information The nearest international airport is in Toulouse. A short navette ride takes you from Toulouse airport to the railway station to catch the train to Cahors. Transfers to and from Cahors railway station is available.

Rates $394 per week, double occupancy. $551 per week, single occupancy. More intensive yoga weeks with visiting guest teachers about $472 per person per week.

Contact Rue de Vivre, 46700 Duravel, France; tel: 011-33-565-36-4351; fax: 011-33-565-36-4347; www.yogafrance.com.

La Maison Verte   Roujan, France

La Maison Verte, built in the 1830s, is a large country house hidden behind huge gates in the middle of Roujan, a small village surrounded by the vineyards of the South of France. Until 1987, the property produced over half a million liters of wine a year. It now belongs to Teddy Hutton and his wife, Nicola Russell, who both speak fluent French and English and are always on hand to assist guests. During the summer, they move into a basement apartment so visiting groups have the run of the 13-bedroom house. The estate's courtyard apartment, green room apartment, gate house, and Limpet house also have guest accommodations.

La Maison Verte has two acres of gardens and a swimming pool. Meals tend to be eaten in the garden, and an old wine press has been converted into a large barbecue.

One-week yoga retreats are held throughout the summer. Yoga class is held twice per day in a barn turned beautiful yoga hall. When not doing yoga, you can swim in the pool, explore Roujan, or borrow one of the bicycles and ride through the surrounding countryside. An on-site gallery displays the work of local artists.

Guest Yoga Teachers? Yes. Including Ken Eyerman, Tim Goullet, Jean Hall, Simona Hernandez, Liz Lark, Sue Pendlebury.

Types of Yoga Classes Ashtanga, Sivananda, flow. Twice per day. No extra charge.

Services Massage.

Other Classes Singing, Thai massage, script writing, pottery, painting.

Recreation Swimming, biking, walking.

Children's Program? No.

Accommodations 13 bedrooms can sleep up to 21 people, plus Courtyard Apartment, Green Room Apartment, the Gate House, and the Limpet House.

Dining Included. Breakfast and dinner. Vegetarian.

Attire/What to Bring Standard yoga attire, swimsuit, walking/hiking shoes, sun/insect protection, beach towel.

Travel Information You can fly to either Montpellier airport or Carcassonne. It is recommended you rent a car and drive to Roujan.

Rates $623–$976 per person per week.

Contact No. 31 Avenue Henri Mas, 34320, Roujan, France; tel: 011-33-46-724-8852; fax: 011-33-46-724-6998; www.lamaisonverte.co.uk; www.freespirituk.com.

Relieve Eyestrain Shut out light and other distractions with an eye-bag filled with hulled buckwheat and scented with lavender; and use a gel-filled eye mask (hot or cold) to reduce swelling brought on by lack of sleep, flying, or dehydration. – K.F.M.

La Maison Verte is somewhat bohemian. For six months in summer the owners move downstairs. It is a three-story house in a quiet little town. There were at least 20 of us doing yoga. The yoga room was incredible, and the yoga teacher, Liz Lark, was from Tri Yoga in London. This woman has written several books about yoga and also has a drama background. She was very knowledgeable and encouraging. She had traveled with a vegetarian cook and a masseuse. There was a chemistry between all of us in the group. We did excursions together to the coast, vineyards, and the town of Pezenas. We also went walking, biking, or just sat by the pool.

—Leia Kline, traveling yoga student, Big Island of Hawaii

Ashrams

Sivananda Ashram Yoga Farm　　　　　　　　**Grass Valley, California**

Sivananda Ashram Yoga Farm is located on 80 acres of rolling hills and meadows in the Sierra Nevada foothills. At an elevation of 1,200 feet, the landscape is dominated by meadows and oak trees. Weather permitting, classes are held on a deck surrounded by a grove of oak trees; meditation is practiced in one of three temples; and the pond is ready for swimming. In the winter, all activities are held indoors in the woodstove-heated farmhouse. A cedar sauna is open year-round. The day begins at 6 AM with morning meditation and yoga. Brunch is served at 10 AM. There is yoga again at 4 PM and a meditation session before bed. Lights-out is at 10:30 PM. All guests are required to attend both yoga classes and both meditation sessions. The schedule is based on Swami Vishnu-devananda's five points for a long and healthy life: proper exercise, proper breathing, proper relaxation, proper diet, and positive thinking and meditation. Guests are encouraged to practice karma yoga (selfless service) by volunteering an hour per day to the upkeep of the ashram. This includes kitchen duties, gardening, cleaning, etc.

Guest Yoga Teachers? No.

Types of Yoga Classes Sivananda. Twice daily. Also studies in raja (yoga of meditation), karma (selfless service), bhakti (yoga of devotion), jnana (yoga of knowledge). No extra charge.

Services N/A.

Other Classes Meditation, pranayama.

The Sivananda Ashram in Grass Valley is in the beautiful rural countryside. The ashram has a feeling of being a farm (minus the barn). I was there 30 days for my teacher training.

I chose to stay in a room in the main building that was shared with three other students. I wanted to make some yoga friends, and it was easy this way. The room had bunk beds. There was excellent vegetarian food and lots of it in great variety.

Sivananda has an excellent teacher training program. We spent four hours a day learning the asanas and how to teach and correct them. Other classes included the study of anatomy, the subtle bodies, the yoga sutras that pertain to hatha yoga, the Bhagavad Gita, Sanskrit prayers, meditation classes, and more. There also was kirtan and wonderful singing of the chants everyday. My favorite part of the training was getting to do concentrated sadhana with no outside distractions for 30 days. My least favorite: The detox that the body, mind, and emotions go through during the second week.

—Marjorie Jackson, hatha yoga and tai chi chuan instructor, Pasadena, California

Recreation Swimming, hiking, sauna.

Children's Program? Yes. Kid's camp in summer.

Accommodations 40 indoor beds. Campsites available.

Dining Included. Two buffet-style, lacto-vegetarian meals daily. No meat, fish, fowl, eggs, garlic, onions, tea, and coffee.

Attire/What to Bring Modest yoga attire, towel, bathing suit, hiking boots, sandals, flashlight, sweater, meditation shawl, sun/insect protection, modest bathing suit.

Travel Information Sivananda Ashram is 150 miles from San Francisco International Airport. Carpools are available; call the San Francisco Sivananda Yoga Center (415-681-2731). The ashram is 57 miles from the Sacramento airport, where you can catch the Foothill Flyer shuttle service (800-464-0808, 530-878-0808). Or take Amtrak to Lake of the Pines and call the ashram for pickup.

Rates $45–$90 per person per night. Dormitory $40–$45 per person per night. Camping $35 per person per night.

Contact 14651 Ballantree Lane, Grass Valley, CA 95949; tel: 800-469-9642, 530-272-9322; fax: 530-477-6054; www.sivananda.org.

The Expanding Light of Ananda   Nevada City, California

The grounds of Ananda Village are stunning and as beautiful as the photos depict them to be. Lotus Lake is a lovely secluded place to spend quiet time. The food has to be experienced to be believed.

I like how the yoga instructors gear the classes toward each person's individual ability to go into the postures. The instructors provide gentle guidance, soothing voices, and good examples, with no pressure to go beyond one's own abilities.

I've been worked on by at least half a dozen [massage] practitioners through the Center for Radiant Health and find them all sensitive to the requests I have for specific attention to different parts of my body.

—Lila Devi, founder, Master's Flower Essences, Nevada City, California

The Expanding Light is part of Ananda Village, a spiritual living cooperative founded in 1968 by Swami Kriyananda (J. Donald Walters). The village has 250 members living on 800 acres of land. Ananda includes homes, businesses (community-owned as well as privately owned), and a school for children. Expanding Light, in the Sierra Nevada foothills, is 20 minutes from the Yuba River and 90 minutes from Lake Tahoe. The daily schedule includes morning, afternoon, and evening meditation, chanting, two or more yoga sessions, three vegetarian meals, and the opportunity to take classes. You can participate as much or as little as you like. All programs are based on the teachings of Paramhansa Yogananda, author of the spiritual classic *Autobiography of a Yogi*.

If it isn't completely booked, visit or stay in Harmony House. Each deluxe guest room is decorated to reflect one of the major world religions.

Guest Yoga Teachers? Yes. Including Nischala Joy Devi.

Types of Yoga Classes Ananda. Twice daily. No extra charge.

Services The Center for Radiant Health offers massage, energy work, counseling, and astrological readings. Call 530-478-7549 for reservations and information.

Other Classes Meditation, pranayama, chanting.

Recreation Swimming nearby, hiking.

Children's Program? No.

Accommodations Deluxe rooms with private baths, rooms with shared baths, cabins, camping.

Dining Included. Vegetarian.

Attire/What to Bring Modest yoga attire, yoga mat, hiking boots, sun/insect protection, swimsuit.

Travel Information Ananda is 80 miles from the Sacramento airport and 100 miles from the Reno airport. Call Foothill Flyer (800-464-0808, 530-878-0808) in advance for shuttle service to and from Ananda.

Rates $68–$206 per person per night. Camping $36–$84 per person per night.

Contact 14618 Tyler Foote Road, Nevada City, CA 95959; tel: 800-346-5350, 530-478-7518; fax: 530-478-7519; www.expandinglight.org.

Mount Madonna Center   Watsonville, California

The Mount Madonna Center is located on 355 acres of meadows and redwood forests in the Santa Cruz mountains, with views of Monterey Bay. The center is inspired by the teachings of Baba Hari Dass and sponsored by the Hanuman Fellowship, a community "designed to nurture the creative arts and the health sciences within a context of personal and spiritual growth." At Mount Madonna Center, the primary goal is to attain peace. Community life is guided by the spiritual discipline of Ashtanga yoga and karma yoga (selfless service). The center hosts both personal and group retreats. Weekend programs with visiting teachers are offered throughout the year.

When not in yoga class, guests can hike, swim, hot tub, and play tennis, volleyball, and basketball. The Kaya Kalpa Wellness Center offers massage, Ayurveda treatments, facials, and acupuncture.

Guest Yoga Teachers? Yes. Including Rama Berch, Edward Espe Brown, Rosalyn Bruyere, Emilie Conrad-Da'oud, Gay and Kathy Hendrick,

Mount Madonna is located on acres of wonderful rolling hills about 10 miles from the ocean. The meals are tasty, simple, and vegetarian. The accommodations are basic but comfortable. Once you're there, you realize that this is a functioning spiritual community, not a resort. There is a main meeting room, hot tub, and rec center, complete with kids running around. When you visit, keep in mind that not all the full-time residents serve guests; you may want to find a guest liaison to handle your requests rather than approaching the first person you see.

—Todd Jones, *Yoga Journal* senior editor

Jack Kornfield, Judith Lasater, Stephen Levine, Dan Millman, Zalman Schachter, Patricia Sullivan.

Types of Yoga Classes Ashtanga. One to two times daily. No extra charge.

Services Ayurvedic treatments, massage, facials, acupuncture.

Other Classes Pranayama, meditation, *Bhagavad Gita*, philosophy, chanting.

Recreation Hiking, swimming, volleyball, tennis, basketball, gym, hot tub.

Children's Program? No.

Accommodations Singles, doubles, triples, and dormitory; private and shared bathrooms. Camping available and tents are provided, if needed.

Dining Included. Vegetarian.

Attire/What to Bring Modest yoga attire, towel, flashlight, alarm clock, swimsuit, hiking boots, sun/insect protection.

Travel Information Mount Madonna center is 40 miles from the San Jose International Airport.

Rates $51–$104 per person per night. Camping $30–$37 per person per night.

Contact 445 Summit Road, Watsonville, CA 95076; tel: 408-847-0406; fax: 408-847-2683; www.mountmadonna.org.

COLORADO

Shoshoni Yoga Retreat   Rollinsville, Colorado

Shoshoni is a residential ashram and spiritual retreat center 35 minutes west of Boulder. If it's high country vistas, pure spring water, and fresh alpine air you're looking for, this is the place. The lodge and cabins are surrounded by wildflowers in spring and summer. In colder months, you'll more than likely spot deer and elk. Shoshoni's founder is Sri Shambhavananda Yogi, a meditation master.

Daily classes include hatha yoga, pranayama, meditation, and chanting. Weekend retreats include three meals daily, accommodations, two yoga classes, and two meditation sessions. Unlike at other ashrams, participation in the daily schedule is not mandatory. Guests can attend as many, or as few, classes as they like.

The health therapies center offers massage, facials, and Ayurveda treatments.

Guest Yoga Teachers? No.

Types of Yoga Classes Hatha. Two to three times daily. No extra charge.

Services Herbal wraps, body treatments, Ayurveda, siddha vaidya (an Indian system of health therapies), shirodhara, massage, facials.

Other Classes Meditation, chanting, pranayama.

Recreation Hiking, horseback riding, skiing.

Children's Program? No.

Accommodations Private and dormitory-style cabins.

Dining Included. Vegetarian and Ayurvedic. Special diets, such as vegan or wheat-free, can be accommodated.

Attire/What to Bring Warm clothing for all seasons, modest yoga attire, swimsuit, slippers, hiking boots, sun/insect protection.

Travel Information The Denver International Airport is about a two-hour drive away. Rent a car or take public transportation to the nearby town of Nederland, where a staff member will meet you.

Rates $75–$155 per person per night. Camping $55 per person per night.

Contact PO Box 410, Rollinsville, CO 80474; tel: 303-642-0116; www.shoshoni.org.

Although the residents at Shoshoni follow a particular guru, he doesn't reside there all the time. They're not dogmatic, but the whole place is wrapped around the teachings of Sri Shambhavananda Yogi. It is definitely more of an ashram setting. There are chants, organized meditation, and devotional practices. But there is also time to enjoy hiking and the hot tub. My wife and I rented a cabin that was very nice and a short walk to the yoga room. Yoga was taught by a member of the Shoshoni community.

—Tim Noworyta, copywriter, editor, and yoga teacher, Chicago, Illinois

NEW YORK

Ananda Ashram   Monroe, New York

Although Ananda Ashram was founded in 1964 by Shri Brahmananda Sarasvati, teachers specializing in different styles of yoga have been holding retreats here since its inception. Jivamukti founders David Life and Sharon Gannon often host Thanksgiving workshops here.

The ashram is on 85 acres of woods, rolling meadows, and orchards in the foothills of the Catskill Mountains, just over one hour from New York City.

Guests can take part in daily meditation programs and ongoing classes in hatha yoga, Sanskrit, and classical Indian dance, as well as weekend workshops, retreats, and cultural performances. A typical day includes three meals, three hours of yoga, and three meditation sessions.

The facilities include guest and resident accommodations, a vegetarian kitchen, classrooms, meditation rooms, a program hall, book and gift shop, natural healing center, swimming pool, and publication center. Three guest houses provide simple dormitories (six people per room) and semiprivate rooms (two people per room), for a total of 45 guests. All bathrooms are shared. Camping available in season.

I've been to the Ananda Ashram twice because my teacher conducts retreats there. It's a beautiful area with great hiking and camping. They even have massage and reflexology, which you wouldn't expect at an ashram. The meals are simple but delicious vegetarian. I especially enjoyed the Sanskrit class and amazing talks at night.

—Denise Canter, prop stylist,
  New York City

Guest Yoga Teachers? Yes. Including Krishna Das, Kudrat Kaur (Vanessa Weinberg), Sharon Gannon, Vasant Lad, Ruth Lauer, David Life.

Types of Yoga Classes Ananda yoga. One to three times daily. No extra charge.

Services Ayurvedic facials and massage, shiatsu, acupressure, foot reflexology, aromatherapy.

Other Classes Meditation, chanting, Sanskrit.

Recreation Swimming, hiking, sauna.

Children's Program? No.

Accommodations Dormitories or semiprivate rooms for 45 guests.

Dining Included. Three lacto-vegetarian meals daily.

Attire/What to Bring Comfortable, modest clothing for meditation and yoga or other exercise, warm clothing and firm shoes for outdoors, sun/insect protection, swimsuit, flashlight, alarm clock, toiletries, notebook, and a mat or blanket for outdoor use. Bring an extra towel if you require more than one per week.

Travel Information Ananda Ashram is located 50 miles from New York City.

Rates $55–$80 per person per night (on weekends).

Contact 13 Sapphire Road, Monroe, NY 10950; tel: 845-782-5575; anandaashram.org.

Shree Muktananda Ashram South Fallsburg, New York

Siddha Yoga's Shree Muktananda Ashram, in the Catskill Mountains of New York, has provided thousands of people with a place to practice yoga and meditation for more than 20 years. Swami Muktananda modeled the retreat after the ashrams of India.

Numerous places on the grounds, such as meditation and chanting caves, silent study areas, and hatha yoga facilities, are devoted to Siddha yoga and other spiritual practices. The ashram is also home to the temple of Baba Muktananda's guru, Bhagawan Nityananda.

Shree Muktananda Ashram offers short spiritual retreats. The ashram schedule is based on a way of life described in the Indian scriptures and includes chanting, meditation, study, selfless service, and contemplation. Hatha yoga classes are also available each day. Check the daily schedule board when you arrive at the ashram.

Accommodations include separate men's and women's dormitory-style rooms furnished with bunk beds. A limited number of single rooms are available. For each visit, ashram guests receive one linen packet including a towel. Guests clean their own rooms and care for their allotted linen. Laundry facilities are available.

Guest Yoga Teachers? Yes. Including John Friend, Kevin Gardiner, Judith Lasater, Aadil Palkhivala, Patricia Walden.

Types of Yoga Classes Hatha. Once or twice daily. No extra charge.

Services N/A.

Other Classes Chanting, meditation.

Recreation Meditation walks, walking.

Children's Program? No.

Accommodations Dorms, single rooms, and double rooms.

Dining Included. Vegetarian.

Attire/What to Bring Modest yoga attire (modest dress is required at all times; shorts, short skirts, and sleeveless or sheer tops are not appropriate ashram attire), warm clothes, rain gear, flashlights, earplugs, battery alarm clock, hiking boots, sun/insect protection.

Travel Information Shree Muktananda Ashram is located in the Catskill Mountains about 90 miles northwest of New York City.

Rates Call for rates.

Contact 371 Brickman Road, South Fallsburg, NY 12779; tel: 845-434 2000; www.siddhayoga.org/shree-muktananda-ashram.html.

At Shree Muktananda, there are three large buildings, former Catskills resort hotels, with about 100 acres of grounds, a lake, and meditation gardens and walks.

Siddha Yoga hatha yoga is similar to Iyengar and Anusara yoga. Generally, several asana classes are taught: beginning and intermediate asana practice, a stretch class, and restorative. The yoga studio is state of the art, holds 200 people, and is often used for ashram-sponsored yoga retreats with visiting teachers like John Friend, Kevin Gardner, Patricia Walden, Judith Lasater, and Aadil Palkhivala.

Shree Muktananda ashram is a spiritual retreat center, offering space for private retreats and holding a number of guided weekend and five-day retreats throughout the year. Weekend meditation intensives, courses, and programs with Siddha Yoga swamis and other teachers are offered.

—A meditation teacher, Carmel, California

Sivananda Ashram Yoga Ranch   Woodbourne, New York

The Sivananda Ashram Yoga Ranch is on 77 acres of woodlands in the Catskill Mountains. Visitors can cross-country ski, hike, or go from the lake to the sauna and back again in summer months. Water for drinking and bathing comes from an artesian well. An organic garden and greenhouse produce many of the kitchen's fruits and vegetables.

The day begins at 6 AM with morning meditation and yoga. Brunch is served at 10 AM. There is yoga again at 4 PM and a meditation session before bed. Lights-out is at 10:30 PM. All guests are required to attend both yoga classes and both meditation sessions. The schedule is based on Swami Vishnu-devananda's five points for a long and healthy life: proper exercise, proper breathing, proper relaxation, proper diet, and positive thinking and

One of the great things about Sivananda Ashram Yoga Ranch is that they have a shuttle bus that leaves from their Manhattan yoga center on Fridays, so it easy to get there. The themed weekends—like Ayurveda, meditation, cross-country skiing—are great. The grounds are very pretty and woodsy. They have an incredible wood-burning sauna and a lake for swimming. There are two guest buildings: a turn-of-the-century farmhouse and a small 1920s hotel. Both have simple shared rooms, with separate baths. Camping is also available.

The food is good, wholesome, fulfilling, and vegetarian, with a slight Indian slant. Salad, a soup, and a cooked grain are always offered.

The dorms are pretty basic, with shared bathrooms. The rooms are a little nicer than the other Sivananda ashrams I've been to. It is modest—they're like the Hindi version of the Amish. They do have a lot of international teachers, because they are always moving their instructors around.

—Susan Cohen, yoga teacher and publicist, New York

meditation. Guests are required to practice karma yoga (selfless service) by volunteering an hour per day to the upkeep of the ashram. This could include kitchen duties, gardening, cleaning, etc.

Guest Yoga Teachers? No.

Types of Yoga Classes Included. Sivananda. Twice daily. Also studies in raja (yoga of meditation), karma (selfless service), bhakti (yoga of devotion), jnana (yoga of knowledge). No extra charge.

Services Massage and shiatsu.

Other Classes Chanting, meditation, lectures, satsang, teacher training.

Recreation Hiking, swimming, sauna, cross-country skiing.

Children's Program? Yes. Children are welcome and encouraged. Teen Camp (July), ages 10–16.

Accommodations Shared rooms, with separate baths. Camping available.

Dining Included. Two buffet-style, lacto-vegetarian meals daily. No meat, fish, fowl, eggs, garlic, onions, tea, and coffee.

Attire/What to Bring Modest yoga clothes; a modest bathing suit for the sauna, sweat lodge, and lake; a towel, house slippers, and shoes suitable for walking in the woods; sun/insect protection; cold weather gear in winter. Bring your own yoga mat or rent one.

Travel Information The Yoga Ranch is 100 miles from New York City. Every Friday at 6 PM a van departs from the Sivananda Yoga Center on West 24th Street and returns Sunday afternoon. Cost is $50 roundtrip. Call 845-436-6492 for reservations.

Rates Shared rooms $55–$60 per person per night. Camping $40–$45 per person per night.

Contact PO Box 195, Budd Road, Woodbourne, NY 12788; tel: 845-436-6492, fax: 845-434-1032, www.sivananda.org.

Pack a Mini Medicine Kit Include Tiger Balm for headaches and muscle tension in the skull and neck. Apply the salve to tender pressure points, according to Sharol Tilgner, N.D., an herbalist based in Creswell, Oregon. An especially active trip may lead to muscle aches, sprains, and strains, and homeopathic arnica gel will come in handy to hasten healing. —K.F.M.

TEXAS

Barsana Dham   Austin, Texas

Barsana Dham is a Hindu temple and retreat center on 200 acres of land, 30 minutes southwest of downtown Austin. It is the main U.S. center devoted to the teachings of Jagadguru Kripalu Parishat and was established in 1990.

A tour of the grounds reveals vegetable and flower gardens, more than 25 resident peacocks, and walking trails. The food is vegetarian, and meals are balanced between American and traditional Indian fare. Typically, participants choose to dine outdoors, weather permitting, at the picnic tables.

More than 60 devotees live here year-round. Accommodations are ashram-style (men housed separately from women). Barsana Dham can accommodate about 180 overnight guests. Accommodations range from dorms with bunk beds to rooms with two or three beds and a shared bathroom to single rooms with a private bathroom. Linens and towels are provided.

At various times throughout the year, Barsana Dham offers special weekend family retreats, mini intensives, and seva weekends (selfless service). In the past, these retreats and special programs have included Hindi and yoga classes or summer dance camp. Individual guests not attending a workshop are expected to attend twice-daily satsang, at 7:30 AM and 7:30 PM.

Guest Yoga Teachers? Yes. Including Swami Atma, Donna Belk, Nina Beucler, Robert Boustany, Lori Chapman, Stacey Childers, Pat Colonna, Mala Cunningham, Dr. Robert Francis, Suzannah Garza, Billie Gollnick, Peggy Kelly, Sat Nam Kaur Khalsa, Barbara Kohn, Charles MacInerney, Natalie Maisel, Sharon Moon, Tara O'Neill, Suzy Shapiro, Katie Smith, Paul K. Smith, Gerry Starnes, David Sunshine, Esther Vexler, Dr. Jackson Wagnon.

Types of Yoga Classes Depends on retreat.

Services N/A.

Other Classes Meditation, Hindi, chanting.

Recreation Walking trails.

Children's Program? No.

Accommodations Dorms and shared rooms for up to 180 guests.

Dining Vegetarian. Included.

Attire/What to Bring Modest clothes and yoga attire (no shorts, short skirt, sleeveless shirts), house slippers, sun/insect protection, walking shoes.

At the ashram, I offer hatha yoga and meditation retreats, yoga and creative writing retreats, 10-day yoga teacher training intensives, and an annual Texas yoga retreat, featuring more than 30 teachers from across the state and beyond and 200 to 300 participants. In addition to practicing hatha yoga, we also practice a wide variety of meditations, including eating, walking, breath awareness, visualization, somatic, and more traditional forms of sitting meditation. We also have workshops on a variety of topics like pranayama (breath control), pratyahara (sense withdrawal), dharana (concentration), mind mapping, and creative writing.

Barsana Dham has an excellent yoga teacher on staff. Chris Dionisi has been teaching hatha yoga since 1986 and is a certified graduate of the Living Yoga Teacher Training Program and is registered with the Yoga Alliance.

The grounds are open for visitors to hike and explore. There are wonderful walkways and trails to explore. When you come over a hill, the temple dome glitters in the distance. The temple is available all day for students to look around or to meditate. Regular Hindu services are open to the public, and guests are invited to participate if they wish to.

—Charles MacInerney, yoga teacher, Austin, Texas

Travel Information Barsana Dham is 30 minutes from the Austin airport.

Rates Contact for rate information.

Contact 400 Barsana Road, Austin, TX 78737; tel: 512-288-7180; www.barsanadham.org.

VIRGINIA

Satchidananda Ashram (Yogaville) Buckingham, Virginia

In 1979, Swami Satchidananda, the guru who opened the Woodstock festival by calling music "the celestial sound that controls the whole universe," acquired 600 acres in Buckingham County, Virginia. He financed the purchase by selling a piece of land in Falls Village, Connecticut, that singer/songwriter Carole King, one of his disciples, had given him. Eventually the ashram acquired more land, and today Yogaville has almost 1,000 acres of woodlands.

A typical day begins at 5 AM with morning meditation, followed by 90 minutes of Integral yoga, then breakfast. Guests can practice karma yoga (selfless service) by volunteering to help with the upkeep of the ashram. This could include kitchen duties, gardening, cleaning, etc. There is an opportunity to walk or relax before the meditation session, followed by lunch. Dinner is followed by an evening program or satsang on Saturdays.

Integral yoga, created by Swami Satchidananda, is practiced here. It integrates the various branches of yoga (hatha, raja, bhakti, jnana, karma, and japa) in order to "bring about a complete and harmonious development of the individual."

Swami Satchidananda, who died in August 2002, believed "truth is one, paths are many." He sponsored many interfaith symposiums, retreats, and worship services around the world. The Light of Truth Universal Shrine (LOTUS), dedicated to all faiths and to world peace, was opened in 1986 on the Yogaville grounds. Built in the shape of a lotus blossom—the ancient symbol for the spiritual blossoming of the soul—the shrine is a sanctuary for silent meditation, contemplation, and prayer.

An organic farm on property supplies some of the vegetables and herbs used in kitchen.

Guest Yoga Teachers? Yes. Including Kam Thye Chow, Kay Hawkins.

Types of Yoga Classes Integral. Once or twice daily. No extra charge.

Services Massage.

My first visit to Yogaville was for rest and relaxation and spiritual renewal. There is a sense of peace pervading the atmosphere. The ashram is in the country, so there are a lot of trees and views of the Blue Ridge Mountains and the James River. The LOTUS shrine is beautifully situated in a valley with exquisite fountains and surrounded by a view of the mountains and river. Yogaville is an oasis of serenity and spirituality.

My room was simple yet clean; anyone can reserve a private room or dorm. The food was beautifully prepared; some days it was simple vegetarian fare, such as tofu, rice, vegetables, and a beautiful salad bar; other days it was more festive, with dessert and tasty side dishes. I'm a vegetarian, so it suited me well. Breakfast always had lots of fruit, warm cereal or cold, different soy milks, and loads of herbal teas.

The yoga was very enjoyable. There were beginning and intermediate classes available along with morning, noon, and 6 PM meditations. The hatha classes were thorough yet meditative. I did karma yoga by working with various departments offering whatever service they needed, from gardening to office work and receptionist.

—M. Mala Cunningham, Ph.D., assistant professor, School of Medicine, University of Virginia, Charlottesville, Virginia

Other Classes Meditation, Indian dance, holiday cooking, Ayurveda, Thai yoga massage.

Recreation Gardening, hiking, sauna, hot tub.

Children's Program? Yes.

Accommodations Dormitories, private rooms, camping.

Dining Included. Three lacto-vegetarian meals daily.

Attire/What to Bring Modest yoga clothes (no shorts), toiletries (including soap), yoga mat, swimsuit (no bikinis), beach towel, flashlight, alarm clock, indoor slippers, slip-on shoes or sandals for walking between buildings, walking or hiking shoes, sun/insect protection, umbrella.

Travel Information Yogaville is 60 miles from the Charlottesville/Albemarle airport.

Rates $40–$95 per person per night. Discount for children under age 11.

Contact Rt. 1, Box 1720, Buckingham, VA 23921; tel: 800-858-9642, 434-969-3121; www.yogaville.org.

CANADA

Yasodhara Ashram   **Kootenay Bay, British Columbia**

Swami Sivananda Radha (Sylvia Hellman, 1911–1995), founder of Yasodhara Ashram, was born in Berlin and was a successful concert dancer. In 1957, after a time in India, she opened the Sivananda Ashram Vancouver in Burnaby, British Columbia, which was relocated in 1963 to its present location on Kootenay Bay in the Canadian Rockies and renamed Yasodhara Ashram.

Yasodhara trains students in the Kundalini yoga system's Hidden Language approach to hatha yoga, which explores the symbolic meaning of postures and their effect on the psyche and spirit. Swami Radhananda, the successor to Swami Radha and the president of Yasodhara Ashram, keeps the teaching alive.

A typical retreat day at the ashram begins at 7 AM with a hatha yoga class or chanting in the temple, followed by breakfast. Then you are asked to contribute two hours of karma yoga (selfless service) toward the upkeep of the ashram. This could include kitchen duties, gardening, cleaning, etc. After lunch, there is time for one of the following classes: hatha yoga, dreams, the divine light invocation, mantra, Kundalini yoga, dance, or karma yoga. Classes may be individual or in small groups. Dinner is followed

I've been going to the Yasodhara Ashram at least once a year since 1993, and I've been there three times this year to participate in both weekend retreats and weeklong events. I practice at the Radha yoga center in Spokane, so that is what initially attracted me to the ashram. But it is also a place of sanctuary, really spiritual, very peaceful, and the people are wonderful. When you take a course there you can be taught by one of the residents or a teacher visiting from any of the Radha centers around the world. I particularly like to go in August, because there are a lot of teachers from all different countries in to renew their certification, so it is a real international gathering. All ages and religions are drawn there—it is a very tolerant place. During the summer, the garden is amazing, and you get fresh vegetarian fare made from its harvest.

Most times I go by myself, but this year I took my kids, ages five and nine. We weren't there during the summer camp, so they took a hatha yoga class with me, and we all participated in karma yoga. They also helped decorate the temple and attended satsang. They are not vegetarians and they didn't like the food that much, so they ate a lot of granola bars. I like that there are a lot of youths there from high school and also in their twenties. It gives me a lot of hope for the world.

—Holli Brown, homemaker, Spokane, Washington

by satsang (chanting) in the temple. Meditation rooms are available for personal practice. The ashram is known for its comfortable rooms and nourishing meals. Family and group retreats are welcome.

Guest Yoga Teachers? No.

Types of Yoga Classes Kundalini/Hidden Language, dreams, the divine light invocation.

Services N/A.

Other Classes Meditation, dance, mantra.

Recreation Hiking, swimming.

Children's Program? Yes.

Accommodations Shared rooms. Single rooms may be available upon request. No camping facilities.

Dining Included. Three vegetarian meals daily, served in silence. Fish, poultry, and meat are occasionally served.

Attire/What to Bring Modest, loose-fitting yoga attire, outdoor work clothes, waterproof footwear, slippers for indoors, a flashlight, an alarm clock, and a phone card if you plan to make calls.

Travel Information Daily connector flights from the international airports in both Calgary and Vancouver go to Castlegar. Except on Sundays, the airport limousine will take you to Nelson and a local bus will take you to the ferry at Balfour. The ashram will pick you up at the ferry landing at Kootenay Bay. Driving takes eight hours from Calgary, four from Spokane.

Rates $95 per person per day plus $25 deposit per day. Deposits are required when you make your reservation. The balance is payable on arrival. The deposit guarantees your place and is usually not refundable.

Contact Yasodhara Ashram, 527 Walkers Landing Rd., Kootenay Bay, B.C., Canada V0B 1X0; tel: 800-661-8711; fax: 250-227-9494; www.yasodhara.org.

Salt Spring Centre of Yoga   Salt Spring Island, British Columbia

The Salt Spring Centre, on 70 acres off Canada's west coast, was established in 1981 by the Dharmasara Satsang Society, a group guided by the common practice of classical Ashtanga yoga as taught by Baba Hari Dass. The Salt Spring Centre holds yoga workshops and classes in the creative and healing arts, offers Ayurveda treatments, massage, and reflexology, and is home to a small residential community and the Salt Spring Centre School. Although the majority of members and center residents are students of Baba Hari Dass, no commitment to a spiritual tradition or teacher is required to participate in any of the activities. Visitors are asked to participate in karma yoga (selfless service). This could include kitchen duties, gardening, cleaning, etc.

Accommodations are for those who are registered for a workshop, so make the proper arrangements before you arrive. The public may attend daily yoga classes or book a health treatment at the Healing Arts Studio without being an overnight guest.

Guest Yoga Teachers? Yes. Including Andrea Kalpana Tabachnick.

Types of Yoga Classes Classical Ashtanga. Once or twice daily. No extra charge.

Services Ayurvedic swedan, massage, reflexology.

Other Classes Satsang.

Recreation Swimming, kayaking, hiking, volleyball, basketball, trail walks.

Children's Program? Yes. Parent-assisted kid's program for ages 3 to 12. Youth program offers yoga classes and recreational activities for teens during annual retreat.

Accommodations Dormitory style. 21 beds, one private room. Camping available.

Dining Included. Vegetarian.

Attire/What to Bring Modest yoga attire, toiletries, slippers or indoor shoes, a bathrobe, swimsuit, walking/hiking shoes, flashlight, rain clothes, sun/insect protection.

Travel Information Fly into Vancouver airport, then take Tswassen Ferry to Swartz Bay on Vancouver Island, transferring to Fulford Harbour Ferry. For information or reservations, call 888-BC Ferry (223-3779) or go to www.bcferries.com on the Web.

Rates $37–$60 per person per night.

Contact 355 Blackburn Rd., Salt Spring Island, BC, V8K 2B8 Canada; tel: 250-537-2326; fax: 250-537-2311; www.saltspringcentre.com.

I decided to go to the Salt Spring Centre because my best friend and I wanted to go away for the weekend to a place that would replenish our flagging energies.

Morning yoga classes were offered, instructed by two different teachers. The first class was restorative yoga. Since most of the female guests were tired (it was a women's retreat), the restorative yoga was a good way to start. I felt the benefits of stress reduction, mental peace, and calmness after the hour class. Not all the guests attended the morning class, since some preferred to sleep in. There was no pressure to participate in center activities. The next morning yoga class was taught by a different instructor and was more active.

The next day, we had reflexology treatments, but the piece de resistance was the swedan treatment, which included a warm sesame oil massage, a sauna session, and exfoliation.

—Connie Gibbs, educational programs coordinator, Vancouver

Sivananda Ashram Yoga Camp in Val-Morin is a large ashram with many buildings spread out over many, many acres. There is both a Subramanya and a Krishna temple on the grounds, plus a meditation hall. There is even a museum highlighting Swami Vishnu-devananda's peace missions.

The accommodations are hotel-like, and camping is available. The swimming pool is for use in the summer. The surrounding area is rural, with low mountains. It is very beautiful. I taught a 10-day program on Ayurveda at the ashram.

The food is vegetarian but not always Indian. Meals occur twice per day and include a large buffet of choices. There is a boutique for the purchase of snacks. In Val-Moran, you can hike, swim, and canoe when not participating in ashram activities.

—Marc Halpern, D.C., founder and director, California College of Ayurveda, Grass Valley, California

Sivananda Ashram Yoga Camp   Val-Morin, Quebec

The Sivananda Ashram Yoga Camp was founded by Swami Vishnu-devananda in 1963 and is the headquarters for the International Sivananda Yoga Vendata Centers. The ashram is located one hour north of Montreal on 250 forested acres. Views of the Laurentian Mountains and the serenity of the camp make this an ideal setting to practice yoga. Free time can be spent hiking, cycling, or swimming in summer, or skiing, snowshoeing, and skating in winter.

The day begins at 6 AM with morning meditation and yoga. Brunch is served at 10 AM. There is yoga again at 4 PM and a meditation session before bed. Lights-out is at 10 PM. All guests are required to attend both yoga classes and both meditation sessions. The schedule is based on Swami Vishnu-devananda's five points for a long and healthy life: proper exercise, proper breathing, proper relaxation, proper diet, and positive thinking and meditation. Guests are required to practice karma yoga (selfless service) by volunteering an hour per day to the upkeep of the ashram. This could include kitchen duties, gardening, cleaning, etc.

Guest Yoga Teachers? No.

Types of Yoga Classes Sivananda. Twice daily. Also studies in raja (yoga of meditation), karma (selfless service), bhakti (yoga of devotion), jnana (yoga of knowledge). No extra charge.

Services N/A.

Other Classes Chanting, meditation, lectures, satsang, pranayama, diet.

Recreation Hiking, cycling, swimming, horseback riding, and canoeing in the summer; skiing, snowshoeing, and skating in the winter.

Children's Program? Yes. Children always welcome but must be supervised. Children's summer camp in July, family week in August.

Accommodations 22 rooms with 62 dormitory beds, cabins, private rooms, camping.

Dining Included. Two buffet-style, lacto-vegetarian meals daily. No meat, fish, fowl, eggs, garlic, onions, tea, and coffee.

Attire/What to Bring Cool weather wear, waterproof jacket, modest yoga attire, yoga mat, slip-on sandals, swimsuit, sun/insect protection, extra towels, flashlight, modest bathing suit.

Travel Information The Sivananda Ashram Yoga Camp is 55 miles from

Montreal. Take a Voyageur bus from downtown to Val-Morin and then a short taxi ride to the camp.

Rates $30–$47 per person per night.

Contact 673 8th Ave., Val-Morin, Quebec JOT 2RO Canada; tel: 819-322-3226; www.sivananda.org.

ASIA

Sivananda Yoga Vedanta Dhanwanthari Ashram   Kerala, India

Sivananda Yoga Vedanta Dhanwanthari ashram was originally an Ayurvedic clinic, built by the late Sri Gopala Vaidyar 40 years ago. The Ayurvedic scriptures on the walls were painted by Vaidyar and remain today. In 1977, Swami Vishnu-devanandaji bought the clinic and opened the ashram in 1978. In the nearby village is a free nursery school run by the ashram.

Yoga vacations begin on the first and fifteenth of every month and last two weeks. The day begins at 6 AM with morning meditation. There is yoga at 8 AM and 4 PM and a meditation session before bed. Meals are served at 10 AM and 6 PM. Lights out is at 10:30 PM. All guests are required to attend both yoga classes and both meditation sessions. The schedule is based on Swami Vishnu-devananda's five points for a long and healthy life: proper exercise, proper breathing, proper relaxation, proper diet, and positive thinking and meditation. Guests are required to practice karma yoga (selfless service) by volunteering each day to the upkeep of the ashram. This could include kitchen duties, gardening, cleaning, etc.

Ayurveda treatments are available. The ashram also offers a three-week tour of the spiritual and cultural centers of southern India.

Guest Yoga Teachers? No.

Types of Yoga Classes Sivananda. Twice daily. Also studies in raja (yoga of meditation), karma (selfless service), bhakti (yoga of devotion), jnana (yoga of knowledge). No extra charge.

Services Ayurveda treatments.

Other Classes Chanting, meditation, lectures, satsang, pranayama, diet.

Recreation Walking, cultural trips.

Children's Program? Yes. Kids' Camp once a year, from mid-April to mid-May, for ages 7 to 14.

Accommodations Kailash (double room with private bathroom), hut (double

Two weeks after I lost my job, I enrolled in a Sivananda Yoga teacher training course in Neyyar Dam, India. I felt the experience would give me the discipline and strength to go inward and, ultimately, provide me with tools to live a happier and more rewarding life. When I arrived, it was quite clear that I was completely unprepared. The bathroom was a dark room with a squat toilet. My Lycra tights, tank tops, and summer dresses were completely inappropriate for an ashram. I was given a uniform of a yellow T-shirt and white baggy pants. All of the classes, lectures, and even meals take place on the floor in the open-air temple, which is a beautiful building in the middle of the ashram. The teacher training was very rigorous and it took me a while to get acclimated to the climate and air quality.

The food is fabulous. It is traditional southern Indian food, which you won't find at U.S. ashrams. There are only two meals a day, but they are pretty liberal with serving sizes. There's a little cafe on site where you can buy lassis, fruit salad, cookies, and candy. The cafe was a social place, and even had Internet access.

—Susan Cohen, yoga teacher and publicist, New York

room with common bathroom), dormitory (about 30 people together) with shared bathroom; men and women separate. Camping available (bring your own tent).

Dining Included. Two lacto-vegetarian meals daily. No meat, fish, fowl, eggs, garlic, onions, tea, and coffee.

Attire/What to Bring Modest yoga attire; no tight or see-through clothing; legs, upper arms, and stomach must be covered at all times. Men are required to wear a shirt. Yoga mat, slip-on sandals, modest swimsuit, sun/insect protection, flashlight, sheets, sleeping bag, mosquito netting, towel.

Travel Information Daily flights from Bombay (Mumbai), New Delhi, and Madras (Chennai) to Trivandrum (Thiruvananthapuram) are available. From the airport, take a taxi ($9) or auto rickshaw ($5) to the Ashram 25 miles (40 kilometers) away.

Rates Two-week stay $8–$13.

Contact Neyyar Dam P.O. Thiruvananthapuram Dist., Kerala 695 572 India; tel: 011-91-471-273-093; fax: 011-91-471-227-2039; www.sivananda.org.

CARIBBEAN

Sivananda Ashram Yoga Retreat   Paradise Island, Bahamas

Because of its location, the Sivananda Ashram Yoga Retreat on Paradise Island is one of the most visited ashrams. Located on five acres of private beach and accessible by boat, the ashram is extremely popular with young urban professionals, especially during special retreats such as the Christmas/New Year event. People who study all types of yoga seem to be drawn to this place. You can even request semiprivate beachfront rooms. The rolling sounds of the sea, the soft breezes, and the daily practice of yoga and meditation combine to produce a spiritual atmosphere. Many yoga classes take place on a wooded platform that overlooks the ocean. When it is hot, yoga is practiced in a covered studio that overlooks the bay.

The day begins at 6 AM with morning meditation, chanting, and yoga. Brunch is served at 10 AM. There is yoga again at 4 PM and a meditation session before bed. Lights-out is at 10 PM. All guests are required to attend both yoga classes and both meditation sessions. The schedule is based on Swami Vishnu-devananda's five points for a long and healthy life: proper exercise, proper breathing, proper relaxation, proper diet, and positive thinking and meditation. Guests can practice karma yoga (selfless service) by volunteering an hour per day to the upkeep of the ashram. This could include kitchen duties, gardening, cleaning, etc.

Guest Yoga Teachers? No. Guest lectures from Bhagavan Das, Krishna Das, Nischala Joy Devi, Marc Halpern.

Types of Yoga Classes Sivananda. Twice daily. Also studies in raja (yoga of meditation), karma (selfless service), bhakti (yoga of devotion), jnana (yoga of knowledge). No extra charge.

Services Massage, reflexology.

Other Classes Meditation, pranayama.

Recreation Swimming, tennis, volleyball, basketball, snorkeling.

Children's Program? Yes. Yoga for children.

Accommodations 103 dormitory beds, beach huts, cabins, camping.

Dining Included. Two buffet-style, lacto-vegetarian meals daily. No meat, fish, fowl, eggs, garlic, onions, tea, and coffee.

Attire/What to Bring Modest yoga attire, towel, bathing suit, sandals, sun/insect protection, yoga mat, meditation shawl, flashlight.

Travel Information Fly into Nassau. Take a taxi to the Paradise Island Ferry Terminal. The ashram will send its boat to meet you, so be sure to call from the airport to announce your arrival.

Rates $59–$99 per person per night. Camping $50 per person per night. Children under age 12 are half price; no charge for children under age 3.

Contact Box N7550, Paradise Island, Nassau Bahamas; tel: 800-441-2096, 242-363-2902; fax: 242- 363-3783; www.sivananda.org.

Paradise Island Sivananda Ashram is very basic, no frills. I got a room of my own (top of the line), and it was incredibly monastic. The beach is fabulous—the view from the beach platform (where some classes are held) is incredible. The food is veggie/ vegan—tons of soy, which I kept tasting throughout the day—and definitely nothing contraband like alcohol, caffeine, processed foods, chocolate, etc. Unfortunately, I went on my own and happened to choose a week during which a six-week teacher's training was happening, so basically almost everyone in the place had already bonded. The agenda is really hard-core—you have to show up to all yoga classes (two a day, including one two-hour class before breakfast) and two satsang (chanting) sessions. This all happened before I studied anything about yoga, too, so it was a real shock. Now I wouldn't see it as extreme.

—Lorie Parch, writer/editor , Woodland Hills, California

EUROPE

Sivananda Yoga Vedanta Seminarhaus   Tyrol, Austria

The Tyrolean village of Reith in the Austrian Alps boasts winter sports, pristine mountain lakes, and numerous hiking trails. Nearby, the Sivananda Yoga Vedanta Retreat House offers the classical yoga teachings of Swami Sivananda and Swami Vishnu-devananda, which emphasize asanas, pranayama, Vedanta philosophy, meditation, and a vegetarian diet. Classes are taught in English and German. A few kilometers away, the health spa at Kitzbühel has an indoor swimming pool, massages, and mud baths.

The Sivananda Yoga Vedanta Seminarhaus is blessed with a stunningly beautiful setting reminiscent of a scene from the movie The Sound of Music. The ashram is surrounded by rolling green hills, with the distant peaks of the Alps rising behind them. There is a meditation temple, administrative building, and hotel-like accommodations. Nearby are several beautiful small Austrian towns to visit.

The food is vegetarian but not always Indian. Meals occur twice per day and include a large buffet of choices. There is a boutique for the purchase of snacks. The nearby skiing is some of the best in the world. I was there in the summer, however, and did not ski, but I did go hiking.

—Marc Halpern, D.C., founder and director, California College of Ayurveda, Grass Valley, California

The day begins at 6 AM with morning meditation and, later, yoga. Brunch is served at 10 AM. There is yoga again at 4 PM and a meditation session before bed. Lights-out is at 10 PM. All guests are required to attend both yoga classes and both meditation sessions. The schedule is based on Swami Vishnu-devananda's five points for a long and healthy life: proper exercise, proper breathing, proper relaxation, proper diet, and positive thinking and meditation. Guests are required to practice karma yoga (selfless service) by volunteering an hour per day to the upkeep of the ashram. This could include kitchen duties, gardening, cleaning, etc.

Guest Yoga Teachers? No.

Types of Yoga Classes Sivananda. Twice daily. Also studies in raja (yoga of meditation), karma (selfless service), bhakti (yoga of devotion), jnana (yoga of knowledge). No extra charge.

Services Massage.

Other Classes Chanting, meditation, lectures, satsang, pranayama.

Recreation Cross-country skiing, skiing, hiking, swimming.

Children's Program? No.

Accommodations Dorms and single rooms for up to 150 people.

Dining Included. Two buffet-style, lacto-vegetarian meals daily. No meat, fish, fowl, eggs, garlic, onions, tea, and coffee.

Attire/What to Bring Modest yoga attire, sandals, swimsuit, sunblock, ski attire in winter, hiking boots, meditation shawl.

Travel Information Fly into the Innsbruck airport.

Rates Dormitory $30 per person. Shared rooms (3 beds) $34 per person. Double room $44 per person. Single room $53 per person.

Contact Reith bei Kitzbühel, Am Bichlachweg 40 A, 6370 Reith bei Kitzbühel, Tirol, Österreich; tel: 011-43-53-566-7404; fax: 011-43-53-566-7405; www.sivananda.org.

Ananda Assisi   Assisi, Italy

The Ananda retreat is located in the Umbrian hills near Assisi. Weekend and weeklong programs focus on how to integrate meditation into your daily life and the Ananda system of yoga postures. All programs are based on the teachings of Paramhansa Yogananda, author of the spiritual classic *Autobiography of a Yogi.*

The weekend program begins on Friday at 4:30 PM with a yoga and meditation session and continues through Sunday lunch. On Saturday and Sunday, the day begins at 7 AM with yoga and meditation. Midmorning classes are dedicated to a particular theme chosen for that weekend. Evening activities include devotional singing and concerts given by the Ananda World Brotherhood Choir. Five- and seven-day programs are also available. Swami Kriyananda (J. Donald Walters), founder of six Ananda communities and one of the few remaining direct disciples of Yogananda, often gives lectures at the ashram. Guests stay in the main activity center or in country houses 15 minutes away.

Guest Yoga Teachers? No.

Types of Yoga Classes Ananda. Twice daily. No extra charge.

Services N/A.

Other Classes Meditation, introduction to chakras, Ayurveda.

Recreation Hiking.

Children's Program? Yes. Family weeks during the summer (June–August).

Accommodations Double and a few single rooms, with and without baths. Rooms with three to five beds and shared bathroom. Sheets, blankets, and towels are provided.

Dining Included. Vegetarian.

Attire/What to Bring Warm, comfortable clothes for yoga and meditation practice, walking shoes, a warm sweater or jacket, rain gear, flashlight, alarm clock, house slippers, sun/insect protection.

Travel Information The closest international airport is outside of Rome (Fiumicino–Leonardo da Vinci Airport). From the airport, you can take the train to Assisi and then a taxi to Ananda.

Rates $39–$76 per person per night.

Contact via Montecchio 61, I-06025 Gaifana di Nocera Umbra (PG) Italy; tel: 011-39-074-281-3620; fax: 011-39-074-281-3536; www.ananda.it.

Scandinavian Yoga and Meditation School   Hamneda, Sweden

Located in southern Sweden, the Scandinavian Yoga and Meditation School was founded by Danish Swami Janakananda, a disciple of Swami Satyananda. Here, you'll learn yoga and meditation based on the Tantric tradition. The three-month sadhana program involves 33 days of silence.

I went to Ananda Assisi because I felt the need to be in a spiritual environment that would offer me beautiful surroundings, comfortable lodging, the opportunity to meditate and be with other devotees, and access to spiritual counseling, inspirational classes, and talks. The retreat is situated in the beautiful hills outside of Assisi.

I participated in the family week, which drew families from all over the world. The theme of the week this year was love. Every morning began with hatha yoga and meditation for those who wished, followed by breakfast and karma yoga or community service for the entire family. Then there were classes in parenting for the adults and activities for the children. In the afternoon, there were outings for everyone, as well as free time and trips into Assisi. The older children participated in a Scout Program that culminated in an overnight campout.

—Helen Purcell, educator, Mountain View, California

I had been working for a marketing firm in Los Angeles that was dissolving, and I thought I really wanted to change direction and become a yoga teacher. I was a practicing Buddhist, so the Scandinavian Yoga and Meditation School was attractive because it incorporates that as well.

You have to adhere to a strict schedule. The day begins at 5 AM with meditation, followed by yoga asanas. Then there is a light breakfast, followed by karma yoga (selfless service). Yoga nidra meditation is next. You are in savasana for 40 minutes. It is said to be the equivalent of eight hours of sleep.

After lunch, you have two hours of free time. It is suggested you walk or do something creative. They didn't want anyone sleeping or resting. There are more asanas and meditation in the afternoon. After dinner, there are lectures about philosophy or meditation.

The diet is a cleansing diet—mostly vegetables and occasional rice, no spices, no caffeine. Once a week we would go on a 20-kilometer walk.

We began with 40 people in my class, but a lot of people dropped out as the schedule became more rigorous. By the end, you are only sleeping three to five hours a night. They are teaching you to see and overcome the limitations in your mind. The program really changed my life.

—Robyn Wotton, hatha yoga teacher, Newport, Rhode Island

To participate in a one-month Kriya course, you must first complete a 10- or 14-day course. (You can attend the three-month course without having participated in one of the other courses, though.) The Kriya yoga course includes advanced meditations and yoga methods.

The 10- to 14-day courses are attended by those who have never tried yoga and meditation and by those who wish to further their experience. Classes are taught in English, supplemented with Danish or Swedish.

Students stay in traditional Swedish red farmhouses near a lake surrounded by forest and fields. In the snowy season, guests might enjoy ice-skating or a ride through the snow on horseback.

Guest Yoga Teachers? No. Occasional appearances by meditation teachers from India.

Types of Yoga Classes Kriya. Twice daily. No extra charge.

Services No.

Other Classes Meditation, philosophy.

Recreation Sauna, horseback riding, rowing, hiking, cross-country skiing, canoeing.

Children's Program? Yes. If space allows, children are welcome at half the course fee. The school looks after the children during classes and karma yoga periods.

Accommodations Five or six houses with rooms in each house. Some are shared rooms, most are individual. Shared bathrooms.

Dining Included. Vegetarian, organic. In the one- or three-month program, no milk, sugar, spices, raw vegetables, and fruit after 10 days. No coffee, chocolate, black tea, and alcohol.

Attire/What to Bring Cold weather attire is provided. Boots are provided if you don't have them. Bedsheets (quilt, pillow, and sheets) and a towel can also be rented.

Travel Information The nearest international airport is in Copenhagen, Denmark, with connecting trains to Älmhult. The center is $15^1/2$ miles (25 km) from Älmhult.

Rates 10- and 14-day program $630–$665. One-month program $1,134. Three-month program $2,650.

Contact Håå Course Center, S-34013 Hamneda, Sweden; tel: 011-46-372-55-063; fax: 011-46-372-55-036; www.scand-yoga.org.

APPENDIX: IN-FLIGHT YOGA

Ravi Malhota & Char Daigle

Once you step aboard an airplane, you confront a number of challenges. There's the tiny economy-class seat, with its two inches of legroom and its attendant problems: claustrophobia, stiffness, cramps, and a slowed metabolism. Other equally menacing monsters lurking in the cabin are invisible. Viruses and bacteria thrive in the recirculated air. Reduced oxygen levels at high cruising altitudes can produce dizziness, fatigue, headaches, tunnel vision, nausea, and tingling of the hands and feet. Lower-than-sea-level air pressure causes the familiar popping in your ears—it also expands the gases in your abdomen and can make you feel uncomfortably bloated. The desert-dry air at cruising altitudes contains so little moisture that the resulting humidity in the cabin is about 10 percent—making it drier than the Sahara. Dehydration sets in quickly; the body loses about eight ounces of water every hour.

And of course, there's the demon of jet lag. Flights spanning two or more time zones disrupt the rhythms of your body's natural clock, besetting you with sleepless nights, drowsy days, and the forgetfulness, confusion, and sluggishness that accompany fatigue. Fortunately, you can minimize these problems with preflight preparations and in-flight breathing and stretching exercises. Try these simple in-flight yoga stretches and survival strategies, and you'll arrive at your destination feeling relaxed and refreshed.

Preflight Preparations

Your first line of defense is preparation. If you observe the simple guidelines that follow, you'll be in good shape to withstand the rigors of your flight.

- Increase your water intake in the twelve to twenty-four hours before the flight. Also, avoid diuretics such as caffeinated drinks (coffee, tea, colas) and alcohol.

- In the day or two before your flight, eat easy-to-digest foods such as fruits and vegetables. Once you're aboard, loss of body fluids from dehydration will impede your digestion. (Actually, if you like to fast, this may be the ideal time to start a juice or water fast.)

- You may want to ask for a vegan meal or fruit platter if you are not fasting. (Almost all airlines require a twenty-four-hour notice for a special meal.) In addition, pack a large bottle of water and some healthy snacks for the flight. Again, eating easy-to-digest foods will minimize demands on a digestive system already taxed by inactivity and dehydration.

- A run, aerobics class, or vigorous yoga workout will bring you to the boarding gate in optimum condition—limbs stretched, lungs rejuvenated, and mind relaxed.

- Remember that cabin temperatures are often uncomfortably hot or cold. Dress in layers you can put on and take off with minimal fuss.

- Make sure your clothes are comfortable. Tight-waisted pants and belts are not a good idea, and you may want to wear shoes or sandals you can slip into and out of easily.

- You might also consider stowing a few small creature comforts: a moisturizing cream for your face and body, a water spritzer to spray on your face and hands, a face cloth, some earplugs, and, of course, a toothbrush.

- Request a more spacious seat. Even in economy class, bulkhead and emergency-exit-row seats offer more legroom than ordinary ones (although you can't raise the armrests in emergency-row seating).

- Get to the flight with time to spare. An extra half hour in the airport is a small price to pay to avoid the stress of running for your flight at the last minute.

In-Flight Strategies

You've made it on board and you've located your seat. Your earlier preparations are sure to serve you well; all you need to do now is continue that good work.

- Keep yourself hydrated during your flight. Try to drink sixteen ounces of water for every hour in the air (dehydration will take away half that amount). The extra water will aid your digestion and help wash away any germs you might have inhaled on the plane.

- Avoid caffeine, alcohol, and salty foods. Eat lightly. Eat healthy. Give your body less work to do, and you'll have fewer problems with jet lag.

- Don't forget the kit you packed before your flight: fruit, moisturizing cream, eyedrops, earplugs, etc. All these can improve your time in the air.

- Whenever you can, take the opportunity for a brisk walk up and down the aisles. On some planes, you can find room near the rear doors for standing poses like Trikonasana (Triangle) and Uttanasana (Standing Forward Bend). (It's always a good idea to check in with the flight attendants to make sure you won't be in their way.)

- Finally, recalling that *asana* can be translated as "steady, comfortable seat," take ten minutes every few hours to stretch and revive your body.

Airplane Asanas

Before you start, remove your shoes and make sure your clothes are comfortable and won't restrict your movements. You may want to introduce yourself to your neighbor and explain what you're about to do—they'll probably be more supportive than if you just begin practicing with no warning. You may even find yourself demystifying yoga for someone who thinks of it as an alien, esoteric cult.

Begin by Centering Yourself Sit up tall, with your sitting bones firmly in contact with the seat, feet parallel and planted hip distance apart on the floor. Keep your spine long, your chest open, and your shoulders released back and down. Allow your neck to lengthen and yet fully support your head. Imagine a pocket of air between each arm and your chest. Close your eyes and let your face be soft—forehead smooth, jaw relaxed. Bring awareness to your breath, observing it as it enters and leaves your body.

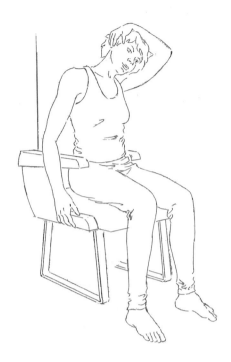

Stretch the Sides of Your Neck Inhaling, lift your right hand over your head. While continuing to stretch your upper arm toward the cabin ceiling, bend at the elbow and place your right fingers (pointing down) on the left side of your head, just above your ear. Exhaling through the nose, let the weight of your right arm stretch the left side of your neck as your right ear moves closer to your right shoulder. Keep both shoulders back and down. Take five breaths and switch sides.

Stretch the Back of Your Neck Interlace your fingers and place your hands on the back of your head (not your neck). Inhaling, sit up tall, with your shoulders relaxed down away from your ears. Exhaling, allow your head and arms to relax forward, with your chin traveling toward your chest. Breathe deeply, letting each exhalation move you more deeply into the pose. After five breaths, release your hands and slowly roll your head up to vertical again.

Stretch Your Arms and the Sides of Your Torso Elongate your lower back, press your belly button back toward your spine, and inhale, stretching your arms overhead. Keep your shoulders back and down. Interlace your fingers and turn your palms toward the ceiling, pressing your sitting bones down while reaching up. Keeping your arms straight alongside your ears, exhale and turn to the right, feeling the stretch on the left side of your ribs and your left hip. Do not collapse on your right side. Take five breaths before repeating to the left.

Stretch Your Upper Back With your arms raised as in the previous pose, inhale and stretch back, opening your chest to the ceiling. Look up toward your hands, being careful not to constrict your neck. Take three breaths and release your arms.

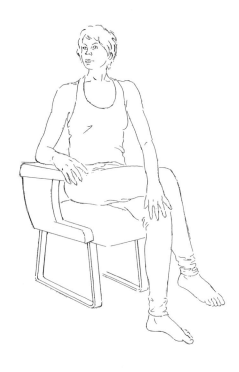

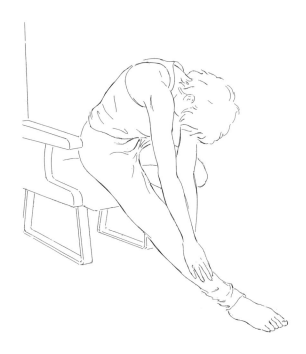

Spinal Twist Cross your right knee over your left knee. Place your left hand on the outside of your right knee and brace your right palm against the right elbow rest. Inhale, lengthening your spine. Then exhale and twist to the right, keeping your left sitting bone firmly grounded. Inhale again, and as you exhale, use your left arm against your knee and your right palm against the elbow rest to push yourself gently further into the twist. Look over your right shoulder, keeping your chin parallel to the floor. Close your eyes. Imagine that your spine is a spiral staircase, and let your breath facilitate the movement: With every inhalation let your spine grow longer; with every exhalation, allow the twist to deepen. After thirty seconds, release from the pose, leading with your head before unwinding the torso. Repeat the twist on the other side.

Modified Forward Bend Sitting toward the front edge of your seat, curl your left leg under so that your left foot is under your buttocks. Stretch your right leg straight out, angling it down so the heel touches the floor. Move your right sitting bone back and flex your right foot. Inhale, elongate your spine, and let your shoulders fall back and down. As you exhale, keep your back straight and bend forward, gently holding your thigh or calf with both hands. Let your head drop toward your knee, keeping your neck relaxed. After sixteen breaths, repeat on the other side.

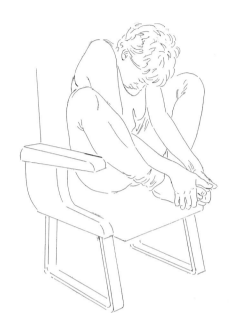

Modified Ankle-to-Knee Pose Sit well back in your seat, with feet planted firmly on the floor. Place your left ankle on top of your right knee. Inhale, straightening your back, and then bend forward as you exhale, trying to touch the center of your chest to your left calf. Place both forearms atop your lower leg. Keep your left sitting bone firmly rooted. You should feel this stretch in your hips and thighs; it also helps tone the lower back. If you want more stretch, gently push your left knee down with your left elbow. After eight breaths switch sides.

Open the Hips If you're lucky enough to have an empty seat on either side of you—or extremely friendly neighbors—you can practice full Baddha Konasana. Sit back so there is room for your feet on the seat. Bring your heels close to your groin, with the soles of your feet touching, and let your knees open outward. If you can lift the armrests to give your legs more room, great; if not, just allow your legs to rest on the armrests. Grasp your feet, inhale, and straighten your back. Exhale and bend forward for sixteen breaths. (If you don't have room for the full pose, scoot over to one side of your seat and practice with one leg at a time: Bring the sole of one foot to touch the other inner thigh, keeping that foot firmly planted on the cabin floor.)

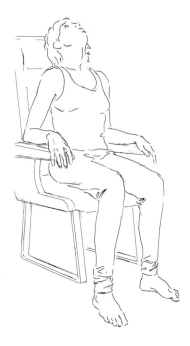

breath, lift your arms up high, and hold your breath for a few seconds. Exhale, letting the arms float down. Repeat this cycle two more times.

Nadi Sodhana (Alternate Nostril Breathing) Make sure your back is relaxed yet extended, your chest open, and your jaw and forehead relaxed. With your right hand, make a gentle fist. Then open your thumb and last two fingers. Press your right thumb into the fleshy part of your right nostril until the passage is closed and slowly inhale through your left nostril. At the top of your inhalation, release your thumb and use your ring and pinkie fingers to close your left nostril. Exhale slowly and completely through the right. Then inhale through the right, release your fingers from the left side of your nose, and close your right nostril with your thumb again. Exhale fully through your left nostril. This completes one round of Alternate Nostril Breathing. To begin a second round, inhale through your left nostril again. Continue this cycle for about three minutes, allowing your breath to become longer and smoother. Then breathe normally, observing the effects of the practice.

Modified Wheel Pose Sit at the edge of your seat with the feet planted firmly on the floor. Place your forearms snugly on the armrests, palms down. Keeping your sitting bones and feet firmly planted, inhale and lift your sternum up toward the ceiling. Let your head fall gently back, taking care not to crunch your neck. Allow your breath to expand your upper chest. After twelve breaths, release back to a relaxed seated position.

Kapalabhati (Cleansing Breaths) Sit in a simple cross-legged position. If space is limited, keep both feet on the floor and sit up tall. Inhale a comfortable breath, letting your abdomen expand slightly. Begin Kapalabhati with a quick, sharp exhalation: Pull the diaphragm in completely and force all the air in your lungs out through your nose. Let your inhalation be effortless. Release your abdominal muscles immediately after your forceful exhalation, and your lungs will fill up automatically. Keeping your focus on the exhalations, repeat thirty times. Then inhale a full, deep

Relaxation Sit comfortably with your feet on the floor. Inhale and contract all the muscles of your body, including your face, lifting your legs and arms a couple of inches into the air. Hold even tighter for another moment. Then exhale and release completely, feeling the muscular relief that comes after sustaining such a strong contraction. Repeat twice. Close your eyes and allow your body to be completely supported by the seat. Let the back of your head release into the headrest, your arms melt onto the armrests, and your sitting bones sink into the seat. Let your jaw relax. Keeping your breath deep and steady, imagine that with every exhalation you are removing toxins from your body; with every inhalation, you are breathing in *prana* (life force). When you are ready, slowly open your eyes and gaze softly into the sky.

Ravi Malhotra and Char Daigle practice and teach yoga, write, and live in New York with their two sons.

GLOSSARY

abhyanga An Ayurvedic oil massage used for healing dry, rough skin and alleviating deep physical and psychological tension.

acupressure This ancient Chinese technique involves the use of finger pressure on specific points along the body to treat ailments and stimulate the flow of qi, or energy.

acupuncture Fine needles are painlessly inserted at specific points to stimulate the flow of qi, or energy, and treat ailments.

ai chi A type of tai chi, done in the water, based on a series of 19 movements.

Alexander Technique This massage technique was created by Australian actor F. M. Alexander in the 1890s. It reeducates the body with an emphasis on breathing, posture, lengthening and widening the torso, and freeing the neck. Practitioners work with clients stretched out on treatment tables or seated on chairs.

Ananda yoga Swami Kriyananda developed Ananda yoga, a series of gentle hatha postures designed to move energy upward to the brain and prepare the body for meditation. Classes focus on proper alignment, posture transitions, and controlled breathing exercises (pranayama) to facilitate an exploration into the inner dimensions of yoga and self-awareness.

Anusara yoga This new system of hatha yoga, created by John Friend, is both spiritually inspiring and grounded in a deep knowledge of outer and inner body alignment. The central philosophy of this yoga is that each person is equally divine in every part-body, mind, and spirit.

aquaerobics Aerobic exercise done in a pool.

aromatherapy The age-old science of using essential oils extracted from botanicals to enhance physical and emotional well-being. Often combined with facials, massages, and body treatments.

asana A yoga posture or pose.

Ashtanga yoga A rigorous series of sequential postures made popular by yoga master K. Pattabhi Jois, who lives in Mysore, India.

Ayurveda A 5,000-year-old Indian healing system that incorporates herbs, diet, oils, massage, yoga, and meditation.

Bach flower remedies A method of healing using wild-flower essences and oils, discovered by Edward Bach in the late 1920s.

balneotherapy The practice of healing through bathing, sometimes with infusions of minerals or scented essential oils.

Bikram yoga This method of yoga was designed by Bikram Choudhury, who sequenced a series of 26 traditional hatha postures to address the proper functioning of every bodily system. Each studio is designed to replicate yoga's birthplace climate, with temperatures pushing 100°F.

bindi A detoxifying Ayurvedic body treatment using heated herbal infused oils.

biofeedback A process for monitoring a body function (such as breathing, heart rate, blood pressure, etc.) and altering the function through relaxation or imagery.

Boxercise A high-energy exercise class incorporating punching and kicking.

Breema bodywork Exercises using nurturing touch, tension-relieving stretches, and rhythmic movements to create physical, mental, and emotional balance.

chi nei tsang The Thai treatment of massaging directly into the navel and surrounding areas, where stress, tension, and negative emotions accumulate. Used in the treatment of digestive problems such as irritable bowel syndrome, bowel syndrome, bloating, constipation, gas, acidity, and for the elimination of toxins in the gastrointestinal tract.

chi yoga Energy and breathwork through flowing movements and centering postures combining hatha yoga and qigong.

circuit-training A workout series combining the use of weight-resistance machines and high-intensity exercises.

Continuum movement Creation of wave motions within the body by using a variety of movements, breaths, and sounds. Created by Emilie Conrad.

craniosacral therapy A gentle, hands-on method of enhancing the function of the membranes and cerebrospinal fluid that surround and protect the brain and spinal cord, with massage focusing on the head and neck. Created by osteopathic physician John E. Upledger.

DansKinetics A blend of creative movement, dance, and yoga, done to music from around the world, created at the Kripalu Center in Lenox, Massachusetts, in the early 1980s.

deep-tissue massage Concentrates on specific areas of the body, relieving chronic pain, knots, and tension.

dosha According to Ayurveda, the universal life force manifests as three different energies, or doshas, known as vata, pitta, and kapha. We are all made up of a unique combination of these three forces. It is important to determine which dosha is prominent before Ayurvedic treatments can begin.

ear candling The burning of a natural candle, with the cool end inserted in the ear, to draw out wax and fungus deposits from deep inside the ear canal.

Feldenkrais Method A hands-on method to retrain the nervous system to send different messages to the muscles, created by Israeli physicist Moshe Feldenkrais in the 1940s. By slowly and gently moving the body in the most efficient ways, these lessons allow the nervous system to learn new and better habits of movement and posture.

Five Tibetan Rites Composed of five flowing movements, this active workout keeps students on the move. Beginners start with 10 or 12 repetitions and progressively work their way up to the 21 repetitions of the full routine.

hatha yoga The physical practice of poses. Term is also used to denote a type of practice that blends two or more yoga styles.

Hellerwork Combines deep-tissue muscle therapy and movement reeducation with dialogue about the emotional issues. Developed by Joseph Heller.

Hidden Language yoga Explores the symbolic meaning of postures and their effect on the psyche and spirit. Developed by Swami Radha.

homeopathy An alternative system of healing based upon the assumption that a medicine that produces a set of symptoms in a healthy person will cure the same set of symptoms.

hot stone massage Heated stones are used in conjunction with massage to bring relief to tense and sore muscles.

hydrotherapy Water-oriented treatments, including underwater jet massage, showers, jet sprays, and mineral baths.

Integral yoga Developed by Sri Swami Satchidananda, Integral yoga uses classical hatha postures, which are meant to be performed as a meditation, balancing physical effort and relaxation. In addition to a gentle asana practice, classes also incorporate guided relaxation, breathing practices, sound vibration (repetition of mantra or chant), and silent meditation.

Iyengar yoga Poses (especially standing postures) are typically held much longer than in other schools of yoga, so practitioners can pay close attention to the precise muscular and skeletal alignment this system demands.

Created by B. K. S. Iyengar, this type of yoga uses props, including belts, chairs, blocks, and blankets, to help accommodate any special needs such as injuries or structural imbalances.

Jin Shin Jyutsu A gentle healing art practiced by placing the fingertips (over clothing) on designated energy meridians to harmonize and restore the energy flow and reduce tension and stress.

Jivamukti yoga A rigorous style of yoga created by David Life and Sharon Gannon that combines Vinyasa-style asanas with chanting, meditation, and affirmations.

kickboxing Competitors use sparring, kicks, punches, kick blocks, shadow boxing, and wood breaking that is learned and applied under professional instruction. Classes might include the use of a heavy bag.

Kirtan Devotional chanting or singing, often with musical accompaniment or drumming.

Kripalu yoga This system of yoga, developed by yogi Amrit Desai, focuses on alignment, breath, the presence of consciousness, a conscious holding of the postures, and meditation in motion.

Kriya yoga A spiritual, meditative type of yoga that incorporates poses, muscular locks (bandhas), hand gestures (mudras), chanting, meditation, and breathing exercises to awaken energy centers, or chakras. A series of 18 postures are taught in stages. Paramahamsa Yogananda, widely known as the author of *Autobiography of a Yogi,* was the first Kriya yoga master to come to the West in 1920.

Kundalini yoga The practice of Kundalini yoga incorporates postures, dynamic breathing techniques, chanting, and meditating on mantras such as Sat Nam (meaning "I am truth"). Practitioners concentrate on awakening the energy at the base of the spine and drawing it upward through each of the seven chakras.

kur A series of treatments based on the use of natural resources, such as thermal mineral water, algae, mud, essential oils, and herbs.

lomi lomi An ancient healing massage practiced by Hawaiians. Traditionally, the massage is done with the receiver laying on the floor or ground on a hand-woven mat. The masseuse uses finger, palm, and elbow strokes. Kukui nut, macadamia nut, and coconut oils are used during the massage.

m'ai chi A water workout that combines the movement of tai chi with the style and dance of the martial arts.

naturopathy A system of medicine that uses natural substances to treat the patient, acknowledging that a patient's mental, emotional, and physical states must all be treated.

NIA (Neuromuscular Integrative Action) A fitness program that combines tai chi, yoga, martial arts, and dance, created by dancers Debbie and Carlos Rosas.

ovo-lacto A vegetarian diet that includes eggs and dairy products.

panchakarma A series of Ayurvedic treatments designed to help the body release toxins and restore balance.

Pilates A series of exercises designed to improve overall alignment, strengthen deep abdominal and back muscles, and encourage good posture, created by German doctor Joseph Pilates in the 1920s. Some exercises are performed on a floor mat, others on a variety of special Pilates machines.

Polarity Therapy A comprehensive health system, developed by Dr. Randolph Stone, involving energy-based bodywork, diet, exercise, and self-awareness. It works with the "Human Energy Field," electromagnetic patterns expressed in mental, emotional, and physical experience.

power ball A strength-training class utilizing therapy balls and weights.

Power yoga A rigorous workout that develops strength and flexibility while keeping students moving quickly from pose to pose.

pranayama Yogic breathing exercises.

qigong Also spelled chi kung. An ancient Chinese health care system that integrates physical postures, breathing techniques, and focused intention.

reflexology A science based on the premise that there are zones in the feet and hands that correspond to all glands, organs, parts, and systems of the body. Applying pressure to these areas is thought to reduce stress and promote physiological changes in the body.

Reiki method An ancient form of energy work. Rooted in Japanese heritage, Reiki means "universal life force" or "universal love." Reiki balances the emotional, physical, mental, and spiritual aspects of the body.

restorative yoga Gentle poses, done with props for support, that allow the mind and body to recover from stress and strain.

sadhana Most often means "spiritual practice."

Sanskrit The language of the Hindu scriptures and thought to be one of the oldest languages in the world.

satsang A spiritual gathering to chant, recite from scriptures, or meditate.

shiatsu A Japanese style of acupressure. Comfortable pressure is applied to all parts of the body with hands and thumbs, elbows, knees, and even feet.

shirodhara An Ayurvedic treatment during which warm oil is continually poured onto the middle of the forehead, or third eye, to quiet the mind and soothe the senses.

Siddha yoga This yoga practice, made popular by Swami Muktananda, focuses on meditation, chanting, selfless service, studying spiritual scriptures, and hatha yoga. The goal is an awakening of the soul, called shaktipat.

Sivananda yoga At its core, Sivananda yoga is geared toward helping students answer the age-old question "Who am I?" This yoga practice, based on the philosophy of Swami Sivananda of Rishikesh, India, emphasizes 12 basic postures to increase strength and flexibility of the spine. Chanting, pranayama, and meditation are also included, helping students to release stress and blocked energy.

Spinning An instructor-led indoor stationary cycling class.

swedana Ayurvedic therapeutic sweating induced by medicated steam, sauna, or plasters of hot substances. Plants such as castor root, barley, sesame, black gram, jujube, and the drumstick plant are often used in the steam or plasters because they encourage the body to sweat more easily.

Swiss shower Fresh water is sprayed over the body from both overhead and side-positioned valves, with varying spray velocity and temperature.

tae kwon do A self-defense martial art.

tai chi An ancient Asian practice of continuous movements combined with breath control to promote relaxation, balance, flexibility, muscle tone, and coordination while improving overall physical and mental health.

Thai massage A practitioner stretches and compresses the body into yogalike postures to create energy, release tension, and allow for relaxation.

thalassotherapy Water-based treatments using mineral-rich components from the sea (algae, seaweed, and sea salt) for therapeutic purposes.

Tragger A massage technique during which the body is rhythmically moved and shaken to release tension.

trigger point release A massage technique using gentle, deep pressure to release tightness and allow muscles to lengthen and function freely. Especially effective in shoulder and neck areas.

TriYoga A slow, relaxing, and rejuvenating practice created by Kali Ray. A typical class, often accompanied by music, focuses on natural alignment and breath within the flow and ends with meditation. A union of asana (postures), pranayama (breathwork), and mudra (seals), this practice is deeply meditative, promoting relaxation and inner peace.

t'ui na A type of Chinese bodywork that includes kneading, rubbing, and gentle traction to relax and tone the body while increasing range of motion.

Vichy shower A collection of custom-designed showerheads that are suspended over a treatment table that create a massaging or "soft rain" sensation.

Viniyoga A gentle practice, created by T. K. V. Desikachar; poses are synchronized with the breath in sequences determined by the needs of the practitioner.

Vinyasa yoga Also called flow. A flowing sequence of yoga poses.

vipassana meditation Also called insight meditation. Buddhist meditation technique dedicated to seeing things as they truly are and understanding suffering and impermanence.

watsu Also called water shiatsu. In a pool of warm water, a practitioner stretches and guides the client through a series of dancelike movements while using shiatsu massage techniques.

White Lotus yoga A flowing Vinyasa practice, created by Ganga White and Tracey Rich, which ranges from gentle to vigorous depending on a student's ability or comfort level. In addition, classes incorporate alignment, breath, and the theoretical understanding of yoga.

Yogilates The integration of Pilates mat work with the therapeutic practice of hatha yoga.

ALPHABETICAL LISTING OF RETREATS, RESORTS, SPAS, B&Bs, AND ASHRAMS